A CLOSER LOOK AT LIFE AND DEATH

BOOK SERIES
VOLUME I

SECOND EDITION

Inspired To and Written By
Tracy Jones

COPYRIGHT 2025 © TRACY JONES
ISBN: 9798999333605

All rights reserved. No part of this book may be reproduced, stored in a retrieval system, or transmitted in any form or by any means, electronic, mechanical, photocopying, recording, or otherwise, without written permission from the author, except for brief quotations in critical reviews or articles. The scanning, uploading, and distribution of this book via the internet or by any means without the permission of the author is illegal and punishable by law. Please purchase only authorized editions that support the author's work.

A CLOSER LOOK AT LIFE AND DEATH

This book provides accurate and authoritative information regarding the subject matter. The information contained in this book is not to render legal or professional advice. All Book Series Volumes and Editions, including this republished are "Inspired to and Written by Tracy Jones." First Edition/Volume I, Copyright © 2022, ISBN: 979-8364749970 (Nov 11, 2022), Republished First Edition Copyright © 2025, ISBN: 979-8999333629; eBook First Edition Copyright © 2025, ISBN: 979-8999333643. Second Edition, Volume I: 979-8999333605; eBook Second Edition Copyright © 2025, ISBN: 979-8999333612; Hardcover Second Edition Copyright © 2025, ISBN: 979-8999333650.

Face Eternity Publications encourages the right to free expression and the importance of copyright laws. The goal of this copyrighted material is to encourage authors and artists to produce profound, innovative works that strengthen our society.

"A Closer Look at Life and Death" Book Series is an imprint of Face Eternity Publication. This publication may not be reproduced, stored in a retrieval system, or transmitted by any means, electronically or mechanically, via photocopy, recording, or otherwise, without the author's prior permission except as provided by USA copyright law. Request permission to use material from all volumes and editions (other than for review purposes), please contact us via email at info@FaceEternity.org or visit us on our contact page at www.FaceEternity.org.

Visit and Follow on Social Media:
X.com/FaceEternity
Instagram.com/FaceEternity
Facebook.com/FaceEternity
LinkedIn.com/FaceEternity

www.FaceEternity.org

This book is an imprint of Face Eternity Publications. The name, content, and Logo are also copyrights of Face Eternity Publications. We are not responsible for websites (or their content) not owned by the publisher. For courses, training, and speaking engagements or for more information, please email us at info@faceeternity.org.

Printed in the United States of America

A CLOSER LOOK AT LIFE AND DEATH

THE NEWER TESTAMENT
SO THAT NONE SHOULD PERISH

"THE LITTLE BOOK"

THE BOOK OF REVELATION
CHAPTER 10

*"I [Apostle John] saw still another mighty angel coming down from heaven…He had a **Little Book** open in his hand…Thou must prophesy again before many peoples, and nations, and tongues, and kings"*

~ **Revelation 10:1-2, 11** ~

CONTENT

Foreword: A Divine Masterpiece…The Best of Its Kind --- 1

Life And Death --- 3

CHAPTER 1

Your GPS Location: Heaven --- 5

What is Eternal Spirit Life Energy? --- 10

What is Death? --- 24

What Does Your Shadow Reveal About You? --- 29

God Called "You & Me" Out of Darkness Into His Marvelous Light --- 34

Our Body: The Vessel That Takes Our Spirit Through God's Redemption Process --- 38

God Went to Great Extents to Redeem You! --- 43

The Big Book And The Little Book --- 53

"Time" Belongs To God Alone --- 59

Returning Home --- 64

Sex Is Worship --- 70

Our Blessed Hope --- 73

Warning! --- 81

Man…God's Masterpiece --- 84

Is Your Soul For Sale or Filled with the Holy Spirit? --- 88

God's Presence Is Everything! --- 91

The Holy Throne of God --- 93

The Good News that Reverberated Around the World --- 97

Jesus… The First Human To Ever Enter into Heaven --- 102

What Would We Do Without "HOPE?" -------------------- 106

What Is The Purpose Of Life On Earth In It's
Fallen State? -- 113

The "Evidence" of Your Betrayal and Rebellion
Against God While You Lived in Heaven -------------------- 116

Your Consequences --- 124

Our Separation From God's Holy Light…Who Created
The Darkness Of Hell? ---------------------------------- 127

Your First Obituary --- 139

Your Second Obituary… Acceptance of Your
Second Death -- 141

Satan Has Always Communicated With Man - He Drives
Man And Technology To Meet His Desires ---------------- 145

Space Force: The Rise of Drone Technology And
Strong Delusion --- 151

Real Intelligence (RI) VS. (AI) Artificial Intelligence ---- 164

CHAPTER 2

Life Is Governance --------------------------------------- 177

Lucifer: The High-Ranked Cherubim Angel -------------- 189

The Art of Deception and Satan's Countermeasures ---- 204

Our Life Is the Lord's Breath of Life ---------------------- 226

Who Are We? And Why Are We Born As Sinners? ----- 231

The Duality of Spirit Life Energy --------------------------- 235

You! Cast Out of Heaven/
Heaven Became Closed to Us ------------------------------- 245

It's Hell being in Hell…Our "Tree" Selection ----------- 248

Truth Revealed --- 259

Motive -- 265

The Big Lie --- 271

Sinner Symptoms -- 276

Works & Deeds Cannot Save You -------------------------- 285

Sinners Are Subject To --------------------------------------- 291

War… We Are At War! -- 334

Modern-Day Persecution Of "The Christ-Like:" The
Seven Noahide Laws -- 338

America: The Second Beast Turns Cruel ---------------- 340

The Vaccine (Snake Bite) ------------------------------------ 346

The Ultimate Death Test ------------------------------------- 357

Depopulation --- 364

Alternate Universes: Is The Metaverse In
Bible Prophecy? -- 371

Recap And Conclusion --------------------------------------- 379

God's Redemption Plan in Action
Diagram: War In Heaven ------------------------------------- 383

Exercises: You Need To Know What You Believe ------ 386

Bibles: King James | New King James Version | Other Versions as Noted
Primary Scripture Searches: BibleHub.com | BibleGateway.com |
Strong Correspondence

A CLOSER LOOK AT LIFE AND DEATH

FOREWORD

A Divine Masterpiece
The Best of Its Kind

There is life before birth and life after birth. The Bible says in the book of ***Jeremiah 1:5, "Before I formed thee in the belly, I knew thee: and before thou camest forth out of the womb, I sanctified thee and ordained thee to be a prophet unto the nations."*** This is specifically talking about our existence before birth (which is eternal), and our existence after birth.

Romans 6:23 says, "For the wages of sin is death, but the gift of God is eternal life through our Lord." So, the greatest gift that we have been given in birth is eternal life through Jesus Christ, the only begotten Son of God. This poses a question: What is the gift of life? Life is simply being aware of your eternal existence.

I am convinced that the original thought of God was that man should never experience death or the transformation thereof; that the same way or state that we were born in was the way we were supposed to live forever. However, Tracy Jones illustrates how death entered the Earth realm through disobedience and not following instructions that have eternal implications.

The wages for not following eternal instructions are death, which is eternal separation of life with our Heavenly Father, but following eternal instructions leads to eternal life with our Father, who is our source through Jesus Christ, His only begotten Son. Life is not an experiment, and you shouldn't experiment with your life, because life is eternal. Once you are born into this earth realm, you have eternal existence, after which, there are two eternal destinations. Broad is the way that leadeth to destruction, narrow is the way that leadeth to righteousness, and few there be that find it.

Moreover, it is recorded in the Book of St. ***John 9:4 "I must work the works of him that sent me while it is yet day for the night cometh when no man can work."*** This statement is not just sobering it is bone-chilling. To understand that life's final common denominator is appointed to all of us. We all only have a certain amount of time before we step out of time into eternity.

Tracy Jones, in such a profound way, vividly illustrates in this book the reasons why setting eternal priorities should be the number one priority in our lives, and having an eternal relationship with our Heavenly Father, through his only begotten Son, ***Jesus Christ. John 14:1 says, "Let your heart be not troubled, ye believe in God, believe also in me."*** Then in ***John 14:6 he says, "I am the way the truth and the life, no man cometh to the father, but by me."***

Not only does this book give us deep insights on how to set eternal priorities, but it is also a prophetic announcement in the Last Days for those who try to comprehend and understand God, through intellectual knowledge, rhetoric, and science, which many have chosen to replace the Word of God as their means for discovering truth.

This book helps to eliminate any separation and confusion among scholars, thought leaders to the common unskilled laborer, about the existence and reality of sin and evil, inasmuch, eternal life in the paradise of heaven or eternal life in Hell and its various chambers.

In over 42 years of active full-time ministry and being the first ecclesiastically endorsed Chaplain for Education in US history, recognized by a Pentagon endorser at the Federal level, I can say that Tracy Jones was divinely selected to write this divine prophetic masterpiece for these last days. This providential work teaches us how to prepare for eternal life with our Heavenly Father or eternal separation from our Heavenly Father – the choice is yours.

Tracy Jones is a prophetic voice, speaking to the nations about life and death.

Bishop Howard M. Lee
Chairman, Global Ministry Business Commission

Life And Death

Heaven = Light = Life | Hell = Darkness = Death

Although the subject matter in this Book Series may appear to be RELIGIOUS, IT IS NOT because neither Life nor Death nor the principles that govern them are Religion. On Earth, religion is centered around man's concept of the worship and teachings of God. However, no matter what Religious Denomination you are affiliated with, including Christianity, none of them can impact your Birth, and none can prevent your certain Natural Death that is to come. Therefore, in the simplest terms, this Book Series is centered around Our Creator, who has lost One-Third of His Creation (you and me), who are now living separated from Him and captive to certain death due to their sins committed in their Spirit and Body. Therefore, God has extended His Grace and Mercy by implementing a Divine Redemption Plan to offer Himself back to those who receive Jesus Christ…His Indwelling Holy Spirit, which is Eternal Life!

DISCLAIMER: The goal is not to dissuade or persuade you to believe in God or Jesus Christ, but to highlight your choices regarding what you have been taught in school (Science) and the "Choice" between eternal life and eternal death (Deuteronomy 30:19) that God puts before you with each breath, along with the respective consequences of your choice.

A CLOSER LOOK AT LIFE AND DEATH

CHAPTER 1

Your GPS Location: Heaven

"In the beginning God created the heavens and the earth [the world]"
~ Genesis 1:1

Infinity (∞) means endless, forever, eternal, everlasting, or words that describe our "Life" with no end. These words are the essence of our Eternal Spirit, which was first created by God in Heaven. Our Spirit is created of pure divine light, in His likeness, and is made from heavenly material and properties known to God alone. Therefore, only He knows how our Spirit was created, how it moves, has its existence, and consciousness of being. Our Spirit, which now resides within our body, consists of our mind…thought, memory, our word, and character, which are eternal; everything else perishes... the body, material things, and the spheres.

Our Creator-God is the purity of Holy Divine Light. He *"...alone has immortality, dwelling in unapproachable light" (1 Timothy 6:16).* His Holy Spirit is the sustenance that defines the word "Light," and thus establishes the Universal Law of Light. According to *John 4:24, "God is a Spirit: and they that worship him must worship him in spirit and truth."*

God = Light = Energy = Spirit = Holy Spirit = Holy Ghost = Spirit of Truth = Breath of Life = Eternal Life

Since God exists as an Eternal Spirit of Divine Light, and we know that light is Energy, consequently, He created our universal presence as Eternal Spirit Life Energy, in His likeness: *"**THE SPIRIT OF MAN** is the candle [light] of the LORD" (Proverbs 2:27).* Spirit Life is created, energized, and sustained by God's Holy Spirit, the Life Energy that He extends to all of His Creation.

God's Exalted Holy Presence of Light is called The Holy Spirit, which is the fundamental nature of His Supreme Being as Divine Spirit, as Divine Immortal Flesh, as well as His Divine Holy Word. His Presence within the Truth of His Holy Word manifests as Divine Universal Law in the form of verbal commands, speech, or spoken and written words... language, thought, and His Holy Word that materialized in the visible flesh as Jesus. The term "Holy" means exalted or worthy of complete devotion as one perfect in truth, goodness, and righteousness.

Hence, God's Divine Word, which flows directly from His Lips, is Truth, and therefore, His Holy Spirit is also called The Spirit of Truth: *"But when He, THE SPIRIT OF TRUTH, comes, He will guide you into all the truth [full and complete truth]. For He will not speak on His own initiative, but He will speak whatever He hears [from the Father--the message regarding the Son], and He will disclose to you what is to come [in the future]" (John 16:13, AB).* Therefore, a Holy God of Truth created our Spirits holy and immersed in His truth. Truth is what personifies Him as Holy. Jesus confirms this as He prayed to God: *"Make them [us] holy by your truth; teach them [us] your word, which is truth" (John 17:17, NLT).*

God's Eternal Spirit Energy exists above the Heavens as an immense, incomprehensible Bright Light that is exponentially brighter than our sun. His Brilliant Light is intangible to us because, like our sun, no one can bear staring into its light. Therefore, no one can bear seeing the purity of God's Glorious Light: *"No one has ever seen God, but the one and only [begotten] Son [Jesus], who is himself God and is in closest relationship with the Father, has made him known" (John 1:18, NIV).*

[Side Note]: *Genesis 32:30 states: "It is because I [Jacob] saw God face to face, and yet my life was spared."* Some disbelieve John 1:18 above; however, Jesus, who is God, said in *John 14:9, "He who has seen Me has seen the Father; so how can you say, 'Show us the Father?'"* It appears that both scriptures are true because of the Triune existence of the Lord: *"For there are three that bear record in heaven, the Father [Jehovah/Intangible Light], the Word [Speech/Jesus/Flesh /Tangible Light], and the Holy Ghost [Spirit/Light]: and these three are one" (1 John 5:7).*

Furthermore, since *John 1:18* reveals that Jesus *"...is himself God...,"* some question John 17:17 above, whereby Jesus is praying to God: "Is Jesus praying to Himself?" Of course, the answer is... Yes! As you continue reading, you will discover that Jesus is God's spoken Word, which became visible in the flesh for the purpose of our redemption. Therefore, since we fell into sin, Jesus came to be our example, thus showing us how to communicate with God, how to conduct our behavior before a Holy God... righteousness, **repentance**; how to receive His Holy Spirit back again, and how to be redeemed back to Eternal Life with our Heavenly Father.

God, through Jesus, brought Heaven to Earth as a gift to the fallen, or all of us, *"...who fall short of the glory of God" (Romans 3:23);* hence, our **GPS location is Heaven**, on Earth, if you **repent** and invite God's Indwelling Holy Spirit (Christ) to live within you. Heaven is wherever God's Holy Spirit dwells... Why not allow Heaven to dwell within you?

We have received an undeserved second chance because of *"God's Divine Mercy and Grace,"* here on Earth, you will discover that you are, redemptively, a Spirit Being having a human experience to ultimately choose between eternal life and eternal death: *"This day I call the heavens and the earth as witnesses against you that [with each breath] I have set [put] before you [eternal] life and [eternal] death..." (Deuteronomy 30:19).* Therefore, if you do not take your next breath, which will be your final destination... Heaven or Hell? I reiterate, your **GPS** location is Heaven, on Earth, through Jesus Christ... **Glory!** [end]

Now, as I was saying, **"Light"** belongs to the Glory of God alone. His Light is so inconceivably and exponentially bright that we cannot endure its intensity; therefore, in order for God to interact with His Creation, He clothed or covered the Magnificence of His Brilliant Light... His Holy Presence, in a Human-Looking Spirit Form, to make His Divine Light bearable to us and also make Himself tangible to our senses, so that He can dwell and interact with us... Angelic Spirit Beings (in Heaven) and Human Beings, whereby the Spirit is held within a body (on Earth).

Your Spirit is the same no matter where you exist...Heaven, Hell, or Earth. God designed, created, and established the human-looking features of the Spirit of those who reside in Heaven, as well as the human look of the Flesh for the Human body. All Life originated as Spirit in the eternal realm of Heaven... our home: *"You alone are the LORD. You made the heavens, even the highest heavens, and all their starry host [us], the earth and all that is on it, the seas and all that is in them. You give life to everything, and the multitudes of heaven worship you" (Nehemiah 9:6, NIV).*

Heaven is where we belong, and where we live completely fulfilled with the fruits of His Holy Spirit... *"...Love, Joy, Peace, Longsuffering, Kindness, Goodness, Faithfulness, Gentleness, [and] Self-Control" (Galatians 5:22).* On Earth, we replicate this feeling of home as we regard our homes as the place where we feel most comfortable and secure. Since our Spirit within our human body, in its purest form, is our first state of existence in Heaven, it is why many call Heaven home when referring to the loss of a loved one. Some say their loved one has "gone home" or is "in Heaven."

What is Eternal Spirit Life Energy?

*"[your] spirit [held within your body]
will return to God who gave it"*
~ Ecclesiastes 12:7

We have and will always exist as Eternal Spirit Life Energy that will never die or be destroyed. Scientists have confirmed this fact in The Law of Conservation of Energy and The First Law of Thermodynamics, which states that ***"Energy [Spirit] can neither be created nor destroyed; energy can only be transferred or changed from one form [state] to another."*** In terms of the subject of life and death, the transfer of Energy or Spirit is its transition from the finite realm of Earth to the infinite realms of Heaven or Hell. Once God created our Eternal Spirits, there is no way of ending Spirit Life. Eternal Spirit Life Energy can only be punished into nonexistence, eternal separation from God in the Lake of Fire and Brimstone, forever (more later). Therefore, in the forever realms of Heaven and Hell, your punishment or reward lasts forever or is without end.

To establish a clear understanding of Eternal Spirit Life Energy in relation to our human body, the most effective method is to examine its presence and absence within the human body. We will analyze the difference between the body of a vibrant living human being and a deceased human body. The two physical body states are, jarringly, different; a living human with the indwelling of Eternal Spirit Energy uses our five senses of sight, smell, touch, taste, and hearing to allow us to function… think, talk, walk, laugh, work, express emotions, and interact with others. Consequently, a dead body is absent of Eternal Spirit Energy; therefore, without this energy, the body cannot do any of the latter. The above reveals the release of Eternal Spirit Life Energy as it exists in the essence of its purest form in God's Holy Presence without any external extremities like a body.

Therefore, what renders a person deceased is the return of their Eternal Spirit Life Energy to God, who gave it, according to ***Ecclesiastes 12:7, "Then the dust [your body] will return to the earth as it was, And the [your] SPIRIT will return to God who gave it."*** And verse 20 confirms what we all know to be true: ***"All [human bodies, animals, everything] go to one place; all come from dust, and all return to dust."*** Consequently, upon death, the body is left behind like a shell, so it lacks all mental and physical functionality that is orchestrated by the mind, which is now gone.

Per the Oxford Dictionary, Life is *"the strength and vitality required for sustained physical or mental activity."* Spirit is light energy that endows functionality to our mind and body through the vibrational flow of energy. However, the real definition of "Life" is defined by the optimal indwelling of God's Holy Spirit **(Christ)** within you or not; without it, we perish; Jesus Christ died and was resurrected by God in Heaven, to give you the option of returning to Eternal Life with the Lord, but it's your decision.

Spirit = Energy = Existence = Eternal Life = Consciousness, that manifests within the human body as the Lord's Breath of Life within the lungs to effectuate respiration (a pulse), as well as our flow of thought energy through our minds that endows communication and interaction with others. We also receive energy from Earth's surface, the wind, and the elements, as well as from God's Sunlight and Moonlight. The Sun represents the Father, and the lesser light, the Moon, represents the Son... the Messiah: *God = Lord = Light = Spirit = Sunlight = Son = Jesus Christ = Messiah = Moonlight (the lesser light).* The Perfect Son or God's Indwelling Holy Spirit **(Christ)** can be invited to dwell within your Soul, or it can be empty of it, then when your life ends, by default, you will experience Hellfire, and the part of Hell called Eternal Death...The Lake of Fire and Brimstone. You will learn more details about this subject as you read along.

God's nature is embedded within all of us. God has imparted His essence into our Spirits... His Holiness, Light, Truth, Righteousness, Goodness, and Love. God's Holy Spirit consumes and surrounds us in the security of His Divine Love. His Eternal Holy Spirit bestows Eternal Life to us, which is why He is called the Living God. He created and defined the words "Life" and "Living," which manifest within all creation in the form of energy. When God created us as Spirit Life, it began our introduction to our Creator and reveals God's story regarding the art of creating Life and the consciousness of living to us. Our Creation marks the beginning of God's story or His-story and the beginning of our Eternal History of living Eternal Spirit Life.

The Lord's Majestic Light illuminates Heaven's architecture as it adorns exquisite landscapes that far exceed Earth's. At the age of twelve, I had what I now know was an "out-of-body" experience that prompted me to research what happened to me. The closest phenomenon that describes what happened to me was my study of Near-Death experiences. Although I did not die and transition into the eternal realms, my Spirit left my body, went up, and hovered over the pizza restaurant, where I could look down and see the expanse of everything inside and out, as well as see myself still eating with my friends.

However, from reading many Near-Death accounts, I did notice that they converge to describe Heaven with gardens draped in unsurpassed beauty and splendid Paradises beyond comprehension. Some describe the leaves of trees that look like pure silver with radiant fruits that appear like gold; the flowers' color appears as vibrant as a rainbow. Some speak of mansions and palaces made of precious gems and the finest stones that are so magnificent that mere words cannot justly describe them: ***"In My Father's house there are many mansions [abodes]" (John 14:2).*** They say that there are plains, mountains, minerals, hills, rocks, valleys; and living waters: *"From the throne of the Lord flows the Fountain of Life with Living Waters" (Jeremiah 2:13),* which flow forth with the sole purpose of giving and sustaining life to all Creation.

Emanuel Swedenborg's book, *"Heaven and Hell,"* states that the Lord allowed him to visit Heaven and Hell. He describes Heaven as inconceivably jubilant, full of nothing but unbelievable delight, blessedness, goodness, holiness, and Divine Love. However, because we now exist in the flesh, away from Heaven's Holy atmosphere, we have forgotten Heaven's light, beauty, blessedness, and our own holiness, to the point that living that way is now beyond our belief. This is why we must attune ourselves to the Spirit or be born again, not focusing on worldly things of the flesh. Jesus said: *"Except a man be born of water [mother's womb] and of the Spirit [Baptism], he cannot enter into the kingdom of God. That which is born of the flesh is flesh; and that which is born of the Spirit is spirit" (John 3:5-6).*

Now, let us behold Heaven's exquisite, brilliant beauty and holiness in our mind, anyway… Sit back, relax, close your eyes for a few moments, and imagine Heaven's excellence: The great purity of God's Glorious Light, Truth, and Living Waters flowing forth as He sits on His Holy Throne with all power and dominion. Now, imagine yourself there before Him, in the Holiness of His Presence. Ahh, it's so refreshing!

Man's life would cease to exist if it were not continually supplied from God's fountain. Heaven's waters are so pure, crystal clear, that it can cleanse the exterior (the body) and the interior (the fallen spirit within your Soul) from the filth and imperfection of sin. On the Earth, God's waters are embedded within the Earth to spring forth our oceans and seas, and flow from Heaven as soft, gentle raindrops. We drink it, use it in our recipes, cleanse our bodies with it, and use it for our earthly needs. Is water man-made? Can you deny your dependence on God's water? Of course not. On Earth, water is not intended to wash away sin, but to sustain life and for our use.

The Lord's Light and Love abundantly fill the Heavens! The abounds of Heaven is Love. Love is the very essence of paradise... for God is Love! He is the origin and the very embodiment of the definition of it. Heaven is not merely a distant place beyond the stars; it is a knowing, a presence of love in abundance. When love fills the heart, kindness flows freely, and when we embrace others with compassion, we touch the divine. On Earth, through love, **"...he who turns a sinner from the error of his way will save a soul from death and cover a multitude of sins" (James 5:20).** Love has the power to transform ordinary moments into something extraordinary, turning the world around us into a reflection of Heaven itself.

In God's Divine Light, there is peace and love, and because of Christ, we find the essence of Heaven on Earth. The heat (internal spiritual heat, not natural heat in the atmosphere) that proceeds from God as a sun, above Heaven, is that of His affection, His Divine Love. The influx of this heat gives all that He creates the ability to receive His Love, enabling us to express His love to each other. In Heaven, the heated affection from God is called love and is implanted by way of influx (happens internally to our being), which manifests on Earth as our nominal body temperature (98.6° F/37° C). This alleviates any chance of doubt regarding the source of love. The heated passion of love is also designed and ordained by God to be expressed between married couples. Love is the foundation of that which is good and true.

The Lord created our universal presence as holy Eternal Spirit Life, in His Presence, and formed our Spirit in His Divine Image to dwell and commune with Him and each other, in truth, forever. Our Spirits are created by the Lord's Breath of Life, which flows from

His Lips as Commands of His Holy Word (Jesus). This is the same Breath of Life that He blew into Adam to cause respiration.

"Word," by definition, means a sound, speech, command, or written language (alphabetic words). God created and established words, commands, or the act of speaking. Therefore, in Genesis 1:1, before God's Word became flesh, on Earth: *"[Jesus was and will forever be] the Word and the Word was with God, and the Word was God" (John 1:1).* This means that Jesus was (and is) God's spoken Word or Command that was "sent forth" from His Lips to create everything that was made*: "He [The Word = Jesus/God's Word] was in the beginning with God. All things were made through Him [The Word], and without Him [God's Word] nothing was made [in Heaven or on Earth] that was made. In Him [The Word] was life, and the life was the light of men" (John 1:2-4).* Jesus was not yet born as the Begotten Son, which only became necessary when we disobeyed God or fell into sin. However, we were eternal life and made of the Spirit of Light until we fell into darkness by our disobedience in both realms. However, Jesus Christ has brought eternal life and the light of God's Holiness back to us by His resurrection.

At this juncture, God forgave us and revealed His prophecies or the blueprint of His redemption plan through His inspired prophets who wrote, thousands of years beforehand, that He would send a Messiah to save us and show us "the way" to be redeemed back to eternal life: *"And I [God] will put enmity [strife] between thee [Satan's church/followers] and the woman [Christ's Church], and between thy seed [Satan's children] and her seed [Christ's Children]; it [Satan's defeat] shall bruise thy head [on Calvary or Golgotha, a skull-shaped hill where Jesus' Cross was driven down into the ground thus crushing Satan's head/skull or mental state] and thou shalt bruise his heel [by nailing Jesus' feet to the Cross]" (Genesis 3:15).* Google "Golgotha" for deeper relevance of this scripture.

Therefore, God sent forth His Word to be born in the flesh as our Messiah to purposely defeat Eternal Death, now called The Second Death, per His redemption plan. And according to His plan, Jesus Christ will return to Earth, in the near future, as King of Kings to rule and reign on Earth. At His Second Coming, He will appear coming down from Heaven on a white horse: *"And his name is called The Word of God" (Revelation 19:13).*

The Triune Presence of God (Father, Son, and Holy Spirit) was not complete until after the Word **(Son)** became flesh…His birth, death, resurrection, and ascension into Heaven for the purpose of our redemption. As a result, and for the sake of carrying out our redemption, in the human form of Jesus Christ, the **Trinity** consists of:

God, The Father (Jehovah/Light) … His Holy Divine Intangible Presence as incomprehensible Bright, Unapproachable Brilliant Light above the Heavens, which no one has seen except the Son.

God, The Holy Spirit (Spirit of Truth/Light) … His Holy Divine Presence that exists in His spoken Word as Truth that manifested on Earth, as Jesus. His Word or Command was within Jesus and raised Him from the dead; His written Word as recorded in the Holy Bible, and His Light that existed as His Divine Human Spirit that resided in a Divine Body, in the Garden of Eden, made of Holy Divine Immortal Flesh.

God, The Son (The Word/Son of Man/Perfect Son/Light) … God's visible Begotten (Born) Word. Jesus, in the Flesh as a Man, *"who was made a little lower than the Angels for the suffering of death" (Hebrews 2:9);* And the risen Christ… The Indwelling of the Holy Divine Spirit that rose to retrieve His same human body and later ascended to Heaven. This feat enables us to invite Christ to live within our human body.

Therefore, **THE TRINITY** does not consist of three persons but is **ONE CREATOR** whose **DIVINE** is **present in** the **SPIRIT**, the **FLESH**, and within **HIS HOLY DIVINE WORD** (each one of the three is referred to as "Lord" and is called "He" because our Heavenly Father is male). While in Heaven, the Word was spoken or sent forth from God's Lips which created everything that was made: *"All things were made by him [the Word/Jesus]; and without him [the Word] was not anything made that was made" (John 1:3).* On Earth, God's Word became written and then came to life from the pages of the Holy Bible; made visible in the body of Jesus Christ. Furthermore, on Earth, the Lord God existed in His Immortal Divine Human Flesh when He was in the Garden of Eden with Adam and Eve; again, at that time, He had not yet been born of fallen flesh or the Begotten Son (*Begotten = Born of fleshly parents*).

As well, He existed in Immortal Divine Human Flesh, which clothed or covered the Divine Light of His Spirit, as was surprisingly revealed from within Jesus at...

THE TRANSFIGURATION: *"Jesus took Peter, James, and John...on a high mountain...and He was transfigured before them. His face shone like the sun, and His clothes became as white as the light" (Matthew 17:2).* *"I [Jesus] am the light of the world" (John 8:12).* Therefore, the "Word" or God's Light unto the World, came to Earth, in physical human form, to defeat the darkness of sin and death, thus giving us the gift of eternal life; also, to give us back God's Holy Spirit that we lost due to our sins that we committed in Heaven.

The "Word" was sent to dwell with us in its Truth, *"And the Word was made flesh, and dwelt among us" (John 3:14).* This is why many say that Jesus was "sent," He is the "Word" sent forth in the flesh for the purpose of our redemption, again, Hebrews 2:9, states: *"But we see Jesus, who was made a little lower than the angels for the suffering of death...that he by the grace of God should taste death for every man."* Therefore, all humans are made a little lower than the Angels because we are no longer in Heaven, so we must suffer our two deaths, Natural Death and Judgment regarding who will experience The Second Death (Revelation 20:10-14). Both of our death sentences and both of our punishments are a result of our sins that we committed in our Spirit, in Heaven, as well as our sins committed in the body, on Earth, to complete the whole of man's composition made of Spirit, Body (flesh), and Bones (which have both a physical and **spiritual** significance); more on this later.

In the redemption plan, since we were extricated from God, we are now allowed through Christ, to be His adopted sons because *"God decided in advance [while planning our redemption] to adopt us [back] into his own family by bringing us to Himself through Jesus Christ" (Ephesians 1:5).* Therefore, the Word came to Earth to be seen as an example of a perfect one of us or **"A Perfect Son."** Hence, the relationship between God and His Son **(Jesus)** is not only a representation of a **"Daddy-Son"** bond, like in our parental relationships here on Earth, but the "Son" represents God's mission in action to carry out our redemption by defeating eternal death through Christ's resurrection so that we might regain our eternal life. The Son of God is an example of a Perfect Son who does NOT *"fall short of the Glory of God,"* whereas all the rest of us do fall short and thus we are His imperfect sons. Jesus is the only Son on Earth who is perfect and sinless, while you and I are fallen sinners.

When the Word of God materialized by birth, an Angel of the Lord spoke: *"And she will bring forth a Son [conceived in her is of the Holy Spirit], and you [Mary] shall call His name Jesus" (Matthew 1:20-21).* God came as His Word to experience life on Earth, like us in our fallen state, to become tangible to us, meaning not abstract or some faraway being that is not real. Therefore, we

A CLOSER LOOK AT LIFE AND DEATH

could see God's written Word as a man who would show us, by example, God's redemption plan in action and the process we will follow to be redeemed. How else would we know how to be saved if we are not shown? There were no YouTube videos back then to show us. This is the very reason that we give examples and provide samples and videos to others, so that we can show or allow them to experience what we are telling them about. We recreate God's method of promotion every time we promote something by example.

God and His Word (Jesus) are ONE (1): *"I [Jesus] and my Father [God] are one" (John 10:30)*, again, as evident during the transfiguration: *"Jesus took Peter, James, and John…on a high mountain…and He was transfigured before them. His face shone like the sun, and His clothes became as white as the light" (Matthew 17:2)*. Therefore:

> Creator God = **Light** AND Jesus = The Word = **Light**,
> equates to: God = Jesus = The Word = **Light** = ONE (1)

Hence, **John 14:9 tells us that "…the one having seen Me (Jesus) has seen the Father"** because they are one and the same… Light! It is this Divine Power of Light Energy through God's **"Word"** that interconnects all things in His Universe. And it is His Holy Spirit Life force within Spirit Beings and within Human Beings (fallen Spirit within a body) that defines and perpetuates His Supreme Universal Power.

Furthermore, *1 Timothy 3:16*, also confirms that Jesus is God: *"And without controversy great is the mystery of godliness: GOD WAS MANIFEST IN THE FLESH, justified [Jesus' Human Body was Gloried or declared righteous in the Light/Sight of God, in Heaven] in the Spirit seen of angels, preached unto the Gentiles [non-Jews], believed on in the world, received [back] up into glory [Heaven]."* Please read that again and let it sink in. This scripture confirms that God did it all for us, Himself! He did not send someone else to Earth to save us from eternal death. He came in the Flesh to save us, Himself... **Glory!**

God, through His Word (Jesus), created the interconnectedness of all things *"that was made" (John 1:3)*, which further equates to how our minds are designed to process thought; **thought is spiritual**. For the purpose of our redemption, the human mind reflects the co-existence of good and evil or "duality" within the nature of all things, and therefore, manifests within our brain to produce thought or our "thought life." Our mental thoughts flow from the duality of the two Spirit realms... Heaven and Hell. The duality of this energy equates to: *Heaven/Hell = Light/Darkness = Eternal Life/Eternal Death = Good/Evil = Truth/Lies = Right/Wrong = Up/Down, 1/0 = On/Off (Light Switch/Electricity, Math and Binary Computer Technology)* and thus our choices, decisions, actions, electrical, mechanical, mathematical functions, hence derive our results, situations, and circumstances. Nevertheless, the thoughts that we ponder originate from the two eternal spirit realms in our Universe, which are foundationally sustained by the opposing spiritual forces of Heaven and Hell.

Therefore, since God and His **Word (called Jesus in the flesh)** are one and the same, so it is that you and your word(s) are one and the same. Your words go forth to represent you; your words are your presence in situations and circumstances because they are an extension of you; they express what you believe. Words can be either God's Truth or a lie; there is no in-between. This is why your words can be used against you in a court of law. Also, the Lord put power in your words as they are expressed with your tongue: *"Death [darkness/evil] and life [light/good] are in the power of the tongue," Proverbs 18:21. The "tongue is a deadly arrow; it speaks deceitfully" (Jeremiah 9:8, NIV).* Therefore, be careful of what you allow to roll off your tongue because you have the power to speak blessings and curses or life and death into your own life and the lives of others.

The Lord's Breath of Life flows through His Words or Commands to create everything that was made. However, He blew His Breath of Life into Adam after forming him out of the dust of the Earth. His Breath of Life within us is what establishes His Omnipotence or His ever-present and all-knowing ability concerning each one of us, because His Spirit is embedded in all of us. We are designed to dwell with the Lord in Heaven and on Earth, so that *John 14:3* will always remain true: *"Where I am, there you may also be."*

God's creation of our Spirits created an endearing relationship **(Creator-Created)**, which establishes the continuity of God's love for each of us: *"We love him, because he first [created us and] loved us" (1 John 4:19).* God loves each of us (His Creation), so deeply, and more specifically, He, incomprehensibly, loves you to the core of your Soul. He created only one Spirit of you, which remains the same whether you are in Heaven, Hell, or Earth (fallen Spirit living internally within your body).

Our divine Spirit Energy and Human Flesh are both created in God's likeness. Therefore, our Spirit Energy is that of His Light, so we unknowingly have electromagnetic energy with light properties that emanate outward from our being. The light of your righteousness or aura intertwines with the incomprehensible brightness of the Light of the Lord; however, if you choose a life of unrighteousness, the darkness of your mind and aura around you intertwines with the pitch-black darkness of Satan and his demented mindset.

Our energy emanates outwards, like Earth's energy as it oscillates and rotates on its axis around its negative and positive poles to generate the flow of electromagnetic energy that expands outward and around the Earth. In a like manner, our energy emanates outwards from us, so when others see our face and body, they also receive our outward flow of energy (protons, electrons, and neutrons, remember those terms from school?) that cannot be seen with the naked eye. Some may call this your vibe **(vibrational energy)**. I am sure that you've noticed that when you are around some people, you feel or receive good vibes, but when around others, you feel bad vibes.

The flow of God's energy between planets or interplanetary power is established and maintained by what Scientists call: Birkeland Current. This is God's Sovereign Power regarding how His Energy powers His Universe. His Divine Light Energy also manifests in the Earth as electricity, which flows throughout all space, including people, machines, everything, and everywhere. Therefore, sometimes when the Earth is mentioned, we refer to the entire interplanetary system, not just the blue ball.

Our Eternal Spirit Energy within our bodies is in constant motion with vibrational characteristics that generate energy waves and signals throughout our entire body. Vibration keeps our Spirit Energy moving with the source being our beating hearts, which causes collisions of particles, molecules, cells, atoms, blood platelets, fluids, etc., that scatter and bump into each other to cause circulation throughout our body. Since our mind is designed to process thoughts from the two spiritual realms, consequently, life is spiritual. It is the **"Duality of Thought"** within our minds that ties all three realms together in our Universe. Recall that Spirit Energy manifests within the human brain as our central control center that processes our flow of thoughts, produces our intellect, and memory, and mobilizes all our body functions. Our **"will"** manifests within our hearts with the ability to love or hate (duality).

Our Spirit Energy flows into Earth's realm as God's Light Waves at high frequencies (Hz), which Scientists call **the speed of light** (186,000 miles per second), so that spiritual things can become visually realized by our eyes. Our eyes are also referred to as the window to the Soul, reflecting your Spirit of righteousness or unrighteousness. Your eternal Soul within your body is where the Lord's Holy Spirit can be invited to reside within you, or your Soul can be filled with the Spirit of your enemy… Satan.

What is Death?

"Yea, though I walk through the valley [Earth/Natural Death] of the shadow of death [The Second Death (Revelation 20:14)], I will fear no evil"
~ **Psalms 23:4**

God's Holy Spirit is what makes Life... Eternal Life! ***"For as the body without the spirit -is dead" (James 2:26)***. And, due to our redemption, without God's Indwelling Holy Spirit, you will experience the Eternal Second Death. God's Holy Spirit is synonymous, or one and the same: His Word is Truth, and He is His Word. Without God's Holy Spirit of Truth within us, we are void (empty) of truth... liars, and certain to die The Second Death. Without His Light, we are darkness; without His Breath, we cannot breathe or exist... There is NO Eternal Life without the Indwelling of the Lord's Holy Spirit within you. Therefore, if you know that you have your Eternal Life in Christ Jesus... **Fear NO Evil or Death!**

As you continue to read, you will gain insight into the purpose of the only two death sentences God has ever issued to His Creation...to our Spirit while we were living in Heaven, and our human body while living on Earth. However, both death sentences are the result of the removal of God's Holy Spirit... His Holy Presence is based upon your righteous or unrighteous standard of living, or your choice to invite the indwelling of the Holy Spirit or Christ, to live within you or not. However, God's Breath of Life remains with fallen Spirits within humans to allow respiration until their death penalty occurs on Earth. Hellfire, in both Gehenna (Hell) and the coming Lake of Fire and Brimstone, will be executed in the Abyss, which consists of both a physical and spiritual atmosphere.

The Hellfire of Gehenna is simply a shadow of our real and

permanent death... The Second Death, according to *Psalms 23:4,* *"Yea, though I walk through the valley [Earth/ Natural Death] of the shadow of death [The Second Death (Revelation 20:14)], I will fear no evil, for thou art with me."* This scripture confirms that Natural Death is simply a shadow, an example, a representation, or a dress rehearsal of our destined, permanent, and Eternal Death, which is now called, according to God's redemption plan, The Second Death: *"...[Natural Death and the Second] Death and Hades [Grave] were thrown into the lake of fire. This is THE SECOND DEATH—the lake of fire"* (Revelation 20:14).

Lucifer = Darkness = Death = Eternal Separation From God = Murderer = Hell = Hellfire = Sheol = Hades = Grave = Gehenna = Paradise = Satan = The Dragon = Serpent = Natural Death = Eternal Death = The Second Death = The Lake of Fire And Brimstone = To Exist No More in the Spirit or Flesh = You, Erased From All Eternal Eternal Memory Forever = You are Eternally Destroyed

In *Psalms 51:11,* David asked the Lord: *"Do not cast me from your presence or take your Holy Spirit from me."* This confirms that God's Holy Spirit is the essence of our life. God's Presence is what gives us Eternal Life. The Lord's Breath of Life that He blew into the human body (Adam) establishes our Eternal Spirit in a visible fleshly body, on Earth. But sin happened in Heaven (Spirit) and on Earth (Body) to change our course.

Spiritual Death is defined as darkness, meaning that we live and operate from a dark mental place. And physically, by living in the Abyss (bottomless pit) where we were first cast down into, upon leaving Heaven. We were cast into the same Abyss that the demons who had possessed a man and begged Jesus NOT to send them to: *"And they [a legion of demons] begged Him [Jesus] that He would not command them to go out into the abyss" (Luke 8:31,*

NKJV). We were cast down into the bottomless, along with Lucifer, and held away from our Heavenly Father by a gravitational pull. Earth's Force of Gravity was created and established by God to hold spiritually dead sinners away from His Holy Presence.

Therefore, being absent from the Lord's Presence or His Holy Spirit means you are spiritually dead. And without His Breath of Life within your human body, you are physically dead. Since our Spirit contains our mind and eternal memory, it is our Spirit that resides within our body that must worship God *"in spirit and in truth" (John 4:24). Genesis 1:2 (NKJV)*, depicts our location after being cast down out of Heaven into the darkness of the Abyss of Hell (see diagram in the index): *"The earth [you and me] was without form [of the Image of God], and void [of truth]; and darkness was on the face of the waters [Abyss]. Revelation 17:15* explains that *"The waters…are peoples, multitudes, nations, and tongues…"*

However, *Revelation 17:15* has a two-fold meaning; let's take a closer look… *Waters = Peoples.* **Firstly, *"the waters" in Genesis 1:2, "And the Spirit of God was hovering over the face of the waters,"*** represent our fallen Spirit, which was as dark and formless as water; void of truth and living in darkness after being cast down from Heaven. Also, consider *Job 26:5,* which states: *"Dead things are formed from under the waters [the Abyss of Hell], and the inhabitants thereof [who were cast out of Heaven],"* more later.

At this juncture, our Spirits, like the Earth, are formless or not formed in the Holy Image of God's Spirit-looking Human Anatomy. Secondly, this same scripture applies to our fallen Human Bodies that was later formed into the Holy Image of God (Genesis 2:7), which are called *"people"* = *"multitudes, nations, and tongues [those of us who were cast out of Heaven, but now are formed into people from the dust of the Earth, by God, in His Holy Divine Immortal Human Image for the purpose of redemption]..." (Revelation 17:15).* The human body gives our fallen Spirit structure that then forms us into a shape that conforms us to God's Divine Order and His Holy Image. Also, by belief in Christ, we can gain God's knowledge and His Supreme Mindset that restores us to our original divine nature. However, your redemption is solely based on your individual lifestyle choice, irrespective of your religious affiliation or lack thereof, because with each breath, we all face death.

Since our Spirit contains our mind (central control) whereby we make all our choices and decisions, then it is our **"Spirit"** within our Body that must worship the Spirit of God, "in Spirit" or with our Spirit... Spirit to Spirit worship. When we genuinely think and act to pray, read God's Holy Word, use our faith, express our belief in Christ, and speak the truth and power of His Word that comes directly from our Lips, as written in the Bible, we use our mind, which is our Spirit worshipping God's Spirit.

Also, according to ***Proverb 23:7**, Mind = Spirit*: *"For as he [Spirit of a Man] thinketh in his heart, so is he [righteous or unrighteous]" For: "Whoever sows [thinketh/doeth] to please their flesh, from the flesh will reap destruction; whoever sows [thinketh/doeth] to please the Spirit, from the Spirit will reap eternal life" (Galatians 6:8, NIV).* However, because of our Spirit's fallen (from Heaven) state, we can no longer worship God *"in spirit and in truth" (John 4:24).* We disobeyed and fell for Satan's sinful lies and rebelliousness, thus we are no longer there with the Lord, in Heaven, so Heaven became closed to us: *"Therefore we are always confident, knowing that, whilst we [our Spirits] are at home in the body, we are absent from the Lord" (2 Corinthians 5:6).*

Also, we are no longer living before God's physical presence of Divine Immortal Flesh, in the Garden of Eden, because *"... the Lord God sent him [Man] out of the garden of Eden to till the ground from which he was taken. So, He drove out the man; and He placed cherubim at the east of the garden of Eden, and a flaming sword which turned every way, to guard the way to the tree of life" (Genesis 3:23-24).* Therefore, both Heaven and the Garden of Eden became closed to us.

Fallen = Fell = Disobedient = Sinned = Believed Or Fell For A Lie = Fallen Spirit = Fallen Angel = Fallen Spirit Within A Fallen Human Body

We have fallen from Heaven because we believed Lucifer's lie, and Genesis 1:2 reveals our location after we were cast out of Heaven. At this juncture, we are without form, or we no longer exist in God's Divine Image. We are now the epitome of darkness and living in mental darkness and chaos; our light from the Lord has been extinguished; we have become void or empty of His Truth. So, we are now living separated from Him in the depths of darkness and chaos instead of living in God's Light and Order. Therefore, God declared, *"You are of your father the devil, and the desires of your father you want to do. He was a murderer [taketh away eternal life; taketh you away from God's Holy Presence] from the beginning and does not stand in the Truth [void] because there is no truth in him. When he speaks a lie, he speaks from his resources, for he is a liar and the father of it" (John 8:44, NKJV).* Therefore, God is the Spirit of Truth, and Satan is the Spirit of Lies.

A CLOSER LOOK AT LIFE AND DEATH

What Does Your Shadow Reveal About You?

*"...because of the tender mercy of our God, by which
the [Day has] Dawn...[on] us from on high, to shine
on those who live in [mental] darkness and in
the shadow of death [The Second Death]"*
~ Luke 1:78-79 BSB

We were cast down below Heaven into the darkness of the Abyss (the bottomless pit, Genesis 1:2), void of God's Truth, living in unimaginable chaos and dense darkness. And this darkness is real; close your eyes; what do you see? The mental darkness that came with you from the Abyss... the darkness that you still are!

Interestingly, your **"Shadow"** that follows you everywhere reveals that you were and are cast down to Earth, and you are living in the shadow of death... The Second Death (Revelation 20:14), as the diagram in the index depicts. Why do you think you have a shadow? You probably never thought about it. Well, let's take a closer look: the word "Shadow" means a dark area or shape produced by a body. Therefore, your shadow reflects your darkness, whereby God's Light casts down the dark reflection of your fallen Spirit to the ground, from whence your Body came and will return upon your death, as your shadow reveals. Your shadow outlines your human body, which contains your fallen Spirit from the darkness of the Abyss and your fallen Body from the darkness of Earth's surface.

Everything, on this fallen Earth, casts the darkness of a shadow in the Presence of God's Light. Look at your shadow, outside in the sun, in an open area, and notice its deep darkness; its color and texture are unlike anything on Earth. Your shadow establishes the darkness of your fallen Spirit... your fallen mind with its sinful and rebellious nature that is now held within your body, which came from the ground, also fell: ***"...the woman [Eve] who was led astray [by Satan] and fell into sin" (1 Timothy 2:14).*** And your shadow establishes that your body will return to the ground from which it came.

Your cast down "Shadow" is the shadow of our eternal, permanent Second Death. Your shadow also follows you around to remind you of that day in our Eternal History when The Second Death will occur, whereby you will either be a witness of our "real death," which is now called The Second Death, according God's Divine Redemption Plan or you will a participant in it as you burn in the eternal Lake of Fire and Brimstone, forever: ***"Don't be afraid of those who want to kill your body; they cannot touch your soul [the Inner Man/Temple where either the Holy Spirit or the Spirit of Satan = Your Selfishness can dwell]. Fear only God, who can destroy both soul and body in hell" (Matthew 10:28).***

Your shadow is shown casting down to the ground because it reflects your dark fallen Spirit that was cast downward vertically from Heaven to the horizontal plane of Earth within the Abyss. However, your body was not vertically cast down; Adam and Eve were cast out or put out of the Garden, but they remained on the same horizontal plane of the ground. Therefore, it is not the body that causes your "Shadow" to cast downward to the ground; it is your fallen Spirit. For this reason, it signifies that all of us who have disobeyed God are considered "fallen," or fell into sin by believing or falling for a lie, whether in Spirit or in the Body, hence the words "Fallen Angels" or humanity fell.

Therefore, you visibly see the undeniable evidence of your Eternal History as revealed by your **"Shadow"**...Eternity Past (Fallen-to-Sin-Spirit cast from Heaven), Present (Fallen-Spirit residing in a fallen Sinful Body created from the ground, destined for Hellfire with a your dark Spirit displayed on the Ground whereby your Body will return), and Future (Your Natural Death and Eternal Second Death to come, unless you choose to believe in Christ). Your shadow is evidence that follows you around everywhere as a constant reminder that you are in a cast-down state. Now, let that sink in.

The fall of Lucifer's Spirit and those of us who followed him are fallen Spirits or Angels. And because of Adam's fall, our Body, which houses our fallen Spirit, is also called fallen and indicates that the complete composition of **Man (Spirit/Flesh)** is now fallen and is ready to participate in the redemption process. Please take a moment to review the diagram in the next few pages. On the diagram in the index, you will discover that the darkness of your **"Shadow"** reveals exactly what is shown, that the Spirit of You and I was cast down from Heaven along with the former Light Bearer. However, for the purpose of providing you and me a second chance or a means of redemption, God chose to form your **"Body"** from the dust of the Earth, in His Image (again), to give your fallen Spirit the ability to choose to accept God's Indwelling Holy Spirit **(Christ),** that leads to Truth, Righteousness, and Eternal Life, or not.

Now, read **Genesis 1:2** again, and notice that we are only being held in the darkness of the Abyss; there is no mention of **"Hellfire."** This is because Hellfire punishment is purposed for the Spirits of Humans who die and leave Earth, as their bodies are preserved in a grave. But the Hellfire of the Lake of Fire and Brimstone or the penalty of **The Second Death** is purposed for both Spirits or Angels and the Human Body. Hellfire punishment is designed to be carried out using the "Body" composition of man.

For the purpose of redemption, there are various chambers or locations within the Abyss of Hell: The Abyss of Outer Space, Outer Darkness, the surface of the Earth, the darkness of our night sky, under the Earth… **the grave (Hades)**, Earth's inner core… Hell (Gehenna and Paradise); the Waters/Oceans, the Lake of Fire, and the darkness of the mind of Man: *"darkness covers the earth, and thick darkness is over the peoples [minds]" (Isaiah 60:2)*. The

Abyss, Earth, and our mental darkness are three parts of Hell that we have already experienced or are experiencing. Those who have passed on are experiencing the grave and one of the two eternal realms; however, the Lake of Fire has not been availed to us yet.

According to God's redemption plan, the secret is that our bodies are used to redeem our fallen Spirits upon the death of our bodies; our Spirit returns to God who gave it, more later. Through your body's composition of Spirit, Flesh, and Bones (see figure), you will experience your Natural Death and receive your judgments or rewards and punishments of Hellfire. Your dark shadow reflects your Spirit, and your Spirits fall from Heaven to Earth, which led to both your Natural Death sentence and your Eternal Second Death sentence being adjudicated in Heaven. Natural Death is carried out on Earth, and subsequently, the Second Death will occur in the Abyss of the Lake of Fire and Brimstone, forever.

So, why do you think that when God or Jesus is mentioned, many automatically think of Religion or Church instead of the fact that **Jesus Christ came as a matter of our eternal life and death**, which applies to everyone on the planet who dies? His coming was not for religious purposes or to indoctrinate you as a Catholic, Mormon, Christian, Baptist, Evangelical, or any religious denomination. Life and death occur regardless of any church or organizational affiliation, your job, financial or power status, or any situation or circumstance on Earth.

THE REDEMPTION PROCESS TAKES PLACE THROUGH THE COMPOSITION OF MAN'S SPIRIT...BODY...BONES TO EXPERIENCE OUR DEATH, JUDGMENT & PUNISHMENT

Hebrews 2:9 "But we see Jesus, who was made a little lower than the angels for the suffering of death...that he by the grace of God should taste death for every man." Therefore, all humans are made a little lower than the Angels because we must suffer our two deaths Natural Death and Judgment in regard to who will experience The Second Death (Rev 20:10-14)

Heaven became **CLOSED** to us as evident by our Spirits being cast out of it; Therefore, **before the Resurrection of Jesus Christ**: ALL our Spirits went to Hell. **After Christ**: Heaven became open to those who believe in Him

SPIRIT

The Vessel of the Human Body is designed to **HOLD our Spirit** that God called from the darkness of the Abyss of Hell as depicted by your **Shadow for the purpose of participation in God's Redemption** process. And the Body is the Temple (Dwelling Place) of God's Holy Spirit within us if we so choose to invite Christ to live within

BODY & SHADOW (FALLEN SPIRIT)

Our Skeletal System represents the last earthly traces of us, and according to Scientists, "seem to last forever." Therefore, Man's Skeletal Structure is designed to experience the Fires of Hell (Gehenna) and the Lake of Fire, The Second Death

BONES

Upon Death: "For man goes to his eternal home [Heaven or Hell], And the mourners go about the streets...Then the dust will return to the earth as it was, And the spirit will return to God who gave it" Ecclesiastes 12:5-7

God Called "You & Me" Out of Darkness

"[God]...called you out of darkness [The Abyss of Hell] into His marvelous light [on Earth]"
~ 1 Peter 2:9

God extended His Divine Mercy to you and me by offering us a second chance, through His redemption plan, which put off eternal death, which is now called The Second Death, to allow the redemptive purpose of Natural Death to redeem us back unto Himself through belief in Jesus Christ; however, the default is the Eternal Second Death (Revelation 20:10-14).

Scientists, in their quest to distract us from the truth of God, have theorized hypotheticals, called **The Theory of Evolution** and **The Big Bang Theory.** They posit that "the bang" is the moment that we were created from a single organism, billions of years ago. And over time, we evolved into **"Apes"** and, subsequently, we evolved into humans... **"Man."** My definition of the word **"Science"** is: *"Science is the study of what God has already created and established."*

The true Big Bang occurred with the explosion of the burst of **"Divine Light"** from God's Holy Spirit, which came down from Heaven, and entered our darkness (Genesis 1:2). And subsequently, He said ***"...Let there be Light [on Earth (Genesis 1:14)."*** Then out of His Divine Grace, He ***"...called you [and me] out of darkness [The Abyss of Hell] into His marvelous light [on Earth]"*** *(1 Peter 2:9)* in order to ***"...set [put] before you [us, with each breath, eternal] life and [eternal] death"*** *(Deuteronomy 30:19).* As well, the truth of our evolution is our universal and eternal evolution from the darkness of our fallen Spirits evolving into repented, forgiven, born again Spirits of light through faith in the blood of Jesus Christ.

"He [God] brought them [us] out of darkness and the shadow

of death [The Second Death]," And broke their [our] chains [the bondage of mental darkness and death] in pieces [by the resurrection of Jesus Christ]" (Psalms 107:14). Thus, God forgave us and called you and me out of darkness to consciously participate in His redemption process, which includes Natural Death and the Eternal Second Death. Our redemption will be effectuated through the composition of our human body, made of Spirit, Body (Flesh), Bones, and a cast down Shadow to remind us of our eternity past.

Your dark shadow reflects your Spirit's fall from Heaven, which led to both your Natural Death sentence and your Eternal Second Death penalty, which was adjudicated in Heaven. Natural Death is carried out in the Abyss of Earth, and subsequently, The Second Death will occur in the Abyss of the Lake of Fire and Brimstone, forever. *"For you were once darkness [formless in the Abyss of Hell], but now you are light in the Lord [on Earth]. Walk as children of light" (Ephesians 5:8). "Then Jesus said to them, 'A little while longer the light is with you. Walk while you have the light, lest darkness overtake you [in death]; he who walks in [mental] darkness does not know where he is going. While you have the light, believe in the light, that you may become sons of light...'" (John 12:35-36).*

"I, the Lord, have called You [out of darkness and unrighteousness] in[to] righteousness, And will hold Your hand; I will keep You [Isaiah] and give You as a covenant to the people [that I formed in my image and follow righteousness], As a light to the Gentiles, To open blind eyes, To bring out prisoners from the prison [of darkness], Those who sit in darkness from the prison house. <u>I am the Lord, that is My name</u>; And My glory I will not give to another, Nor My praise to carved images. Behold, the former things have come to pass, And new things I declare; Before they spring forth I tell you of them [in my written Word

and in my visible Word, Jesus]" (Isaiah 42:6-9).

"He [God] has rescued us from the dominion of darkness and brought us into the kingdom of His beloved Son (Jesus)" (Colossians 1:13). The end result of God's redemption plan, for those who choose to believe in Jesus Christ, is that "...*you [believers in Christ] are a chosen generation, a royal priesthood, a holy nation, His own special people, that you may proclaim the praises of Him who called you out of darkness into His marvelous light; who once were not a people [formless, not in the image of God (Genesis 1:2)] but are now the people of God [created in His Image], who had not obtained mercy but now have obtained mercy" (1 Peter 2:9-10)*... **Glory!**

The 90-year-old, famed Canadian "Star Trek" actor William Shatner, confirms the validity of our darkness when he returned from his eleven-minute space flight on Blue Origin with Jeff Bezos on October 13, 2021. He said that he often fantasized about actually going into outer space; he thought it would be very exciting and an awesome experience, but upon his return to Earth, he reported that he felt quite the opposite. He shared his experience in multiple reports, stating that the space flight filled him with sadness and profound grief that caused him to cry. In Variety and other interviews, he stated: *"Outer Space always fascinated him but he was surprised by his own reaction to the experience. He said there was no mystery, no majestic awe to behold . . . all I saw was death."*

Furthermore, CNN posted the following statement by Shatner: *"I saw a cold, dark, black emptiness. It was unlike any blackness you can see or feel on Earth. It was deep, enveloping, all-encompassing. I turned back toward the light of home [where in the Abyss of our darkness (Genesis 1:2), God came down and said Let there be light]."* Ironically, this darkness that Shatner saw in the Abyss is the same darkness from the Abyss of Hell that we see when we close our eyes, which is the darkness that we still are! And the Lord said: *"I have come as Light into the world, so that no one who believes in Me will remain in [mental, spiritual] darkness" (John 12:46).*

Our Body: The Vessel That Takes Our Spirit Through God's Redemption Process

"[If] Christ lives within you, so even though your body will die because of sin, the Spirit gives you life because you have been made right with God"
~ Romans 8:10

Our body is the vessel that takes our Spirit through the redemption process, which also includes Hellfire. Since our Spirit is eternal, and is in constant motion, and never dies, upon death our Spirit enters the temporary part of Hell **(Gehenna and Paradise, see diagram in the index),** which is designed to receive the Spirit of humans who die from the Earth. And our bodies (and bones) enter the grave **(Hades)** where they sleep **(1 Thessalonians 4:13)** until they are resurrected to conjoin back with their or your same Spirit, as Jesus did upon His resurrection. The permanent part of Hell which burnth forever... The Eternal Second Death or the Lake of Fire is designed to receive the Spirit of Satan, his chief Angels, other Angels/Spirits, and Human Bodies. Some Angels, who remained in Heaven after we were cast out, fell later, like those who were attracted to beautiful women on earth and came down to mate with them: *"When the sons of God came into the daughters of men and they bore children to them" (Genesis 6:4, NKJV).* Their children were giants and are called Nephilim.

Unlike us, some Angelic Spirits are denied access to a body to participate in God's plan of redemption, like Satan. Some will remain in various places within Hell: in the darkness of the bottomless pit, in the pits of Gehenna's Hellfire, in outer darkness, etc. Some will be released during the Tribulation/Great Tribulation: *"So the four angels, who had been prepared for the hour and day and month and year, were released to kill a third of mankind" (Revelation 9:15).* After the Last Judgment, The Second Death or the eternal Lake of Fire and Brimstone will be availed to Satan and all unbeliever; it is prepared for all eternity.

The Second Death = The Lake of Fire will receive all unbelievers… Spirit Beings and resurrected Human Beings after their final appearance before God at **"The Great White Throne Judgment" or "The Last Judgment"** (Revelation 20:12-15).

Our bones represent the last earthly traces of us, and according to Scientists, they "seem to last forever." Therefore, man's skeletal structure is designed to experience or go through the fires of Hell and the Lake of Fire, which will burn forever. *"For my days [my life] disappear like smoke [upon my death]. Yes, and my bones burn like red-hot coals [in the fires of Hell]" (Psalms 102:3).* We will explore this topic more as we go along, and in greater detail once we change **GPS** locations.

Most importantly, God's Presence is everything! Please get this wisdom: His Presence sustains our Spirit Life, for He is Life! So, to be cast out or expelled from His Presence, in Heaven, and in the Garden of Eden, on Earth, or to live in the body without God's Holy Spirit through Christ, means Hellfire punishment in Sheol (Hell) and the Lake of Fire and Brimstone (Revelation 20:14). These two punishments await you upon the death of your body.

The removal of God's Holy Spirit can occur instantly or gradually. Still, the death of your body comes at an appointed time determined by God alone. Because of redemption, the death of your body is, purposely, not instant upon your spiritual death. Still, it does mean that the death of your body is coming. For instance, Lucifer's eternal, permanent Hellfire punishment in the Lake of Fire and Brimstone, as described in Revelation 20:10, has not occurred yet. It did not happen the moment that he experienced his death or separation from God, and subsequently, was cast out of Heaven. However, he became spiritually dead and is still awaiting his eternal punishment. You will come to understand the delay of his punishment as you continue reading.

Similarly, the temporary Hellfire punishment designed for the Spirits of Humans who die from the Earth did not occur the moment that Adam and Eve experienced their spiritual death or separation from God and were cast out of the Garden of Eden. They, too, immediately became spiritually dead, but their bodies did not immediately perish. However, their deaths did eventually occur; in fact, Adam lived to be 930 years old before his death.

But since they acknowledged their sin with overwhelming sorrow, God accepted their gift of atonement, which was animal blood sacrifice at that time (Leviticus 17:11, NLT), but now our **blood sacrifice** is Jesus Christ **(once and done)**. He is our means of atonement, or the act of setting things right with God. So, when you turn away from righteousness or choose not to invite Christ to live within your Soul or body, rest assured that your consequential punishments await you.

According to God's Divine Redemption Plan, the death of your human body occurs when the Lord's Breath of Life, which allows you to breathe, is removed from your body upon your death. At this time, the respiration of your lungs stops, which causes your heart to stop beating then you are declared dead, as your Spirit departs to return to God who gave it (Ecclesiastes 12:7). However, as fallen human beings who lost the God's Indwelling Holy Spirit from within us when we sinned, in Heaven, however, on Earth, we must invite or ask to receive God's Indwelling Holy Spirit **(Christ)** during the redemption process. Have you thought about asking or inviting Christ to dwell within you today?

You see, after we fell from God's Glory… His Presence of Divine Light and Truth, which is eternal life, was no longer automatically embedded within our Spirits as it was upon our heavenly creation; as well as in the Garden, we lost the Lord's embedded Holy Spirit from within us, thus our Souls became empty. And although we lost God's Holy Spirit, His Breath of Life remains with us until our judgments and punishments are executed. However, some choose to disbelieve in the afterlife because they believe that death is simply the natural cycle of life; therefore, death just happens, and there is no **"afterlife"** beyond Earth. While life and death are a natural cycle of life for us, you must realize that there is more to our death than just being a natural cycle. Logically, none of us spend time and money thinking, planning, and bringing creative ideas, inventions, improvements, and technological advancements to life, just for them to fail or die off.

We create for the progression of the betterment of all with the goal of advancement and establishing a lasting legacy. Do you believe that the inventors of the light bulb, heating and air, airplanes, trains, kitchen oven, computers, etc., designed their inventions to last or to fade away or die off? Of course not, because these things are essential for living; we still use them today. Therefore, the same is true with God's Creation of us; He did not invest His love, His Word, or His Eternal Breath of Life into creating us just so that we will die off. No! God created us to live with Him forever, in Heaven and on Earth.

Consider this question: "What is the first thing that you do when you go into a dark room or space?" Turn on the light so that you can see. So, of course, light is essential; we need and depend on light. We evolved from using fire to candlelight to the light bulb because of our dependence on light due to the darkness of the Abyss in which we live. However, navigating through our life's choices, decisions, situations, and circumstances requires spiritual light within our minds that only Jesus Christ can provide.

Always remember that our **"afterlife"** exists because although your body dies, your **"Spirit"** is your eternal legacy and never dies:

"[If] Christ lives within you, so even though your body will die because of [your] sin [that you committed in Heaven], the [your] Spirit gives you life because you have been made right with God" (Romans 8:10, NLT). Consequently, God has a plan, specific to your eternal life and eternal death, so the manner of thinking that death is simply the natural cycle of life and that there is no **"afterlife"** beyond Earth may require reevaluation, don't you think?

God Went to Great Extents to Redeem You!

"In Him we have redemption through His blood, the forgiveness of sins, according to the riches of His grace"
~ Ephesians 1:7

Although our Eternal Spirits sinned against God's Holy Spirit...His Being of Truth, Goodness, and Love, the Lord, overwhelmingly loved us enough to develop a redemption plan to save us from eternal death. God's redemption plan has no concept of reincarnation, although the former Light Bearer may fool you with his lies and antics. But according to the Lord, **"...there shall be a resurrection of the dead, both of the just and unjust" (Acts 24:15).** Therefore, you will always be the same Spirit that God first created of you, the same "You" that He wants back in His Eternal Life.

[Side Note]: When speaking with those who believe and teach reincarnation, in comparison to God's redemption plan, I ask: *"If God's plan calls for all men to be resurrected, meaning that your Spirit will conjoin back to your same body, as Jesus did upon His resurrection; then which reincarnated body will your Spirit be resurrected too?"* Silence ensues... A valid question, don't you think? **[end]**

God's redemption plan is centered around God's priority objective to give us back His Holy Spirit within us, which is eternal life. Therefore, a means had to be created for the Holy Spirit to enter and dwell within our fallen human bodies so that we can receive Eternal Life. This was accomplished through Jesus Christ, who was resurrected and returned to Heaven to send us His Indwelling Holy Spirit: **"... when He, the Spirit of truth, has come [within you], He will guide you into all truth" (John 16:13, NKJV).**

Do you realize how much money we spend on getting to the truth, which belongs to God alone? We spend much time, effort, and thousands of dollars on investigations, attorneys, court costs, witnesses, etc., so that we can obtain the truth of a matter to make a final judgment whereby our very lives hang in the balance.

We place our hand on the Word of God...The Holy Bible and raise our right hand to God **(signifying His righteousness)** as we are instructed to say, under sworn oath: *"I (name) solemnly swear to tell the whole truth, and nothing but the truth, so help me God."* The oath communicates to God and invokes His authority to help us tell the truth. And if he or she knowingly lies in a statement, orally or in a written deposition, the individual can be held accountable and prosecuted under the crime of perjury or lying under oath. We, ceremonially, call on God **(even atheists)** at the very beginning of testimony in every court proceeding to indicate that we rely on, and value God's Truth, as it holds the individual personally accountable to the Truth of God.

When the truth comes into God's Light, it is undeniable and indisputable...no further arguments, Your Honor...case closed. Truth is the end-all of every situation: **"...we can do nothing against the truth, but [stand] for the truth" (2 Corinthians 13:8).** Ironically, you must lie to try to get around the truth. However, the truth always ends up catching up with you. In fact, every time we tell the truth, honestly, what we are saying or revealing is using His Truth. Even confessing your sins reveals what God already knows about you: His Truth.

Still, the consequence of unbelief awaits you unless you accept Jesus Christ. However, many of us do not want to hear the truth about Jesus Christ, Satan, Heaven, Hell, or Eternal Life; we would rather believe the **"big lie"** that they don't exist. But I will continue to remind you that they are as real and true as God's words to Adam and Eve: *"Thou shalt not eat of it [the tree/fruit]: thou shalt surely die" (Genesis 2:17).* Therefore, aren't you awaiting your turn to die, right now?

A CLOSER LOOK AT LIFE AND DEATH

God's Eternal Holy Spirit is His Divine Presence that exists in Heaven, on Earth… throughout His Universe. The Lord's Holy Spirit dwelt within our Spirits in Heaven, as well as in a Divine Immortal Body in the Garden of Eden with Adam and Eve. His Holy Spirit also dwelt within the body of Jesus and dwells within the human bodies of all believers in Christ as the Indwelling Holy Spirit that Jesus Christ sent down to us once He returned to Heaven. Some speculate, "Do we live in a computer simulator or a matrix?"

Although it may seem like it, as the totalitarian Antichrist, and his computer-controlled global Beast System, will ensure that everything and everybody is connectable (via metal implants under the skin, vaccine technology, digital tattoos, etc.) and is connected to his World Wide Web. This will make Satan all-knowing and in control, like God. So, the above answer is yes when you consider Satan's plan for humanity, but the answer is no, according to God's plan to save us. The reality of the bigger picture is that we live within God's Divine Redemption Plan, which is designed to save us from Eternal Death. God may be trying to tell you something; pay attention!

Ultimately, the "Word" is God's spoken Word materialized as Jesus to make His Word come true before our eyes. His Word came to show us the defeat of death by His resurrection and to give us God's Holy Spirit back, which is the resurrection to Eternal Life within us; the same Holy Spirit that raised Jesus to eternal life. Thus, we will follow the Word's living example of Eternal Life, as the Word says: *"I am the way and the truth and the life" (John 14:6).* Beware of those who say that there are many ways back to eternal life except through Jesus because **"there is no other name under heaven given among men by which we must be saved" (Acts 4:12).**

Just as there is only **"one way"** to pay your taxes to your government or the IRS, there is only one way back to eternal life.

A CLOSER LOOK AT LIFE AND DEATH

To pay your taxes, you must go to the tax office or mail your payment to the tax office, as instructed. You cannot go to multiple, unaffiliated places to pay…other government offices, businesses, etc.; likewise, God has instructed us to follow Jesus Christ as **"the only way"** back to eternal life with Him.

Originally, God's Holy Spirit dwelt within our Spirits, in Heaven, where His Truth resides. However, this is not the case concerning humans because after we sinned in the Garden and were expelled or separated from God's Presence **(death)**, our Spirits lost the indwelling of God's Holy Spirit within our bodies. This is why, within God's redemption plan, it was purposed that He would give Jesus, the **"Perfect Son"** (or perfect human being), His Holy Spirit to give to us: *"the Holy Spirit descended [from Heaven to Jesus on Earth] in a bodily shape like a dove upon him" (Luke 3:22).*

Christ already had God's Holy Spirit indwelled within Him according to *Luke 4:1, "Then Jesus, full of the Holy Spirit, returned from the Jordan and was led by the Spirit,"* and also according to **Matthew 17:2**, Jesus is God…the Truth of His Holy written Word shown visibly in the flesh. Therefore, it would be quite the process to give God's Holy Spirit back to fallen human beings with their fallen Spirits now housed within a body. It would take someone sinless to accomplish it. The process entails Jesus receiving the Holy Spirit from our Heavenly Father, who is in Heaven, in order to then give it to us.

Therefore, Jesus' birth, death, resurrection, and His ascension into Heaven would be required. When God's Holy Spirit came down from Heaven, like a dove, it rested upon Jesus, but it did not enter and dwell within Him. This is because the purpose and focus was for Jesus to receive the Holy Spirit, and thus by His ascension into Heaven would make God's Holy Spirit of Light and Divine Truth available and embeddable into our fallen human bodies with a fallen, sinful Spirit within. Nevertheless, it was not until after

Christ was resurrected and had returned to Heaven that God's Indwelling Holy Spirit could be sent down to us to be capable of entering the human body to dwell within. Jesus told His disciples who did not want Him to leave Earth: *"...it is to your advantage that I go away; for if I do not go away, the Helper [Comforter, Advocate, Intercessor, Counselor of Truth, Strengthener] will not come to you; but if I go, I will send Him (God's Indwelling Spirit) to you [to live within you]" (John 16:7).*

God's original embedded Holy Spirit that was created within us in Heaven and the Indwelling of the Holy Spirit that Christ sends down to dwell within a Spirit that resides within a human body are used interchangeably because they are both God's Holy Spirit; however there is a distinct difference between how God's Holy Spirit is embedded within Spirit Beings, in Heaven, and how it is designed to be given back to those Spirits who lost it, and now, reside in a human body due to sin and expulsion from Heaven. However, due to the fall of both our Spirit and our Human Body, God's Holy Spirit could not enter and dwell within us anymore. His Holy Spirit could only "rest upon" or "come upon" us, but not enter us and remain.

When Jesus came to Earth, God, the Father, in His intangible form, sent down His Holy Spirit to "rest upon" the body of Jesus, confirming that the Holy Spirit did not enter Jesus because He already was the Holy Spirit internally. Also, when the Holy Spirit came down from Heaven to the disciples, it came down around and about their bodies (Acts 1:25, 19-16, 10:44), but it did not enter them or continuously dwell within their bodies. Therefore, these scriptures address and reveal that there is a process that must be followed whereby He would use Jesus to accomplish the receipt of His Holy Spirit to give to us. However, His ascension into Heaven would be required to make God's Holy Spirit embeddable or indwelling within the souls of fallen Human Beings.

The process of making God's Holy Spirit indwelling within Human Beings or Spirits, housed in a body, would require Christ's ascension into Heaven with His resurrected Body and Spirit intact so that the human body could be glorified or deemed accepted by the Light of our intangible Heavenly Father. Essentially, the above are the steps that had to take place before the Indwelling Holy Spirit (Christ) could be sent down to us so that it would be capable of entering our Souls within our fallen bodies in preparation for our coming resurrection, like Jesus Christ.

Since Jesus Christ is the first Human to ever enter Heaven, it is why He said that He would go to prepare a place for us in Heaven: ***"I go and prepare a place for you [your repentant Spirit housed in your human body]" (John 14:3).*** Once Jesus returned to Heaven, He made the human body fit for eternal living in Heaven and on Earth by converting our mortal bodies into immortal bodies: ***"Our physical bodies will be changed into spiritual bodies" (1 Corinthians 15:44, CEV).***

However, from Heaven, Jesus sent down to us the "Indwelling of the Holy Spirit" that can now enter and dwell within the fallen or mortal human body. The name Jesus Christ represents: Jesus (Body), Christ (The Indwelling of the Holy Spirit). The Christ Spirit embeds God's Holy Spirit within our fallen Spirit (held in a Body) like when we were, originally, created in Heaven: ***"For God wanted them [us] to know that the riches and glory of Christ are for you…And this is the secret: Christ lives in you. This gives you assurance of sharing his glory" (Colossians 1:27, NLT).***

After much research trying to figure out what happened to me, I concluded that what I physically encountered one day was the Indwelling of the Holy Spirit before me. I, actually and astoundingly, witnessed this with my very own eyes. His Holy Spirit of Light was not a glowing light, but it looked like a pure white, see-through human shape in bodily form; the purest white that I have ever seen. He came towards me, looked directly into my eyes, then entered my body, and has never left me.

So, to this day, the Holy Spirit continues to dwell within me: ***"The LORD himself goes before you and will be with you; he will never leave you nor forsake you. Do not be afraid" (Deuteronomy 31:8).*** I was bewildered but not afraid. I thought, "How can I explain this to anyone?" **"Who would believe the LORD, Himself, in Spirit, actually came "before my eyes," and that I literally saw the pure white shadow shape of His human-looking Spirit-form standing before me, then entered my body?** The incident occurred just as the latter scripture described. The Lord is within me, **OMG... WOW!**

God's Word became truth to life within me. After discovering **Deuteronomy 31:8,** I realized that it explains exactly what happened to me. I couldn't contain my joy and tears. Every time I think about it, I tear up and rejoice...Hallelujah! In retrospect, I did not see Christ in a white robe with His hands stretched out; it wasn't a dream or vision; I, physically, saw His Spirit figure...His Holy Spirit in bodily form.

However, my experience was different relative to feeling the **Holy Spirit** coming upon me in church. I also did not speak in tongues, as many say they do or must do. None of the latter are indwelling; they only **"come upon"** you. But of course, everyone has their own encounters with the Holy Spirit that they can attest to; there is no right or wrong experience. Nevertheless, the bottom line is that God is redeeming you back into His Eternal Life by His Indwelling Holy Spirit that was transferred to us through Jesus Christ. Now, you have the choice to invite Christ **(Indwelling Holy Spirit)** to dwell within you, or not. This was done so that you might choose to have the power of God's Truth and Light within you again, which are essential to Eternal Life. We are redeemed through death...our resurrection to Eternal Life. Now, I hope that you can begin to see the blueprint of God's redemption plan in action…His Word in the flesh, to make us redeemable! Therefore, when you call on Jesus Christ, you are calling on the Indwelling Word of God, which made everything that was made **(John 1:3).**

The former Light Bearer has guided many religious leaders of the world to only recognize or accept Jesus Christ as a prophet, a teacher, or merely a good man. But when you say that Jesus is the Word who is God dwelling with us in the flesh, it becomes a huge problem. Some refuse to believe that God's Word is also Human in Jesus or that God, our Creator, would love us enough to, undeservingly, save us after we turned against Him. We turned away from or left God; He has NEVER left us or turned away from us! It is as if some of us can't believe that God could come to exist in the flesh, as a man…Jesus, even though we are made in His Image.

All Heavenly Beings are made in His image, and all humanity is made in His Fleshly image. God lived on Earth as Divine Human Immortal Flesh when He created Adam and Eve. Before and after the fall, He walked and talked with them in the Garden of Eden, beginning in **Genesis 5:2.** Could it be that this mindset of Satan is projected upon us to distract us from believing and worshiping the one and only true God who created Heaven, Earth, you, and me? When we each stand before God, there is one thing for certain that none of us will ever be able to say to Him: *"How can You judge me as a man when You have never existed as a man, Yourself?"* Hmm.

Satan has led many of you to believe in and worship something or someone that you can see with your eyes, like idols, other gods, False Prophets, Popes, Pastors, Antichrists, and eventually, there will be public worship of Satan as god. But realize that it is written that *"…**every spirit that does not confess that Jesus Christ [the Word] has come in the flesh is not of God…this is the spirit of the Antichrist"* **(1 John 4:3).** Now, can you see through this religious lie regarding who Jesus is? This lie is perpetrated upon you to trick you out of your Eternal Life back with the Lord. So that when your body eventually dies, you will go to Hell. Therefore, given the fact that we were created by the Spirit of God, as Spirit, and because of the duality of the Spirit on Earth **(truth and lies),** we must *"test the spirits [to see if they believe that God has come in the flesh as Jesus to determine], whether they [people] are of God" (1 John 4:1)*. And be very grateful that *"In Him [Christ Jesus] we have redemption through His blood, the forgiveness of sins, according to the riches of His grace" (Ephesians 1:7).*

A CLOSER LOOK AT LIFE AND DEATH

The Big Book And The Little Book

"He [A Mighty Angel] had a little book open in his hand"
~ Revelation 10:8

As we have overtly established, we are living in the end times and last days, watching Biblical Prophecy unfold quickly before our eyes. You will discover the technology that is now in place to bring the **Big Book… The Holy Bible's** Prophecy to life, the Gog and Magog War of Ezekiel chapters, 38 and 39, that is leading us towards World War III and eventually to the final War of Armageddon, the fall and destruction of Damascus, Syria **(Isaiah 17:1)**, etc.; as well as the writing of volumes of His Divine Revelations that He has chosen to inspire through me, to my overwhelming amazement, is just as prophetic.

The Lord, very noticeably, had His hands on my life from a young age, and you will later discover how His Holy Spirit came to me and literally, entered my body to dwell within me in order to write down what He has to say, and reveal directly to His Creation, during these critical **"End Times,"** that began when Israel became a state in 1948, and the "Last Days" of the Tribulation and Great Tribulation.

The Holy Spirit, on several occasions, took me to the Book of Revelation, Chapter 10, where it speaks about the **"Little Book"** (*Scroll = Book*): *"I [John] saw still another mighty angel coming down from heaven, clothed with a cloud…He [A Mighty Angel] had a little book open in his hand. And he set his right foot on the sea [the Abyss of Hell] and his left foot on the land [the Abyss of Earth], and…seven thunders uttered their voices. Now when the seven thunders uttered their voices, I was about to write; but I*

heard a voice from heaven saying to me, "Seal up the things which the seven thunders uttered, and do not write them…
And the voice which I heard from heaven spake unto me again, and said, Go and take the little book which is open in the hand of the angel which standeth upon the sea and upon the earth. And I [Apostle John] went unto the angel, and said unto him, Give me the little book. And he said unto me, take it, and eat it up; and it shall make thy belly bitter, but it shall be in thy mouth sweet as honey…Thou must prophesy again before many peoples, and nations, and tongues, and kings" (Revelation 10:8-11).

Thus, the Lord confirmed that my work, from Him, is eternal and has profound eternal implications. After the Rapture of the Body of Christ or the Church is taken out of the Earth before the **"Last Days"** of the Tribulation and Great Tribulation, God, through unprecedented measures, will continue to reach out to unbelievers because He wants none of us to perish **(John 3:16)**. Therefore, during these times, God said *"…it shall come to pass in the last days, says God, That I will pour out of My Spirit on all flesh; Your sons and your daughters shall prophesy, your young men shall see visions, your old men shall dream dreams [to share with others so that none should perish]" (Acts 2:17).*

He will fiercely reveal His truth to unbelievers and will provide safety, care, and protection to converted believers in Christ. He will relentlessly share **"The Gospel"** with all believers and unbelievers, to accomplish this, He will unleash the contents of the **"Big Book"** and the **"Little Book" (Revelation 10:8- 11),** which will bring about understanding and usher in His Light and Peace to believers as the books are prophesied to all peoples, nations, and tongues.

The Lord will allow His divinely sealed 144,000 Saints, the Jews who became believers in Christ after witnessing the Rapture. They are from the **"Twelve (12) Tribes of Israel,"** 12,0000 from each tribe, totaling **144,000** (Revelation 7:4-8), who will teach and aid believers and minister to unbelievers. These shall be rewarded in Heaven with white robes (Revelation 7:9). They are the redeemed from the Earth, standing before God's Throne in Heaven **(Revelation 14:3).**

And God will send His Two Witnesses **(Revelation 11:3)**, to prophesy for 1,260 days, dressed in clothed in sackcloth, preaching the Word of God and performing the wonders of the Lord in the sky. As well, according to ***Revelation 14:6***, the Lord will have an Angel flying, in the midst of Heaven, ***"…having the everlasting gospel [The Big Book…The Bible AND The Little Book] to preach unto them [all men] that dwell on the earth, and to every nation, and kindred, and tongue, and people."***

After **Lucifer** sinned and rebelled, God could have destroyed him or begun his eternal punishment, but He wanted all of His Creation to see Satan… the great dragon, that old serpent that he had become, for ourselves. Consequently, none of us will ever be able to say that God didn't reveal Satan's true nature…darkness, evil, chaotic, destroyer, hideous in appearance, a murderer **(taketh away eternal life)** … the father of lies, death, Hell, and the grave. He also reveals his cunning, blasphemous, and extremely rebellious ways through his followers.

Satan is responsible for every evil against God and you; His intent is to steal your eternal life, kill you and your joy in the Lord, and destroy your chance to receive God's free gift of eternal life. Satan's main agenda is to ensure that you will not accept Jesus Christ so that you will experience **Hellfire** for following and worshipping him, either knowingly or unknowingly **(by default)**. The Lord has warned you in His written Word in great detail about Satan and what is to come for humanity, but oh yeah, you are too busy with your daily life to read His Holy Word. Yet, God is still willing to forgive you and reach out to your heart, mind, and Soul within you… Pay attention!

Again, God didn't send someone to save you; He put off our Eternal Death, now called The Second Death, per His redemption plan, so that He could intervene and come save you, Himself!!! His Holy Word was seeded by the Father or conceived within Mary so that His Word/Jesus could come into the Earth in the form of a baby to save you and me from the Hellfires of eternal death. He gave us His only begotten Son (Jesus), with His Holy Spirit within Him, that He might die and be resurrected for the forgiveness of our sins… **Glory!**

God has provided His Prophets to get His Divine Word out to all who live on the Earth, so there is no doubt of the extent to which He has gone to save you, that you may have **no excuse** to use against Him **when it is your turn to stand before Him**. Again, God has gone to great lengths to save you from the eternal Second Death! Now, what are you going to do about your eternal life? This individual decision has absolutely nothing to do with your religion because this is solely about your **"Life"** and **"Death,"** which is between you and God alone.

The Lord led me to the scripture about the **"Little Book"** to show me the significance of the magnitude of this extraordinary, eternal work that He is revealing, through me, to save His Children from the eternal Second Death, is unprecedented. From the simplistic, layman to scientific or scholarly, He wants the entire world to know the truth regarding their Eternal History from His perspective as Satan's lies and deceptions become stronger during the end times and last days. These writings beget an understanding of Eternal Life and Eternal Death from God's perspective so that we might know that everything God has done through Jesus Christ is regarding giving us back His precious gift of Eternal Life, which has nothing to do with religion. However, your lifestyle choice must exemplify **repentance**, and you must exercise your freedom of choice and choose between Eternal Life through Christ or Eternal

Death through Satan to solidify where you will spend eternity.

The compilation of my volumes of work (since 1996) is the content of His **"Little Book,"** which chronologically-explains the essence of the Big Book... The Holy Bible. According to Bible Prophecy, both books explain your Eternal History and our eternal redemptive choice, and they must be preached to all peoples, nations, and tongues. And I reiterate, it has nothing to do with the **"business model" called religion;** this is about our life and death. According to scripture, during the end times and last days, both the Little Book and The Big Book MUST be preached throughout the entire Earth to all inhabitants. During these critical times, this book serves as a **"Last Call"** from Heaven to come to **repentance** because God's redemption plan will soon come to an end. The magnitude and gravity of realizing that my work of the Holy Spirit is prophesied in the Bible is incomprehensibly monumental to me!

Revelation 10:8-11 reveals the duality of the Little Book, describing it as *"bitter, but...sweet as honey."* It tastes sweet, like honey, in that it represents the awesome sweetness of our salvation through Jesus Christ, yet is bitter from the perspective that all unbelievers, who reject Christ, will experience Hellfire punishment and the permanent, Eternal Second Death or the Lake of Fire and Brimstone. The Second Death and the everlasting, unquenching flames of the Lake of Fire are enough to exponentially sour any stomach...Hmm. **YOUR CREATOR-GOD HAS GONE TO GREAT EXTENTS TO SAVE YOU AND ME... GLORY!**

A CLOSER LOOK AT LIFE AND DEATH

"Time" Belongs To God Alone

"To everything there is a season, and a time for every purpose under heaven..."
~ Ecclesiastes 3:1 BSB

By God's Grace, you are, undeservingly, allowed to participate in God's redemption process, which is designed so that the Natural Death of your body does not occur until a certain time that is determined by God alone. He has provided you and me with a Grace Period of **"Time"** or opportunity (a second chance) to ask for forgiveness (**repent**) of your sins, change your ways, or change your mind up until the death of your body occurs. I refer to this grace period as God's Divine Redemption Plan to save us from The Eternal Second Death through choice **(Deuteronomy 30:19)**. Therefore, **"Time"** is the element in God's redemption plan that takes us from the beginning of His plan (the creation of Adam and Eve) to the end, the resurrection of all humanity from the grave, and the execution of Satan's death penalty, the Lake of Fire and Brimstone or The Second Death.

Yet, **"Time"** is personal because, upon your death, it is said that your time is up and you are buried, but **"Time"** marches on according to God's purpose, alone. However, you can **avoid The Second Death** if you have the Indwelling of the Holy Spirit... Christ, within you, so that you will be resurrected back to Eternal Life with the Lord. Those who die without Christ are also resurrected to eternal life... your fate is sealed to experience both Hellfire and the Eternal Lake of Fire and Brimstone.

God's **"Time"** marks the exact juncture when the events on His Divine Calendar will take place on Earth and have eternal effects within His Universe. According to *Ecclesiastes 3:1-8, BSB,* there is a time for every purpose on Earth: ***To everything there is a season, and a time for every purpose under heaven: a time to be***

A CLOSER LOOK AT LIFE AND DEATH

born and a time to die, a time to plant and a time to uproot, a time to kill and a time to heal, a time to break down and a time to build, a time to weep and a time to laugh, a time to mourn and a time to dance, a time to cast away stones and a time to gather stones together, a time to embrace and a time to refrain from embracing, a time to search and a time to count as lost, a time to keep and a time to discard, a time to tear and a time to mend, a time to be silent and a time to speak, a time to love and a time to hate, a time for war and a time for peace."

 The Bible is evident in that **"Time"** is designed to give the fallen from Heaven, sinners, a second chance over time to be redeemed. God said that He would save us by sending a Messiah (Genesis 3:15); therefore, **"Time"** reflects this fact based on the birth intervention of Jesus Christ… the Perfect Son (Matthew 1:1), who came into the World and proved God's Holy Word to be true. "Time" is designated according to before the birth of Jesus, His advent into the world, and subsequently, His death. **"Time"** rules and governs our finite state of existence, here on Earth.

 We constantly keep up with time as we look down at our wristwatch, cell phone, or wall clock. We are always wondering… ***"What 'Time' is it?"*** We live by the hands of Time. However, Time and Death have replaced the infinity of life for us. Their finite elements have distorted our concept of living life forever, but the fact remains that our Spirits live forever, and so will our Human Bodies when Jesus Christ returns to restore the Earth and rule and reign.

 The seconds of **"Time"** accumulate into minutes, hours, days, weeks, months, and years, hence the idea of counting years, decades, and centuries, which yielded the invention of the calendar that, in fact, surrounds God and His Son (Himself in the Flesh). The Word's intervention into the world was visibly portrayed in Bethlehem and on the cross to die for our sins. The advent of Jesus into the world is the focal point of Eternal History, as we refer to His birth which is symbolized in our calendars as **"Before Christ"** came to Earth **(BC)** and **"After Christ,"** or His advent into the world **(AD). R**ecall that we learn about this in school. However, for official business and government purposes, most countries use the Gregorian Calendar to count years. This calendar was established by Pope Gregory XIII in 1577, using the abbreviations B.C. and A.D.

Today, the international standard designates years based on the Gregorian Calendar with a traditional calculation of years surrounding the time before and after Jesus was born, hence the **"A.D."** and **"B.C."** system. **"A.D."** stands for Anno Domini in Latin and means **"In the Year of Our Lord,"** as it refers specifically to the birth of Jesus Christ and onwards. Consequently, **"B.C."** stands for **"Before Christ,"** before the birth of Our Lord, Jesus Christ.

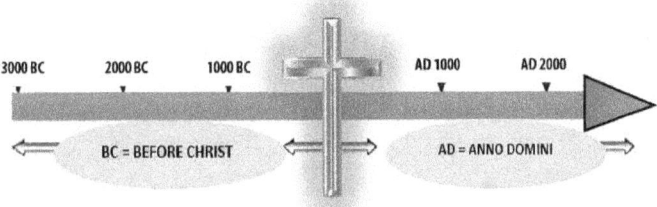

In English, it is common for **"A.D."** to precede the year, so that the translation of **"A.D. 2014"** would read **"In the year of our Lord 2014."** This is how we relay time according to Jesus, but since we have exiled God from our lives, we do not use these same rules of writing years anymore. Nevertheless, although we no longer say **"In the Year of Our Lord 2025,"** the rules of **"Time"** remain the same... all about Jesus Christ! Therefore, when you write or say any year, you are unknowingly saying "In the Year of our Lord" ... Hmm.

During the end times and last days, it will be a time, like we are living in now whereby: *"The nations [people] are angry, and Your [God's] wrath has come, And the time of the dead, that they should be judged [at the Last Judgment], And that You [God] should reward Your servants the prophets and the saints, And those who fear Your name, small and great, And should destroy those who destroy the earth" (Revelations 11:18). "And do this, understanding the present time: The hour has already come for you to wake up from your slumber, because our salvation is nearer now than when we first believed" (Romans 13:11).*

While we live on Earth, we have a calendar that we use to plan things and events, according, to ***Proverbs 19:12, BSB: "Many plans are in a man's heart, but the purpose of the LORD will prevail"*** and the Lord says in ***Psalms 33:10, NASB: "The LORD nullifies the plan of nations; He frustrates [confuses/delay/stop] the plans of peoples.*** Therefore, we must know that the Lord is always in control and we must follow God's End-Time Calendar of Events and timeline, according to His Divine Plan of Redemption in the Earth, per the following figure.

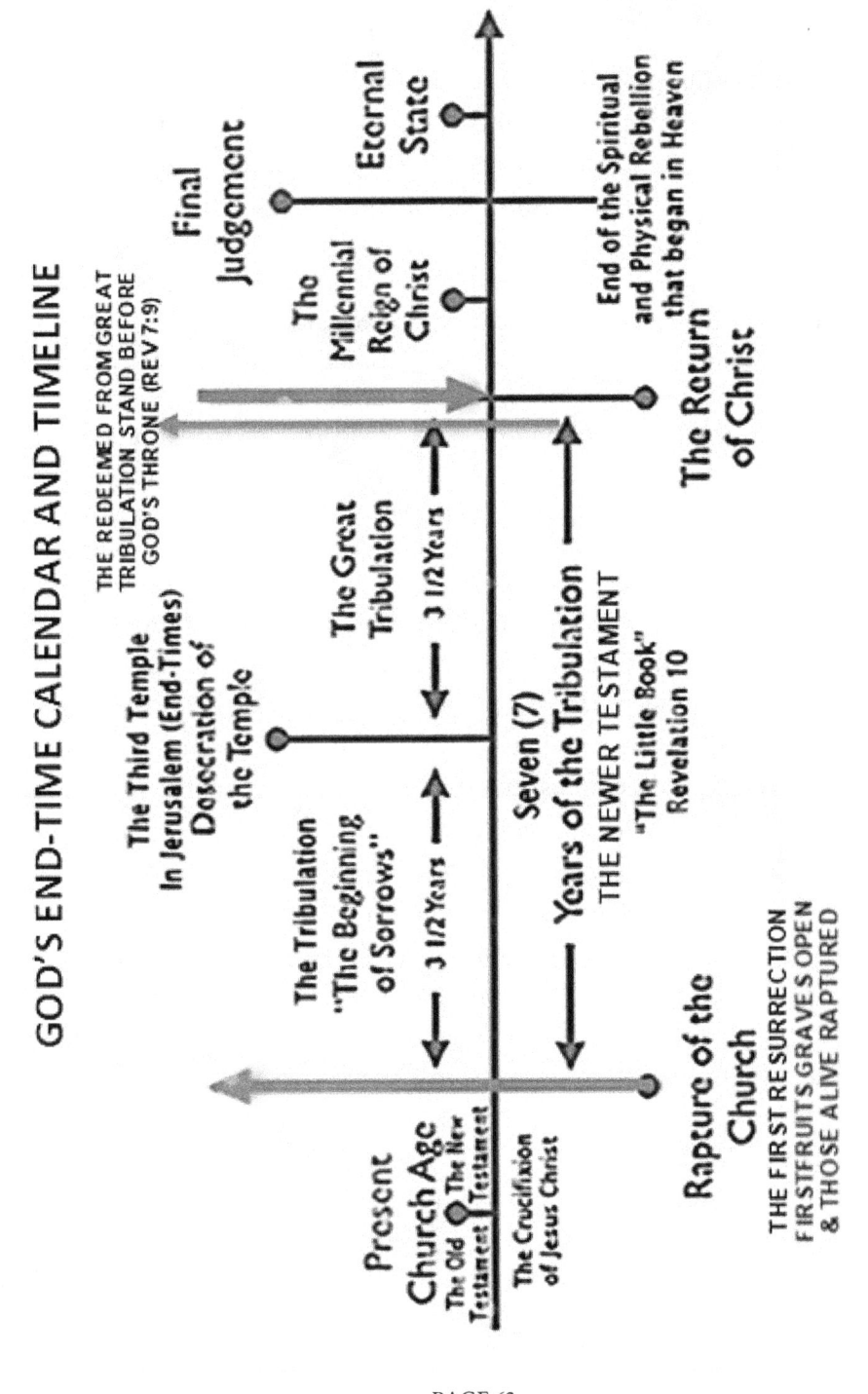

Returning Home

*"...your dead will live, LORD; their [our] bodies will rise
let those who dwell in the dust **wake up** and **shout for joy**"*
~ Isaiah 26:19 NIV

Jesus said: ***"And I also say to you that you are Peter, and on this rock, I will build My church, and the gates of Hades [Hell] shall not prevail against it" (Matthew 16:8).*** Therefore, all believers from all denominations, kindreds, and tongues from around the world are within the body of Christ, according to ***1 Corinthians 6:15, "...Do you not know that your bodies are members of Christ himself?"*** Believers are members of Christ's Spiritual Body, called the body of Christ or His Church, which is not specific to a church building or religious denomination. Although the Church has its place in our lives, we are instructed to fellowship with one another **(Hebrews 10:29).** Nevertheless, DO NOT allow anyone to deceive you into believing that attendance at a specific church or denomination is essential to your being saved.

"Christ-like" became known as the religion that we call Christianity; however, Christianity, nor any religion, can impact your birth **(life)** or prevent your Natural Death, which is to come. To be Christ-like is less about a church building or denomination affiliation and more about the intimacy of a personal relationship with Jesus Christ, who is the **"Head"** of His Church. **"The Rapture"** (Harpazo -Greek: to be caught up or taken away) is the juncture in our Eternal History when Christ will unite with us, His Church Body, from the Earth through Holy Matrimony. This will complete the form of Christ as a Divine Immortal Man that includes us within, and this reveals one of the purposes that the Rapture will fulfill, reuniting Christ, as the Head, of His Church to complete His Divine Body.

Therefore, according to the redemption plan, God has specific purposes for the Rapture. Another purpose is the **"First Resurrection,"** where our graves will open and the bodies (Spirit and Flesh) of believers with the Holy Spirit therein will be changed from mortal to an immortal **(Spiritual)** state, worthy of returning home to Heaven and prepared to see and receive the glorious, brilliant, bright light of your Heavenly Father. It begins with Jesus Christ returning to retrieve His Indwelling Holy Spirit within His Church Body from the Earth when He comes in the clouds at the Rapture to unite with His Church **(believers)**: *"And if I go and prepare a place for you [in Heaven], I will come back [to Earth] and take you to be with me [in Heaven] that you also may be where I am" (John 14:3)*.

To be Raptured into Heaven while alive, on Earth, means your body avoids going into your grave; instead, your body is changed to immortality, and you are immediately transferred to the spiritual realm. This is why it is said that Enoch and Elisha did not die; they were taken up or Raptured to Heaven; their bodies did not go into a grave. To be Raptured after death means that your body is raised or resurrected from your grave, then your body is changed to immortality, and you immediately appear before the Lord. The Rapture will occur in conjunction with the **"First Resurrection"** of the dead (Isaiah 26:19).

The Rapture and Resurrection are similar, but they are distinct and are defined by the timing of their occurrence. The Rapture is to be taken up to Heaven or downwards to Hell (more later), and the Resurrection is the act of being raised from one's grave. The first fruits are those who are first to be raised from their graves, in mass, and their bodies will be changed to immortal bodies, fit for living in Heaven and in the coming restored eternal Earth. At the Glorious appearance of the Lord in the clouds, the First Resurrection and the Rapture of the dead will occur just before those believers in Christ who are still alive are also raptured up to Heaven.

The Lord describes exactly how He will return to Earth in "the clouds" at the First Resurrection, which is conjoined with the Rapture, so that you will know how He will come, you will be prepared, and not deceived by false Christs that will appear during the end times and last days. He tells us in *1 Thessalonians 4:16-17*, *"For the Lord Himself will descend from heaven with a shout, with the voice of an archangel, and with the trumpet of God. And the dead in Christ will rise first [The First Resurrection]. Then we who are alive and remain shall be caught up together with them in the clouds to meet the Lord in the air. And thus we shall always be with the Lord."*

Furthermore, *Revelation 1:7* explains: *"Behold, he [Jesus] is coming with the clouds, and every eye will see him, even those who pierced him, and all tribes of the Earth will wail on account of him. Even so. Amen."* Now notice that the latter scripture says every eye will see Him, even those who pierced Him, who have been dead for thousands of years. This reveals the fact that those who are resurrected so that their Spirits are conjoined back with their body are raptured up to meet Him in the air.

At this moment in our Eternal History, all those who are NOT resurrected from their graves will conjoin with their Spirits from the caverns of Hell to restore sight and awareness to their body in the grave, purposefully so that those who will remain in their graves can see Him in the clouds (there are no clouds in Hell). Thus, all Spirit Life in Heaven and Hell will see Him. Satan, through his false Christs, will try to create this monumental event using lying signs and wonders, but not even he can produce the authenticity of this insurmountable supernatural event. The Lord warns you to see to it that you are not deceived: *"Watch out that no one deceives you!" Matthew 24:4*.

Some say that the word **"Rapture"** is not in the Bible; however, the word "Bible" is also not in the Bible, but we understand what is meant by each word. When Christ returns in the clouds, it will signify that Christ has prepared dwelling places for us in Heaven and that He is ready to provide us with new glorified human bodies made in His likeness and fit to dwell with the Lord forever. Christ's coming will show us that He is ready to take us back home to be reunited with Him. Are you ready?

Christ will come down from Heaven to take His Church (or those of us with His Holy Spirit within us) away from the Earth to attend our Glorious Wedding Ceremony and Wedding Reception Celebration with the Lord. We will unite with Christ through the **"Bond of Holy Matrimony**,' then we will feast with Him in celebration, in the realm of Heaven, our home. This is declared in ***Revelation 19:9, NLT: "Blessed are those who are invited to the wedding feast of the Lamb [Jesus Christ]." And he [the Angel speaking to John] added, "These are true words that come from God."*** Can't you feel the exhilaration?

This heavenly wedding of believers uniting with Jesus Christ, the true definition of marriage, which is why it is Holy and called Holy Matrimony. Our marriage union is representative of conjoining Christ with His Church together, or the two becoming one in Christ Jesus. God taught His chosen people, the Jews, the significance of Holy Matrimony so that the world might know its relevance to God's Eternal Kingdom. This fact is symbolized and represented throughout all wedding ceremonies. The wedding ceremony, the reception celebration, and the act of lovemaking, which completes the marriage, have eternal implications. The Groom lifting up his Bride to carry her over the threshold symbolizes the Rapture or the lifting up and taking away of Christ's Church from the Earth.

The Wedding Ceremony consists of the Service Officiant, standing at the Altar, representing God the Father, in Heaven, there to oversee the union of His Son... Jesus Christ uniting with His Church (Humanity), or those Raptured from the Earth. This union consists of one woman and one man, whereas the Groom represents Jesus Christ, and the bride or woman represents His collective

Church from the Earth...those who have God's Indwelling Holy Spirit residing within them. The ceremony continues with the Groom coming to stand before God at the Altar, ready to receive his Bride. The Groom stands on the right side of the altar, representing the right side of the Father or His righteousness, and then the bride comes down to stand on the left side, representing Christ's Bride or His collective Church. Together the two, stand before God's Holy Altar to recite their vows or promises unto God and to one another as they merge to become **"One Flesh."**

After the Wedding Ceremony, the Wedding Reception begins, symbolizing the celebration of the couple's reception into the Eternal Kingdom of God. Lastly, the couple must complete their marriage by consummating their union with sex, but first, the symbolism of the Rapture of the Church occurs as the **"Groom"** lifts up His **"Bride"** and carries her over the threshold. This monumental moment represents the removal, the lifting up and away from the Earth, or the Rapture of God's Holy Spirit that is within each believer's body within His Church. He will resurrect and remove all believers or His collective Church, both dead and alive, out of the Earth, thus transferring us from darkness into God's Holy Divine Light; or the transfer from Satan's Kingdom into the Eternal Kingdom of God... Hmm. I can't wait. God is Love! Therefore, the two will consummate or complete their holy marriage by retiring to the bedroom to intertwine in God's love, which merges the two into one flesh.

And you thought you were simply attending a wedding to witness the happy couple's union and to celebrate their blissfulness, but you did not realize that you were witnessing an eternal event that will actually take place when we return home to Heaven. Marriage was created, established, and ordained with a specific purpose. This sacred ceremony is our reunion with God and has universal significance. Wedding Ceremonies are purposefully designed to be symbolic of our heavenly union with Christ, which is soon to come. Again, are you ready?

Sex Is Worship

"Marriage is honorable among all, and [keep] the bed undefiled [sexually pure]; but fornicators [unholy marriages] and adulterers God will judge"
~ Hebrews 13:4

The word **"worship"** is derived from the Old English word weorð, meaning **"worthy" (worth + ship)** or worship, which is a **"condition of being worthy, dignity, glory, distinction, honor, renown."** However, in Heaven, worship is a mutual expression; just as we show our praise and love to the Lord before His Throne, from His vantage point, looking down upon His Holy Creation, He reciprocates His Divine Love for us deeper and more profoundly than we can ever imagine or comprehend. He takes pride in His Creation... His Creation of you, more specifically, He delights in the light of your glory before His Throne. You are worth everything to Him; He would sacrifice His Life for you: *"...I [Jesus] give myself as a holy sacrifice for them [you] so they [you] can be made holy by your [God's] truth" (John 17:19)*... Glory!

"Divine Worship" is manifested to humanity through a sexual experience within the holy bond of matrimony. Sex, when it occurs as God designed, established, and ordained, specifically between one man and one woman, is sacred worship to God, and it is His gift to us, declaring us holy and worthy to partake in the intimacy of two becoming one in holy worship before His Throne.

Marital sex is designed to consummate or to make a marriage complete. Normally, the act of lovemaking takes place in the sacredness of the married couple's bedroom or on their **"honeymoon,"** whereby consummation normally occurs in bed. This is a holy, private affair solely between you, your spouse, and God. In Biblical days and per our court system even today, upon marriage, the bride and groom must consummate their marriage with the intimacy of sex. Some old customs required witnessing the consummation, and others required that you let others know that the marriage had been consummated through sex. Some revered the blood-stained sheets as a cause for celebration when a woman's hymen is broken and blood seeps out onto the sheets to reveal and confirm the consummation of marriage. The Lord says: *"Marriage is honorable among all, and [keep] the bed undefiled [sexually pure]; but fornicators, [unholy marriages] and adulterers God will judge" (Hebrews 13:4).*

Now, I hope you understand the purpose of the marital union that God created and ordained, according to His redemption plan. It is my hope that you can understand why marriage unions, other than what God created and ordained, greatly upset Him, as evident by the destruction of Sodom and Gomorrah, and why He deems unholy unions as an abomination (detestable and unforgivable without changing behavior and **repentance**) before His Holy Face. However, if you have engaged in abominable behavior, you can **repent** and ask for and receive His forgiveness, right now, while there is still time (more later as the book series progresses).

Divine worship is manifested to humanity through a sexual experience within the holy bond of matrimony, whereby the husband and wife intimately share their bodies with each other while praying together, being humble, grateful, and praising God for who He is… the Creator of all. He wants us to *"…understand what the will of the Lord is. And…be filled with the Spirit, speaking to one another in psalms and hymns and spiritual songs, singing and making melody in your heart to the Lord, giving thanks always for all things to God the Father in the name of our Lord Jesus Christ, submitting to one another in the fear of God" (Ephesians 5:17-21).*

The couple should rejoice as they thank the Lord for their eternal union and eternal life through Christ Jesus. Praise and honor should be upon their lips, praising the Lord for their acceptance into the Kingdom of God through Holy Matrimony, while expressing their deep love and affection for Him through prayer, and also expressing passionate love for one another.

The holy, sacred act of lovemaking is designed to be spiritually meaningful and holy unto God; however, we have fallen for Satan's definition of sex, which is lust of the carnal body without the spiritual or godly component that is meant to be. It is the private, sacred spiritual component of love making that sustains a marriage, inside and outside of the bedroom, not the physical, lustful act of sex and the carnality of "bed hopping" that only defiles your body before God. Sex, when it occurs as God designed and ordained it, specifically between one man and one woman, is sacred worship unto God and is His gift to us. Our holy union through Christ declares us holy and worthy to partake in the intimacy of two becoming one in holy matrimony and worship before His Throne. The act of godly marital love making is the true definition of "having church" that makes you want to shout.

In the holy union of marriage, the husband provides a spiritual covering of protection, provision and leadership over the woman, as he is the head of the union and is directly accountable to God, according to *1 Corinthians 11:3, "But I want you to understand that the head of every man is Christ, the head of a wife is her husband, and the head of Christ is God."*

Our Blessed Hope

"Looking for the blessed hope and glorious appearing [in the clouds] of our great God and Savior Jesus Christ"
~ Titus 2:13

Our **"Blessed Hope"** of the Rapture will reward us with our new immortal bodies, whereby we will unite with Christ, which will occur just before God pours out His wrath on all unbelievers, particularly the Jews. They rejected Jesus Christ because they were not expecting their King to be born in a manger. Unfortunately, they didn't know that the plan, at that time, was for Jesus to ultimately come to defeat death **(which prevents eternal life)** by His resurrection to make eternal life possible for us again… **Glory!**

Jesus Christ will come back to remove His Church from the Earth or those who are filled with the embodiment of His Holy Spirit within them because ***"God hath not appointed us [His Church/believers in Christ] to wrath, but [we are called] to obtain salvation [redemption] by our Lord Jesus Christ" (1 Thessalonians 5:9).*** *The Lord will remove His Church before **"…the day of the LORD cometh, cruel both with wrath and fierce anger…" (Isaiah 13:9).*** He will pour out His extraordinarily fierce anger upon all unbelievers, not believers in Christ. While God's wrath is being poured out upon the Earth, believers in Christ, who were raptured up to Heaven, are told: ***"Go, my people, enter your rooms and shut your doors behind you. Hide yourselves a little while until the wrath has passed. For behold, the LORD is coming out of His dwelling to punish the inhabitants of the earth for their iniquity" (Isaiah 26:20-21).*** I humbly suggest that you take heed to God's warnings and make a decision regarding your eternal future so that you will not experience His wrath and Eternal Hellfire. Then you will reside in the safekeeping of the Lord for all eternity.

Therefore, the Rapture is a very real event set by God; it is not escapism, as some believe. God planned to save us because He desires our reunion with Him. Again, He is not angry at those of us who believe in Christ; He will not subject us to the suffering of the Tribulation and Great Tribulation *"...such as has not been since the beginning of the world until this time, no, nor ever shall be" (Matthew 24:21).* So, the Rapture is our reward because for those who are alive when it occurs, it eliminates us from experiencing death altogether. Those who remain alive at His coming in the clouds will be saved or Raptured from both Natural Death and The Second Death... **Glory!!** We should therefore be *"looking for the blessed hope and glorious appearing of our great God and Savior Jesus Christ" (Titus 2:13).* Anyway, why is God called a Savior if He is not going to save us from anything? You must come to know and understand the dichotomy of God's plan of salvation.

However, some ministers and others believe that the Church will go through the Tribulation because they refer to scriptures that mention "the Saints" during that period. For instance, **Revelation 6:9,** at the beginning of the Tribulation, as identified by the opening of seven (7) seals: *"I saw under the altar the souls of those who had been slain because of the word of God and the testimony they had maintained."* This confirms that mid and post-tribulation believers do not consider that many will become believers in Christ or Saints right after the Rapture takes place, as well as those who will be converted throughout the Tribulation and Great Tribulation.

However, no matter how you explain that believers in Christ are not appointed to go through the Tribulation period, die-hard believers remain very adamant that all of us must experience the horrors of God's wrath. They insist that this is our fate based on **Matthew 24:13,** *"But he who endures to the end shall be saved..."* This means that we all must endure until the end of our lives. So, then I ask, *"What about my ancestors, my grandparents and great-*

great-grandparents, etc., who were devout believers in Christ, "How will they endure the Tribulation, now that they are deceased? And *"What if I pass away before the Tribulation occurs, how will I endure until the end of it?"* So, again, I ask: *"Why is Jesus called a Savior if He is not going to save us from anything?"*

Most come to realize that there must be an alternate meaning to this scripture. The meaning correlates to enduring the darkness and chaos of Hell in this life until the end of your life. Furthermore, we must endure hard times, working to feed ourselves and our families; some must endure working two and three jobs, and some must endure homelessness, failure, and illness. Some endure caring for the sick and the dying, orphans, and widows. We must endure evil from various people in our lives…at work, at home, or anywhere, and from any source.

We, ultimately, must endure the death sentence (for some, it's two death sentences) that is always in the back of our minds, daily. The fact that you could die at any moment, leaving your children, significant others, friends, and family behind, as well as preparing for your final expenses, does take some real enduring to get through. We live and breathe with the fear of facing death with each breath. And we face the loss of loved ones, which is extremely difficult and heart-wrenching, and requires some "enduring" through the pain. If you come to the natural end of your life by overcoming your daily trials, hardships, stresses, tribulations, and challenges without committing the act of suicide. This means that you have endured this section in the Abyss of Hell on Earth to the end of your life.

Therefore, the only choice that you are required, by God, to make before you leave Earth, is whether you will believe in Jesus Christ or not for your Salvation. The latter is the only determining factor of your eternal future, which includes determining whether or not you are going through the Tribulation and whether you will reside in Heaven or Hell forever… that's it. Your **repentance**, belief, and trust in Jesus Christ is the only choice that will save you from facing, not one, but two death sentences and the penalties of Hellfire, and more specifically, the eternal, unquestionable Lake of Fire and Brimstone. It is up to you, no one can make this choice for you, only you will stand before King Jesus to give an account of your life...the lifestyle that you chose to live.

The Rapture or the lifting away of the Church (those filled with the Indwelling Holy Spirit or Christ) from the Earth, our "Blessed Hope," is the only thing that will save us from death and its Hellfire punishments. The Rapture will be both a very audible and visible event for everyone on the planet: *"Then will appear the sign of the Son of Man in heaven. And then all the peoples of the earth will mourn when they see the Son of Man coming on the clouds of heaven, with power and great glory. And He will send his angels with a loud trumpet call, and they will gather his elect from the four winds, from one end of the heavens to the other" (Matthew 24:30).*

No one will ever be able to deny hearing the prophesied global **"Trump of God"** announcing the glorious appearance of Christ, nor can any of us deny the Magnificence of His Power. There will be those who will be defiant and loyal to Satan for all eternity, who will plant doubt and explain away this monumental event. It is amazing how God shows us things that we see with our own eyes, like those who witnessed the death and resurrection of Christ, and still we fall for lies that the death of Christ never happened. After seeing the stone where Jesus was buried, rolled away, revealing that His Body was no longer there, some still fell for Satan's lies and his seeds of doubt. When will you stop falling?

At the Glorious appearance of the Lord…from that moment on, new Saints will emerge, some will be prosecuted, and others will, willingly, give their lives **(Martyrs)** after they realize God's Word to be true, yet again; no matter how Satan will use his elite's counter- narrative that UFOs and Aliens have taken away those who are unfit to enter his New Age of enlightenment or New World Order. However, the converted new Saints will be wholehearted believers in Jesus Christ forever. Especially, the Jews who rejected Jesus in the manger will finally recognize Jesus Christ as their true Messiah. In fact, **the Jews are the reason for the Tribulation/Great Tribulation** because when you reject Christ, you get the opposite... the Antichrist. And so it is that the Tribulation will occur at God's appointed time, and then their long-awaited false messiah will make his appearance.

Christ will come to retrieve His Holy Spirit from within the righteous dead **(believers),** which is the power within us that will resurrect each of us to Eternal Life, in the same manner Jesus was resurrected. This is also why Natural Death is a temporary state and is really a blessing in disguise, per His redemption plan. All graves will be opened as all men will be resurrected to reward or judgment... to determine who will experience the Second Death. This you can be sure will occur, surely as your Natural Death to come.

Then the righteous who remain alive at His coming will be given a new immortal body that is fit for Eternal Life: *"In a moment, in the twinkling of an eye... the dead shall be raised incorruptible, and we shall be changed [receive a new glorified body like Jesus received when He ascended into Heaven]" (1 Corinthians 15:52).* Christ's Holy Spirit is within every believer, on Earth, and is the only thing that is restraining or holding back the Hell that will come upon the Earth during the Tribulation and Great Tribulation: *"For this lawlessness [Satan's evilness] is already at work secretly [secret societies/the elite], and it [the Antichrist/Beast System] will remain secret until the one [The Holy Spirit] who is holding it*

[The Tribulation] back steps out of the way [or is removed from the earth]" (2 Thessalonians 2:7). This scripture also speaks of the secrecy of the elite and their secret societies who direct, control, and manage Satan's earthly government.

The elite are now moving us towards the realization of their planned New World Order or One-World Government and One-Religion Totalitarian Beast System that will unify the world, under the guise of Climate Change. Follow the money: Climate change has caused nations to allocate large budgets to handle their manufactured crisis. This crisis will eventually usher in the forced worship of Satan's image and his appointed Antichrist via a mandated Sunday Law. Due to the knowledge that the elite have gained from Satan, they have successfully discovered how to control the weather through programs like The High-Frequency Active Auroral Research Program **(HAARP)**, cloud seeding, weather ships, airplane storm navigation, etc.

The elite's goal is to control our weather in order to use catastrophes to bolster their Climate Change agenda that will unify the world to worship Satan, as mentioned above. They seek to own all land/farmland, real estate, control food, water reserves, etc., so that the world's population is completely dependent on them. In the coming digital age beast system, the elite have embarked on the use of the tokenization of all real-world tangible assets (real estate, land, trees, artwork, cash, bonds, water reserves, etc.) to represent digital ownership of physical and financial assets. These asset captures can then be digitally used within NFT(s) (non-fungible tokens) transactions and digital banking currencies, like cryptocurrencies. The goal is…they own everything, and we…the people, own nothing. This is Satan's precursor to control our ability to "buy or sell" unless we have the **"Mark,"** per **Revelation 13:17**.

However, to be very clear, let's sum up the Rapture and the revealing of the Antichrist: When the Lord comes to Rapture His

Church or removes His Holy Spirit which is designed to restrain us from doing evil, it will be God's appointed time for the Antichrist to reveal himself to the world: *"And you know what [The Holy Spirit] is now restraining him [The Antichrist], so that he may be revealed at the proper time" (2 Thessalonians 2:6).* Then and only then will God's wrath be poured out upon Satan and all unbelievers.

Therefore, for the mid-tribulation and post-tribulation Rapture believers, remember it is for God's specific purpose and will occur at His appointed time; He is always in complete control of His redemption plan. Only He gives the appointed time for Satan's Antichrist to make himself known in the Earth; no others have a say. Some may confuse the Rapture with the Resurrection; however, they are distinctly different, with their own specific purpose. The Lord has made it clear that once all believers who have received His Indwelling Holy Spirit (Christ) within them are removed from the earth (both dead and alive), then and only then will the Antichrist be revealed. This also confirms that God's Holy Spirit is removable based on your righteousness or unrighteousness.

Lastly, returning home to live Eternal Life with God is also the function of Natural Death, which is the transfer agent of our Spirit. Natural Death transfers our Spirit from the finite realm of Earth back to the infinite realm of Heaven, thus fulfilling **Deuteronomy 30:19** or God's promise to us through Jesus Christ to give us back our Eternal Life. Although Natural Death is devastating and we miss our loved ones, given what you have now learned about death, we can be thankful for our undeserved second chance to regain our Eternal Life, but it is at the expense of our death. We must understand that for those of us who believe in Christ, Natural Death is truly a blessing in disguise because according to the redemption plan, we will ALL be resurrected whereby we will get to see our loved ones again: *"…and behold, a great multitude that no one could number, from every nation, from all tribes and peoples and* *languages, standing before the throne [of God]" (Revelation 7:9, ESV).* Therefore, prepare!

But hold on, I was taken aback to learn about Satan's sinister plans to use Heaven **(sky)** to trick us into believing that the Rapture has occurred, to make believers think that we are left behind. As well, he will also stage other seemingly miraculous events through Project Blue Beam. Remember, when it comes to evaluating how end-time prophecy will materialize, we are considered **"Conspiracy Theorists."** However, we know that if the Bible prophecies it, it will certainly come to pass with 100% accuracy. So, now we can see how Project Blue Beam can be utilized to fulfill Bible Prophecy to display lying signs and wonders in the sky to deceive us.

A CLOSER LOOK AT LIFE AND DEATH

Warning!

"...every kind of sin and slander can be forgiven, but the blasphemy against the Spirit will not be forgiven"
~ Matthew 12:31

Take heed and understand that since the Truth of God's Words, flows directly from His Lips as Truth, He warns us that ***"...every kind of sin and slander can be forgiven, but the blasphemy against the Spirit [His "Word" as energy, in speech, writings or His word made visible in the flesh as Jesus] will not be forgiven" (Matthew 12:31).*** Blasphemy in one word is DISRESPECT of scared things. The act of showing your disrespect, the same as you would towards any human, but aimed directly at God. Also, mockery and asserting false claims against God seal your fate in Hell **(Gehenna)** and subsequently, the Lake of Fire and Brimstone.

Many have made public vile statements that blaspheme the Holy Spirit, for instance, calling the Titanic "unsinkable." And we know how that turned out… God replied. Now, you know the real reason that the ship sank. The Roman Catholic Church claims to represent Jesus Christ or God on Earth. Is this biblical, or even going to the Catholic Church to confess your sins to them and ask them for forgiveness instead of Jesus? Cardinal Sarto, Pope Pius X, said: ***"The Pope represents Jesus Christ Himself…,"*** and in 1302 Pope Boniface, stated the following in a letter to the Catholic Church: ***"Furthermore, we declare, we proclaim, we define that it is absolutely necessary for salvation that every human creature be subject to the Roman Pontiff."***

Therefore, through their Popes, the Roman Catholic Church has also asserted itself as Vicarius Christi or **"Vicar of Christ."** In the Greek language, Vicar means Anti (Strong #473). In Latin, it means deputy, agent, or substitute for Jesus Christ. Therefore, according to their own statements above, the Roman Catholic Popes have asserted:

Pope = Christ (on Earth) = Vicar = Substitute (Latin) = Anti (Greek) = Are they calling themselves the Antichrist, what do you think?

There is no substitute for Christ in the Universe! According to *1 John 2:18: "…As you have heard that the Antichrist is coming, even now many antichrists have come."* Therefore, there have always been Antichrists and Antichrist organizations on Earth. Bible prophecy is designed to be played out on the stage of planet Earth by those who reside there, so who will be the global Antichrist and False Prophet during the end-time prophecy according to Revelation 13:15? Will it be the Roman Catholic Church that, through its Popes, claims to be Jesus Christ, on Earth, which is a claim that is contrary to the Bible? More on this subject as the book series progresses.

Also, John Lennon stated that the Beatles were **"more popular than Jesus,"** which is to say that their music has more acceptance with the world population than Jesus, who is God's Holy Word that made everything that was made…WOW! So now, we know Mr. Lennon's eternal fate (without **repentance**) because trespassers of God's Word, in any form… speech, writing, or actions, will never be forgiven **(God's words, not mine)**.

As of late, the Golden Globe Awards that aired on January 5, 2025, were scripted to take direct aim at God. The host introduced a **"Tally Board"** that tallied who the celebrity winners thanked during their acceptance speeches:

CAST & CREW – 11 | MOM – 3 | GOD – 0

The host read the tallies with a resounding smile. It is reported that it was approximately 48 hours to a few days later, the most apocalyptic Wildfires began in Los Angeles, California; the most destructive fire in history... a Coincidence or what do you think?

However, one of the most abominable and blasphemous acts in our modern-day society is the duality of the Bible. As you know, most of us study the Word of God using the **"King James Bible."** However, the LGBT+ community has come up with its own bible, called the **"Queen James Bible."** I have no words for the utter depth of Satan and his followers' ungodliness and blasphemous mindset and behavior.... Oh, but surely Hell awaits! Speech or actions that disrespect, defy, and mock God will NOT be tolerated!

Man... God's Masterpiece

"What is man that you [God] are mindful of him, and the son of man [Jesus] that you visit him?"
~ Psalms 8:4

Since **Genesis 1:1 (NIV)** states: **"In the beginning, God created the heavens and the earth,"** and **2 Peter 3:5,** states **"...that by the word of God the heavens were of old, and the earth standing out of water and in the water...;"** and lastly consider, **Proverbs 8:23 NKJV, "I [God] have been established from everlasting, From the beginning, before there was ever an earth."** These scriptures confirm that Heaven was created first and is our home, long before land mass was ever formed on Earth. However, the Lord desired to create His Paradise on Earth, and a new life form made of both Spirit and Flesh... Man, God's Masterpiece: **But there is a spirit in man, And the breath of the Almighty [God] gives him understanding" (Job 32:8).** And for the purpose of redemption, your Spirit will either reflect righteousness or unrighteousness, which will ultimately determine your eternal future of Heaven or Hell.

Again, because of our sin and rebelliousness, we fell and became unworthy of the Light of the Holy Presence of God, so the Psalmist, in **Psalms 8:4-8, wrote of his wonder, and of course Satan wonders: "What is man that you [God] are mindful of him, and the son of man [Jesus] that you visit him? [Answer: Our fallen Spirit's Redemption is provided through the vessel of the "Body of Man" ...Glory!] For you have made him [Jesus] a little lower than the angels, and you [God] have crowned him with glory and honor. You have made him to have dominion over the works of your hands; you [Holy Father] have put all things under his feet, all sheep and oxen, even the beasts of the field, the birds of the air, and the fish of the sea that pass through the paths of the seas."**

Therefore, humanity is God's Masterpiece (remember this statement).

In a coming volume, we will explore God's original plan for the creation of Earth and the eternity of the vessel of Man, in comparison to changes that He made to Earth and Man in order to carry out our redemption. However, for now, just know that our Creator-God originally designed the human body to be an eternal vessel to hold our heavenly Spirits as we dwell in the Earth with the Lord forever, but then sin occurred; therefore, His original plan changed; we will explore both plans.

From the creation of Heaven and the laying of the foundation of Earth before land was called forth, the Lord desires to dwell in the Earth with man forever. However, His dwelling on the Earth has been delayed in order to allow time for His redemption plan to be complete. Then He will return to Earth to rule and reign as King of Kings (to rule over all those who call themselves King) and Lord of Lords (to rule over all those who call themselves Lord). He will dwell with man in the restored earth: **"God's dwelling place is now among the people [on Earth]" (Rev 21:3 NIV).** Therefore, God repurposed the Earth and Man for the purpose of redemption,

And the King, the Supreme Judge of all Creation...Jesus Christ will judge Humanity...each one of us, and He will judge the Nations: *"In those days and at that time, when I restore the fortunes of Judah and Jerusalem, I will gather all nations and bring them down to the Valley of Jehoshaphat. There I will put them [the Nations] on trial for what they did to my inheritance, my people Israel, because they [kings/rulers] scattered my people among the nations and divided up my land..." (Joel 3:1-2, NIV).*

[Side Note]: Ironically, we are on the precipice, in Earth's Eternal History, where dividing up God's land is front and center as never before. With the recent Hamas-Israel War that began on October 7, 2023, with devastating destruction in Gaza, President

Donald Trump's announcement (February 6, 2025), during President Benjamin Netanyahu's visit to the Whitehouse, stated that the United States will own or "take over" the Gaza Strip and rebuild it. President Trump seeks to remove the Palestinians from the region and is actively recruiting Arab countries to take in two million new residents, but his request was met with a resounding NO!

President Trump declares that his Gaza solution will bring peace and security to Israel. **"The Abraham Accords"** is a peace agreement that was introduced and signed on September 15, 2020, in Washington, DC. This agreement that many nations are now signing sets the theme for **"Peace and Safety"** between Israel, its Arab neighbors and the world, according to the Abraham Accords Declaration: *"We, the undersigned, recognize the importance of maintaining and strengthening **PEACE** in the Middle East and around the world based on mutual understanding and coexistence, as well as respect for human dignity and freedom, including religious freedom."*

1 Thessalonians 5:33 tells us, ***"For when they say, "PEACE AND SAFETY!" then sudden destruction comes upon them, as labor pains upon a pregnant woman."*** This scripture refers to officials just simply "saying it," or merely talking about peace and safety with Israel, which means that the Rapture is at hand, occurring just before "The Day of the Lord," when the sudden destruction of God's wrath is poured out on ALL unbelievers... Hmm.

However, with other countries refusing to take Gazan refugees, naturally, leaders will revert to discussing a **"Two-State"** solution, emphasizing dividing up God's land. Bible prophecy states that there will eventually be a 7-year covenant signed between Israel and the Antichrist (not inferring to President Donald Trump), reflecting the agreement of land division. As well, the Third Temple will be built whereby the Antichrist will enter and declare himself as God: *"For one week [7 years] this foreigner [Antichrist] will make a firm agreement with many people [and Nations], and halfway through this week [7 years], he [the Antichrist] will end all sacrifices and offerings. Then the "Horrible Thing" [Satan's Antichrist or his image enters the Temple and declares Satan as god] that causes destruction will be put there. And it will stay there until the time God has decided to destroy this one who [defiles and] destroys [the Temple]" (Daniel 9:27, CEV).* [end]

Now, as I was saying regarding judging the Nations: When *Jesus = God in the Flesh*, comes back to Earth as Immortal Flesh, He will judge the Nations, and subsequently, there will be Nations of believers in the restored Earth and *"The nations will walk by its [God's] light, and the kings of the earth will bring their splendor into it. On no day will its gates [New Jerusalem] ever be shut, for there will be no night there. The glory and honor of the nations will be brought into it [the Holy Light of the Lord]. Nothing impure will ever enter it, nor will anyone who does what is shameful or deceitful, but only those whose names are written in the Lamb's book of life" (Revelation 21:24-27, NIV).*

God will dwell with man in the restored earth: *"God's dwelling place is now among the people [on Earth]" (Revelation 21:3, NIV).* Therefore, God repurposed the Earth and Man for the purpose of our redemption, more on this later. According to your choice and your lifestyle, will your name be found in the Lamb's Book of Life? This choice is yours to make, right now, while there is still time.

Is Your Soul for Sale or Filled with the Holy Spirit?

*"All these things [in the world] I [Satan] will give You
if You [Jesus] will fall down and worship me"*
~ Matthew 4:9

Please know that Satan will take your Soul or inhabit it by any means necessary, so that you will worship him. He will use you, against you, through your sinful thoughts, attitude, compulsive behavior, and your belief system. In addition, he will cause your reactions in situations and circumstances to lead to conflict that may cause destruction and death.

The former Light Bearer will offer you the world like he did Jesus: *"...the devil [Satan] took Him [Jesus] up on an exceedingly high mountain and showed Him all the kingdoms of the world and their glory. And Satan said to Jesus: "All these things [in the world] I [Satan] will give You if You [Jesus] will fall down and worship me" (Matthew 4:8-9)*. What was Jesus' reply? Read Matthew 4:10, to find out. However, note that you cannot offer someone something that you don't own, meaning that Satan could not offer Jesus "the kingdoms of the world," if they were not his to offer, right? Nevertheless, the latter scripture confirms that the Former Light Bearer is truly the ruler over this fallen Earth and that he has an insatiable desire to be worshipped.

Satan uses this same approach often, whereby he will have one of his agents approach you to offer you the desires of your heart, like fame, material things, status: **"The heart [of man] is deceitful above all things, And desperately wicked**...I, the Lord, search the heart, I test the mind, Even to give every man according to his ways, According to the fruit of his doings" (Jerimiah 17:9-10). So, the old saying follow your heart requires rethinking... Hmm. And of course, the power they seek is substantiated by money: *"For the love of money is a root of all kinds of evil..." (1Timothy 6:10, NKJV)*. It is the **"love of money"** that Satan uses to lead our hearts to insatiable greed followed by corruption; however, to obtain it, his agents will require that you deny Jesus Christ first. This demand will be put to your ears, and your reply to them is completely up to you at this critical point. And although it's your choice, just be aware of the eternal consequences of each of your two choices.

Since we established earlier that Lucifer was over music and performance or entertainment in Heaven (more later), isn't it ironic that his agents run Hollywood/Bollywood or the movie and music industry around the world? It is the entertainment industry where **"Soul"** propositions are more prevalent. Gospel singer, Tye Tribbett, exposes the Gospel Music industry, saying that ***"God didn't establish Gospel Music,"*** search for his testimony on YouTube.

And many other entertainers have come forth to expose their industry, see ***"Over 70 Black Male Entertainers That Said "Yes" To The Dress And Made It To The Top"*** on YouTube, featuring Dave Chappelle, in an interview with Oprah discussing the industry's push for him, as well as other men to dress up as women. Also, former Christian singer, Katy Perry, admitted to selling her Soul for the betterment of her career, view: ***"Katy Perry Admits to Selling Her Soul,"*** and singer Bob Dylan's admission to making a bargain with the "chief commander in this Earth and in the world that we can't see," ***"Bob Dylan – Sold his Soul."*** Look up these titles on YouTube.

Once you deny Jesus Christ, due to Satan's angelic abilities and human agents, he will give you opportunities to advance you to the perception of success. But it will be only a temporary gain because your Life on Earth is temporary. Your death is certain, and you cannot take your material gains with you. Also, be aware that the moment you sell your Soul, just like the moment that you confess your sins and express your belief that Jesus is Lord and that God raised Him from the dead, is recorded in the library books of

Heaven. This way, when you stand before the Lord, you cannot deny the why, when, and where you made your decision. So, if you have used your Soul as a bargaining chip to get your desires or **"sold your Soul,"** you can take this opportunity to **repent**, right now, and ask Christ to come live within you. Then you will receive the Lord's forgiveness of your sins and be destined to return to Eternal Life with your Heavenly Father.

However, if you have not compromised your Soul, but you still are an unbeliever, it would be wise for you to examine what you believe regarding your life, death, and eternal future before your certain date with death. Consider choosing Jesus Christ now, while redemption is still available upon the Earth.

God's Presence Is Everything!
"For as the body without the spirit —is dead"
~ *James 2:26*

God alone is Heaven; His Divine Holy Presence is what makes Heaven... Heaven! Therefore, Heaven is wherever God is...His Throne, or His Holy Spirit. Presence, by definition, means to exist where His Throne and/or His Holy Spirit are located. This is an especially important key point because it defines our location within all three realms of our Universe... Heaven, Hell, and Earth, based on our holiness, unholiness, or need for redemption.

Presence means that you are where a person or Spirit exists or is located; you are in a particular place where they are. Our heart's desire should be to be in the Presence of the Lord, like the Angel Gabriel who identified himself to Zacharias, saying, *"...I am Gabriel, which stand in the Presence of God..." (Luke 16:18).*

The Father's Divine Human Immortal Presence manifested in the visible world, in the Garden of Eden, when He created Humanity, and manifested in His written Word... The Holy Bible as well as in the physical body of Jesus. The Presence of God's Holy Divine Spirit within Jesus, at the command of God, resurrected the body of Jesus, which conjoined to the Eternal Spirit of Christ (The Indwelling Holy Spirit) to make up the totality of the "Perfect Son," so that *"...whosoever believeth in him should not perish but have everlasting life" (John 3:16).* *"For as the body without the spirit —is dead]" (James 2:26).*

Our Life, created and sustained by God's Holy Spirit, is the most precious gift ever given! Since God is Life, He created us to eternally live in His Presence and without His Holy Divine Presence... His Holy Spirit, we are eternally dead in the Lake of Fire: *"For as the body without the [Indwelling Holy] spirit [Christ] —is dead [and your body and Spirit will experience*

Hellfire]" (James 2:26).

However, before our fall from grace, we stood before His Throne, giving Him thanks, praise, and adoration for who He is… our Creator. This precious act of holy worship before His Throne is in reverence to His Holiness, Truth, Goodness, and Love, on Earth, many of us pray and thank God for what we have… houses, cars, or material things- but in Heaven, we had no material things, so our focus was only on the Lord. We thanked Him for being who He is and for our Eternal Life; something we should continue to do. We must: *"Enter into His gates [by faith and through prayer] with thanksgiving, And into His courts with praise. Be thankful to Him, and bless His name. For the Lord is good; His mercy is everlasting, And His truth endures to all generation's [forever]" (Psalms 100:4-5).*

"For Christ has not entered [a Temple] the holy places made with [human] hands, which are copies of the true [Temple of God], but [Christ entered] into heaven itself, now to appear in the presence of God for us [humans made of fallen Spirit and flesh]" (Hebrews 9:24).

In **Psalms 42:2**, the Psalmist wrote: *"My soul thirsts for God, for the living God. When shall I come and appear before God?"* Jesus Christ came to Earth as a matter of our eternal life and eternal death (Deuteronomy 30:19), not based on man-made religious denominations. For this reason, as believers in Christ, we look forward to seeing our Heavenly Father again soon; to live with Him forevermore… **Glory!**

The Holy Throne of God

"Thus says the LORD: 'Heaven is My Throne and Earth is My footstool'"
~ Isaiah 66:1

All of Heaven is God's Throne that sits to the far North, ***"On the farthest sides of the north" (Isaiah 14:13).*** All of His Creation looks up to Him in the Magnificence of His Divine Glory. His northern location also establishes and defines our compass of direction… North, South, East, and West.

The Apostle John describes the glorious sight of God's Throne, ***"Behold, a door was opened in Heaven: and the first voice which I heard was as it were of a trumpet talking with me, which said, come up hither, and I will shew thee things which must be hereafter. And immediately I was in the Spirit: behold, a throne was set in Heaven, and one sat on the Throne. And he sat to look upon like a jasper and a sardine stone: and there was a rainbow round about the Throne, in sight like an emerald. And round about the Throne were four and twenty seats: and upon the seats, I saw four and twenty elders sitting, clothed in white raiment; and they had on their head's crowns of gold…And before the Throne, there was a sea of glass like crystal: amid the Throne, and round about the Throne, were four beasts full of eyes before and behind" (Revelation 4:1-6).***

"His head and his hairs were white like wool, as white as snow; and his eyes were as a flame of fire; And his feet like unto fine brass, as if they burned in a furnace; and his voice as the sound of many glasses of water" (Revelation 1:14). And Ezekiel 1:26, describes his vision of God's Divine Glory, ***"And above the firmament that was over their heads was the likeness of a throne, as the appearance of a sapphire stone: and upon the likeness of the Throne was the likeness as the appearance of a man above***

upon it."

Again, God's Spirit exists in a human-looking form; subsequently, the body is patterned after this likeness. *"And I saw the color of amber, as the appearance of fire round about within it, from the appearance of his loins even upward. From the appearance of his loins even downward, I saw as it were the appearance of fire, and it had brightness roundabout. As the bow's appearance, this was the appearance of the likeness of the glory of the LORD" (Ezekiel 1:26-28).*

Enoch, *"the seventh from Adam" (Jude 1:14),* Noah's great-grandson, also described his visit to the Lord's Throne room: *"And I observed and saw inside it a lofty throne—its appearance was like crystal and its wheels like the shining sun, and there was the vision of cherubim, and from beneath the Throne were issuing streams of flaming Fire. It wasn't easy to look at it. And the Great Glory was sitting upon it—as for his gown, which was shining more brightly whiter than any snow. None of the angels could come in and see the face of the Excellent and the Glorious One, and no one of the flesh could see him— the flaming Fire was round about him, and a great fire stood before him.*

No one could come near him from among those that surrounded the tens of millions (that stood) before him. He needed no council, but the holiest ones near him neither go far away at night nor move away from him. Until then, I was prostrate on my face, covered and trembling. And the Lord called me with his mouth and said, "Come near to me, Enoch, and to my holy Word." And he lifted me and brought me near the gate, but I continued to look down with my face…" (1 Enoch 14:18-25).

Although many question the validity of the Book of Enoch and other scripture-related books outside of the King James version of the Bible, during my research, I found that you must follow Truth wherever Truth leads you. Even though some books were not included in the King James Cannon, these books serve to fill in missing pieces of the puzzle of our Eternal History. I found that many of these books align with the King James Bible, and therefore, cannot be denied as Truth. **[Side Note]:** Some ministers instruct you to only study and use the King James Bible, and they tell you not to believe or read anything else. From my research, I conclude that it is Satan's goal to suppress the truth about himself and your eternal consequences, which the Book of Enoch explains in detail.

Now, you can understand that the truth about Hell has been replaced with "prosperity preaching." However, as you study, you must pray and ask to be led by the Holy Spirit because *"…when He, the Spirit of truth, has come, He will guide you into all truth" (John 16:13, NKJV).* Therefore, if a passage from the Book of Enoch, The First and Second Books of Adam and Eve, and other books fits a piece of the puzzle that explains our eternal past, life, death, and our eternal future, why not include it? Unless there is something to hide, like the truth. Only allow the Holy Spirit to lead and guide you! **[end]**

God's Majestic Voice: Surprisingly, many of us do not realize that we hear the majestic voice of the Lord during thunderstorms: *"At this also my heart trembleth and is moved out of his place. Hear the noise of his voice attentively and the sound that goeth out of his mouth. He directeth it under the whole Heaven and his lightning unto the ends of the earth. And after it a voice roareth: he thundereth with the voice of his excellency, and he will not stay [does not restrain] them when his voice is heard. God thundereth marvelously with his voice; great things doeth he, which we cannot comprehend" (Job 37:1-5).*

Also, **Psalms 18:13, NIV** says, *"The LORD thundered from heaven; the Highest voice resounded."* I am certain that a strong thunderbolt or the might of His voice has jolted your heart to tremble in terrifying fear. There is no denying God, even atheists and agnostics cannot deny their dependence on Him for every breath of His air that we take, or we _ _ _, right?

The Good News that Reverberated Around the World

"And now we are here to bring you this Good News The promise was made to our ancestors, and God has now fulfilled it for us...by raising Jesus. This is what the second psalm says about Jesus: 'You are my Son... For God had promised to raise him [Jesus] from the dead, not leaving him to rot in the grave"
~ Acts 13:32-34

Some try to deny it, but everyone knows God because His Word tells us: **"...it is written, As I live, saith the Lord, every knee shall bow to me, and every tongue shall confess to God" (Romans 14:11).** Therefore, the word "every," means everyone on the planet, all of God's Creation in every realm of the Universe, including yourself, me, Satan, and all believers, and unbelievers. All will confess, with their mouths, unto God. But what everyone does NOT know is **"The Good News"** of God's redemption plan whereby the birth, death, resurrection, and Christ's ascension into Heaven opened Heaven back up to us (the fallen), again... giving us back our eternal life which saves us from an Eternal Second Death. It is God's Holy Spirit within Jesus that raised Him from the dead, as He will someday raise you.

This absolutely, phenomenal Good News is called **"The Gospel"** which shows us that God has fulfilled His promise to us and that we can now follow Jesus Christ's example to retrieve our eternal Life with the Lord: **"And this gospel of the kingdom will be preached in all the world as a witness to all the nations, and then the end [of God's Redemption Plan] will come" (Matthew 24:14).** There aren't enough adjectives to describe this historic, phenomenal, extraordinary, unbelievable, supernatural event that defeated our common enemy... Death. None of my relatives or friends has ever returned from the grave. What about yours? Everyone in this world dies, but Jesus is the only one who overcame

A CLOSER LOOK AT LIFE AND DEATH

death and ascended into Heaven. This is why ***John 16:33 says: "I [Jesus, by my resurrection] have overcome the world [where everyone dies]."***

Jesus' resurrection was the talk of the town and eventually the world. This great news has been preached about and written about; archeological findings give credence to it, and landmarks and even the constellations in the sky attest to the Glory of this Good News. This news was written by different prophets who lived at various times in history for thousands of years. God shares His plan, pinpoint-accurate prophecies, and stories about the sinners who lived during biblical times, with us in the oldest and longest bestselling book on the planet... The Bible.

As time drew near for Jesus to fulfill God's prophecy to avail us eternal life by His death, He felt overwhelmingly heavily laden, and ***"...he fell with his face to the ground and prayed, "My Father, if it is possible, may this cup be taken from me. Yet not as I will, but as you will" (Matthew 26:39).*** Imagine knowing that you have to die for the sins of the world, and you know that the time has come for you to face death, how would you feel? But of course, neither you nor I have ever experienced such a monumental task of enormous pressure.

At this juncture, Jesus had freedom of choice and could have refused to die for our sins, but He said let God's will be done, not His will. We could never comprehend or understand dying for the sins of each one of us, even those who hate *God = Jesus*, but Jesus did succumb to God's will, even for those who do not believe in Him, so they might have the opportunity, one day, to change their minds and their ways. How overtly powerful is that?

As Jesus Christ ate with His disciples at what is called the "Last Supper," He told them of things to come, encouraged them, prayed for them, and washed their feet. He also warned and taught them about dealing with their (our) enemy... Satan, or fallen Spirits within a body, as well as demonic, unclean spirits. Then *"...He [Jesus] looked up towards Heaven and prayed: "Father, the time has come. Glorify your Son, that your Son may glorify you. For you granted him [the Son] authority over all people that he might give eternal life to all those you have given him [through birth into the Earth to participate in the redemption process].*

Now this is eternal life, that they may know you, the only true God, and Jesus Christ, whom you have sent [as the Word made flesh]. I have brought you glory on earth by completing the work you gave me to do. And now, Father glorify me [accept me into your Divine Light, in human form, made from the darkness of the dust of the fallen Earth] in your presence with the glory I had with you [as your spoken Word] before the world began" (John 17:1-5). **[Side Note]:** As Jesus is praying to God, you are witnessing His human praying to the Heavenly Father, the same as we all must communicate with our Creator. **[end]**

"...The god of this age has blinded the minds of the unbelievers to keep them from seeing the light of the gospel of the glory of Christ, who is the image of God" (2 Corinthians 4:4). Therefore, the Roman soldiers, who crucified Jesus, mocked and lashed Him as they paraded Him through the streets carrying a heavy cross, representing the insurmountable weight of the sins of the world on His shoulders. And on His head was a crown of thorns representing all the thorns and thistles of our burdens and tribulations that we endure... everyone in the entire world! I know that my burdens are sometimes very heavy, even unbearable, so I can't imagine Jesus carrying and feeling the weight of my burdens, and yours too, let alone everyone's burdens who was ever born on Earth. Can you dare envision the gravity of that moment? **GOD HAS WENT TO GREAT EXTENTS TO SAVE YOU AND ME!**

The resurrection of Christ broke the stronghold that the former Light Bearer had over our eternal lives through death, is now gone.

Therefore, we no longer have to fear death because we know God's plan has visibly defeated death through the man (Jesus) on the cross and by His resurrection (Christ). Jesus remained dead for three days, then returned to Earth to retrieve His same body that housed God's same Holy Spirit. God accomplished the resurrection of Jesus by activating His Holy Spirit within Him to raise His body to eternal life.

[Side Note]: The word "activating" regarding humans causes me to think about the Antichrist's coming worldwide Beast System because, through this system, the Antichrist will exercise this kind of strict control over all of us as metal implants within us will allow us to be connectable and connected to his World Wide Web so that he can activate and deactivate us at will, and our money will be as well. The end of fiat money or cash is our last freedom to fall, whereby a cashless society will usher in true total population control. **[end]**

Again, *1 Timothy 3:16*, confirms that Jesus is God: ***"And without controversy great is the mystery of godliness: God was manifest in the flesh, justified in the Spirit, seen of angels, preached unto the Gentiles [non-Jews], believed on in the world, received up into glory."*** Therefore, again, God did not send someone to Earth to save us from eternal death. He, by virtue of His Word, came in the Flesh to save us Himself... **Glory!**

Also, know this: ***"In the past God spoke to our ancestors through the prophets at many times and in various ways, but in these last days he has spoken to us by his Son [Jesus], whom he appointed heir of all things, and through whom also he [The Word/Jesus] made the universe"*** *(Hebrews 1:1-2)*. And, ***"Do not forget to show hospitality to strangers, for by so doing some people have shown hospitality to [God's] angels without knowing it"*** *(Hebrews 13:2, NIV)*.

Also, notice that as always, God kept His Holy Word: ***"For God had promised [the ancestors] to raise him [Jesus] from the dead, not leaving him to rot in the grave" (Acts 13:34),*** and He certainly DID NOT leave Jesus to rot in the grave. He has risen… **Glory!**

"Behold, I stand at the door and knock. If anyone hears my voice and opens the door, I will come in to him and eat with him, and he with me" (Revelation 3:20, ESV). The most amazing part of this verse is the location of the doorknob—it's on the inside of you… Your Temple. Christ, in His infinite love and respect for our free will, does not break the door down. He stands patiently and knocks, waiting for an invitation from you. His knock is not always loud; sometimes it's a gentle whisper in a moment of quiet, a nudge from a friend, or a longing in our spirit. However, hearing His voice is the first step, but the act of opening the door is a conscious choice, a personal decision to welcome Him into every room of your life.

A CLOSER LOOK AT LIFE AND DEATH

Jesus... The First Human to Ever Enter Into Heaven

"No one [human] has ever gone into heaven except the one who came from heaven—the Son of Man"
~ John 3:13 NIV

Jesus Christ is the first human to be resurrected with both His fallen Body and Spirit. Then, forty (40) days later, He ascended into the eternal realm of Heaven. Can you imagine the shock, and yet the glory of those who actually saw Him after His resurrection, and then witnessed His body's ascension into Heaven? **Glory!** Only a few chosen people beheld it, and they were never the same. This news was so extraordinary that they had to tell everyone they knew, even strangers, and the entire world about **"The Good News!"**

Therefore, our ultimate two eternal choices, according to **Deuteronomy 30:19, "I have set [put] before you [with each breath, eternal] life and [eternal] death,"** have come from written truth to life. Christ's resurrection made both options available to us. Since we were cast out of Heaven, Heaven had become closed to us; there was no way for us to return there, where our Eternal Life with the Lord exists. As a result, our Spirits had no choice but to automatically go to Hell for the punishment of our sins. And when Adam fell, our bodies descend into the grave, upon our Natural Death: *"For all men have one entrance into life [birth], and the like [death] going out" (Wisdom of Solomon 7:6).* Consequently, the following rule applies to all who enter Earth by birth, **Earth Rule (1):** To come to Earth, you must be born or have a body; to leave, you must die, and upon your death, your body goes into the grave and your Spirit goes into Hell. This rule was in effect for all humans until the birth, death, and resurrection of Jesus Christ. Nevertheless, people are dying to leave here.

Therefore, upon Jesus' death, He had to follow this same rule, which explains how God's Holy Spirit ended up in Hell. God intended to release His Holy Spirit from the body of Jesus to enter the gates of Hell to defeat death. He then released the Spirits of all believers in God, from Adam up to Jesus, who resided in the **"Paradise"** section of Hell, to Heaven **(see diagram in the index)**. Therefore, Christ emptied Paradise as He released the Spirits of the Saints back into Heaven, their original home. Hallelujah! **[Side Note]:** Recall the reference to Paradise within the Earth in Luke 23:42 as Jesus hung on the cross between two thieves, one of them recognized Him and confessed his belief in Him; then Jesus said to him, *"...today you will be with Me in Paradise."* Study the diagram in the index to see how this verse became true. [end]

However, since we were cast out of Heaven, this means that we are banned from there and that there is no more Eternal Life with God, for us, ever again. And if you think about it, there is no other way for us to know that Heaven has been opened back up to us (the fallen) again, unless God somehow communicates this fact to us.

Therefore, He sent His Word to Earth, in the flesh, to tell and show us this truth by the resurrection of Christ. Words are our means of communicating with each other; therefore, God sent His Word (Jesus) to tell us that Eternal Life, in Heaven, is available to us again after we die from the Earth. According to the redemption plan, for believers, our Spirits will return home to Heaven, and our bodies will go into the grave.

How else would God bring forth the Truth of His Word, ***Deuteronomy 30:19, which gives us the choice between "[eternal] life and [eternal] death?"*** Jesus! Before the death and resurrection of Jesus, the latter scripture had not been fulfilled because we no longer had Eternal Life in Heaven. Therefore, **the visual display of the birth, death, and resurrection of Jesus Christ is the ultimate means of communication from God to Man.**

Upon Jesus' resurrection, whereby He returned to Earth to retrieve His same Human Body and then ascended into Heaven, Heaven had never received or accommodated a human body before, because only Spirit Beings reside there. Jesus Christ's ascension into Heaven with His earthly Body was necessary to make our fallen Spirits and fallen Bodies acceptable to our Heavenly Father, who is an intangible Spirit of pure Brilliant Light. So now, for the first time, a Man in both Spirit and Body, entered Heaven to dwell before the Holy Presence of God. Again, the Word (Jesus) is God's Light clothed in a Spirit-looking human form. Subsequently, upon the Earth, Jesus, is God's Spirit of Light, clothed or covered with a Body made of Flesh (Matthew 17:2). The human body has now been made ready to receive the incomprehensible Majesty of the Divine Light of our Heavenly Father… **Glory!**

Thus, Christ's Indwelling Holy Spirit within us provides God the ability to dwell within us… our Temple or Soul, and we can dwell in the Divine Light of His Holy Presence, in Heaven. God can now interact with you… His Creation, both in Heaven and on Earth. The Lord's ultimate goal is to dwell with man, according to ***Revelation 21:3, "And I heard a loud voice from heaven saying, 'Behold, the tabernacle [dwelling place] of God is with men, and He will dwell with them, and they shall be His people. God Himself will be with them and be their God…'"*** Amen and amen.

Although our two eternal choices as recorded in **Deuteronomy 30:19** were written thousands of years before the resurrection of Jesus, both options, eternal life and eternal death, were not available to us until Jesus. Still, the Lake of Fire **(The Second Death)** is not currently available to us; only the Abyss and the Hellfire of Gehenna are available to receive our fallen Spirits, and the grave is available to receive our fallen Bodies. It was not until the birth, death, resurrection, and ascension of Jesus Christ into Heaven that Heaven became open to fallen humans. Therefore, the ascension of Jesus Christ has literally availed to us both options in **Deuteronomy 30:19**. Now, upon our death, Heaven (Eternal Life with God) and Eternal Death (Eternal Life in Gehenna, which leads to the coming Eternal Second Death) are now both available to us.

God through Christ has put the reality of our two eternal choices, which weigh in the balance of our belief system, before you and me. Once again, God's Word, as always, has brought truth to life, in the same manner He brought **Genesis 2:17** to life, the realization of your death that is sure to come. God's Grace and Mercy created **"Hope"** for us in Jesus Christ for our redemption, which changed the course of our Eternal History. As a matter of fact, we were headed straight toward the permanency of Eternal Death. Therefore, the birth, life, death, and resurrection of Christ is the greatest news on the planet... the greatest **"Hope"** of our sinful lives!

What Would We Do Without "HOPE?"

"And if we are [God's] children, then we are heirs: heirs of God and co-heirs with Christ—if indeed we suffer with Him, so that we may also be glorified with Him"
*~ **Romans 8:17***

Our future glory in Christ is freedom from sin and death, based on our **FAITH:** *"Faith makes us sure of what we hope for and gives us proof of what we cannot see [yet]" (Hebrews 11:1, CEV).* Since the Abyss of Hell is eternal, I don't think you realize that Hell is real and that there is no way out… whatsoever! Similarly, in our Criminal Justice System, some face life sentences while others face death sentences… with no way out. Subsequently, some have sentences with the hope of parole. However, in Hell, there is no hope, just the inconceivable, unquenchable burning flames of Hellfire along with the thoughts of your every sin constantly running through your mind, without end. There is no way out of Hell because it is in a forever realm.

We will live with our Heavenly Father in the absence of sin and death: *"But in keeping with God's promise, we are looking forward to a new heaven and a new earth, where righteousness dwells" (2 Peter 3:13, BSB).* Therefore, you will never exist to dwell with the Lord in His New Heaven and New Earth. Consequently, since we are all facing two death sentences while we are down here in the Abyss, what would we do if we didn't have the **"Hope"** of a Savior who is telling us the following:

Our Hope is in Christ: *"Therefore, there is now no condemnation [for your sins and rebelliousness] for those who are in Christ Jesus. For in Christ Jesus, the law of the Spirit of life [in Heaven] set you free from the law (Romans 6:23) of sin and death [The Second Death]. For what the [earthly] law was powerless to do in that it was weakened by the flesh, God did by sending His own [born] Son [His Word from Heaven, which is*

Himself in the Perfection of Sonship, to live] in the likeness of sinful man, as an offering for sin. He thus condemned sin in the flesh, so that the righteous standard of the law might be fulfilled in us, who do not walk according to the flesh but [we walk] according to the Spirit [by freedom of choice].

Those who live according to the flesh set their minds on the things of the flesh; but those who live according to the Spirit set their minds on the things of the Spirit [the truth and righteousness of God]. The mind of the flesh is death, but the mind of the Spirit is [eternal] life and peace, because the mind of the flesh is hostile [hatred] to God: It does not submit to God's law, nor can it do so. Those controlled by the flesh cannot please God.

You, however, are controlled not by the flesh, but by the Spirit, if the Spirit of God lives in you. And if anyone does not have the Spirit of Christ, he does not belong to Christ. But if Christ is in you, your body is dead because of sin, yet your spirit is alive because of [your] righteousness. And if the Spirit of Him [the Indwelling Holy Spirit] who raised Jesus from the dead is living in you, He [God] who raised Christ Jesus from the dead will also give life to your mortal bodies through His [Indwelling Holy] Spirit, who lives in you.

We are Heirs to the Kingdom with Christ: Therefore, brothers [and sisters in Christ], we have an obligation, but it is not to the flesh, to live according to it. For if you live according to the flesh, you will die; but if by the Spirit you put to death the deeds of the body, you will live. For all who are led by the Spirit of God are sons of God. For you did not receive a spirit of slavery [to death] that returns you to fear, but you received the Spirit of sonship, by whom we cry, "Abba! Father!" The [Holy] Spirit Himself testifies with our spirit [those who invited Christ's Spirit to live within them] that we are God's children. And if we are [His] children, then we are heirs: heirs of God and co-heirs with Christ [God with us in Immortal Human Form]—*if indeed we suffer with Him, so that we may also be glorified with Him.*

Our Future Glory is in Christ: *I [The Apostle Paul] consider that our present sufferings are not comparable to the glory that will be revealed in us. The creation waits in eager expectation for the revelation of the sons of God. For the creation was subjected to frustration [Tribulation, Death, Hell and the Grave], not by its own will, but because of the One [God] who subjected it [for the purpose of our Redemption], in hope that the creation itself [by freedom of choice] will be set free from its bondage [to sin] to decay [in a grave] and brought into the glorious freedom of the children of God [back to our original state].*

We know that the whole creation has been groaning together in the [increasing] pains [similar] to childbirth until the present time. Not only that, but we ourselves, who have the firstfruits [called the "First Resurrection," the first of God's Children to be resurrected from their graves] of the Spirit [those who have the Indwelling Holy Spirit (Christ) within them as they lay dead in their gave, will be the first or first fruit to be resurrected and raptured to Heaven], groan inwardly as we wait eagerly for our adoption as sons, the redemption of our bodies [the very purpose of the Rapture]. For in this hope we were saved; but hope that is seen is no hope at all.

Who hopes for what he can already see? But if we hope for what we do not yet see, we wait for it [the Rapture] patiently" (Romans 8:1-25, BSB). **"Blessed and holy is the one having a part in THE FIRST RESURRECTION! Over these [firstfruits resurrected from their graves] THE SECOND DEATH has no authority [power], but they will be priests of God and of Christ, and will reign with Him a thousand years" (Revelation 20:6).** This scripture means that once you are dead, you remain dead until you are resurrected, which again nullifies the concept of reincarnation.

A CLOSER LOOK AT LIFE AND DEATH

You only need one lifetime to choose between eternal life and death... that's it!

Now that you see the blueprint of God's Divine Redemption Plan for your Eternal Life, as well as the past, present, and future events on His heavenly calendar. You must renew your mind and start thinking eternal. Start imagining, feeling, and acting like you are eternal, and wonder and contemplate in your mind about eternal things. Jesus Christ brought the Kingdom of God and its righteousness to you, on Earth, so start living in God's Kingdom, right now. You must understand that you are not your dying body, which is temporal and will surely retire to a grave, as your Eternal Spirit, like God, will conjoin to your immortal body so that you can get back to living life eternally, in Heaven, and the restored Earth.

Therefore, we must prepare now to welcome the Lord of Lords and King of Kings who will descend back to Earth to dwell with us forever. After the final war, on Earth, the "War of Armageddon," which will be the completion of the War that began in Heaven, then there will be a general resurrection when all graves will open whereby those who were not Raptured will be raised to meet Christ at "The Last Judgment" to determine who will experience "The Second Death." God will then usher in a New Heaven and Earth for us to inhabit for all eternity, for old things will have passed away.

It is my prayer that you are getting this wisdom: ***"Wisdom is the principal thing; therefore, get wisdom: and with all thy getting get understanding" (Proverbs 4:7).*** Truth is, you did not evolve from an Ape nor did a Big Bang bring your intelligent life into existence. And the fact that your "Shadow" is casting down to the ground, right now and continually, is your evidence. However, if you still do not fully understand that your life is your Spirit within your body and is eternal and that you need God's Indwelling Holy Spirit through Christ, then please repeat the read...repeat, re-evaluate, and **repent** because your eternal future depends on you getting "understanding" of God's Truth.

Now that we have established tangible evidence of God's Divine Plan to save us, which includes the reality of God's Holy Spirit, His Presence in Heaven, and on Earth, His appearance, His voice, His Handiwork… all that He has created; and even what your shadow reveals about you, it is impossible for you to deny the great extent to which your Creator has gone to redeem you and His Divine Love for you.

You cannot deny His extended grace and mercy to give you a second chance, nor His coming to Earth to die for your sins to save you from your deserved consequences. This is unconditional love to the nth degree! Again, it is designed to be your choice. I can only present my research and revelations to you; however, it is up to you to do your own research so that you can make an informed decision about your eternal future.

However, no matter if you are a Christian or belong to any denomination or church; no matter how much you love and believe in God, His Word that materialized as Jesus Christ, in the flesh, or the fact that you have **repented** and prayed Roman 10:9-10 to confess Christ as your Savior, there is no way around *Romans 6:23, "the wages of sin is death" and Hebrews 9:27, "…it is appointed unto men once to die…"* And you know that there is, absolutely, no denying these truths because you know and understand from experience that as sure as you are born into the Earth, you will die. Therefore, you must pay your sin debt, for when you lived in Heaven, with your Natural Death. This is why you are awaiting your turn to die, like me, right? However, you can avoid a Second Death, but again, it's your choice!

We, the fallen, should establish a personal relationship by communicating with God or Himself as Jesus, through *"Prayer."* He instructs us to pray to God, the Father, in the name of the Son, Jesus, or His tangible humanism, as He dwelt with us in the flesh as a Perfect Son: *"And whatever you do in word or deed, do all in the name of the Lord Jesus, giving thanks to God the Father through Him" (Colossians 3:17).*

God came to Earth as His Word (Jesus) to exist in the Spirit and Flesh, just like you and me, so that He can relate to you, Spirit to Spirit and Man to Man. Through Christ, *"so is my word that goes out from my mouth: It will not return to me empty [void], but will accomplish what I desire and achieve the purpose for which I sent it [for your redemption]" (Isaiah 55:11, NIV).* God's goal is to show you…your fallen Spirit, by example, so that you might have the option to *"choose"* to establish a personal relationship, by way of communication with your Heavenly Father through *"Prayer,"* and as well regain your Eternal Life back with Him.

Now, since we are on the subject matter of *"Prayer,"* ironically, one day, I was looking through a few old Bibles and I saw photos of Jesus kneeling in prayer while looking upwards (His eyes were open) unto God, from which cometh His help. His face was not looking downwards towards the darkness of Hell, nor were His eyes closed… Hmm. Now, consider ***Psalms 121:2, which says, "My help comes from the LORD [in Heaven], Who made heaven and earth,"*** meaning that the God of Heaven, above, is whom we depend on.

However, we know that Hell is located below Heaven or downwards, in the darkness of the Abyss, so when it comes to our prayer posture, it appears that we have been globally conditioned by religion to **"bow our heads"** downwards and **"close our eyes"** when we pray, instead of looking upwards towards the God of Heaven. This is certainly not a coincidence; it's an agenda.

Although Pastors, Popes, etc., have profound messages to deliver, they instinctively instruct us to **"bow our heads,"** and **"close our eyes."** I know that, on occasion, we may fall on our faces to pray, as Jesus did, in **Matthew 26:39**, or we may lie on the floor to pray, but we must be mindful of Satan's agenda to teach the masses to do the opposite of what our Creator teaches.

Jesus looks up to Heaven as He prays, per ***John 17:1, "Jesus…lifted up His eyes to heaven."*** I recalled the prayer posture of Muslims or those who kneel, close their eyes, then bow completely downward to the floor or ground to pray. But think about it, normally, when we communicate with others, we speak with our eyes open and towards their direction, or we look them in their eyes, so the question becomes: ***"When we close our eyes and bow our heads or our bodies downwards to pray, who is down there…who are we directing our prayers towards?"***

It dawned on me that deception is at play and that a change to my prayer posture is warranted… **"eyes open, looking upwards"** unto the God of Heaven, whence cometh my help. Is it just me, or what do you think? As you will discover, we were cast down from Heaven, so God utilized Jesus to avail us access to the Light of Heaven again.

What Is The Purpose Of Life On Earth In Its Fallen State?

"I have set before you [eternal] life and [eternal] death"
~ Deuteronomy 30:19

The answer, in one word, is Redemption. Let it sink in that God ***"called you [the fallen from Heaven] out of darkness [The Abyss of Hell] into His marvelous light [on Earth]" (1 Peter 2:9, NKJV)*** to participate in His Divine Redemption Plan. And to add three more words: the purpose is to **Choose** our eternal future, receive our judgments, which is the death of our body or Natural Death, and "The Last **Judgment**," as well as our **Punishments** of Hellfire.

During my research, I traced the purpose for "Life" on this fallen Earth to ***Deuteronomy 30:19, "This day I call the heavens and the earth as witnesses against you that [with each breath that you take] I have set [put] before you [eternal] life [through Jesus Christ] and [eternal] death."*** And the more I researched, the more I concluded that this powerful scripture may well explain the only reason we are here, on Earth, living without being able to see God's face or being in His Immortal Physical Presence. Our Creator calls the entire spheres and all inhabitants of both Heaven and Earth to be a witness against you and me that He has put our eternal choice before us... WOW! Read that verse again and let the gravity of it sink in; this is very serious.

We chose to live in a fallen state that is filled with darkness, chaos, lies, deception, tribulation, and death. Now, choose your way back to God through Jesus Christ. He died to give us the opportunity to invite Him to live within us so that we will avoid eternal death and thus live in God's Holy Presence again. **Deuteronomy 30:19** brought revelation to the premise that there is definitely a grand plan in place, specifically designed to offer us back our Eternal Life with God. Recall that I call this grand gesture,

A CLOSER LOOK AT LIFE AND DEATH

God's Divine Redemption Plan, whereby Heaven, Hell, Earth, Jesus, Satan, all the Angels (us), Death, and Time, each have a role to play. God's plan allows for the summation of our life's choices and decisions to make our eternal choice for us. This is why death is designed as a surprise element and not a planned event; you cannot plan your choice, you must live your choice!!

I hope that it is now apparent to you that God repurposed the Earth to become the venue whereby He would give us "Time" to be offered a second chance to regain our eternal Life with Him. Still, while you are awaiting your turn to die for your sins, you are being offered eternal life. However, I often wondered why Satan, evil, and death are allowed to happen to you and me, but I didn't know that it was because of my own sinful behavior towards God. My research, coupled with God's astounding revelations, revealed so many answers to many unanswered questions. Keep reading, and you will certainly find out more details when we discuss the design phase of the Lord's redemption plan. I want you to grasp the full enormity of the great extent to which God went to save, undeserving, eternal beings like you and me.

However, we no longer have eternal life because we are separated **(death)** from the Lord, whereby Earth's gravitational pull is holding us away from His Holy Presence due to our sins. However, we desire our lives to last forever. We value life, and when it's threatened, we fight, beg, and plead for our lives. When babies are born, we celebrate the birth of new life, and when our loved ones pass away, we mourn the passing of Life. We pray for the Lord to heal the sick because we want them to live; no one wants their life to end.

Death is the most hurtful, earth-shattering, constant, recurring event we will ever face or experience. So, the question becomes: If we were, originally, living eternal life with the Lord, how did we transition from living an infinite life in Heaven with God to living a finite life on earth, captive to certain death? We have already established the answer, which is the fact that we each, individually, sinned against God. This occurred after **Genesis 1:1** and just before **Genesis 1:2,** while Earth was in the initial foundation stage of being created, according to **Hebrews 1:10** and Job 38:4. Earth's foundation had been laid, but light, land, oceans, inhabitants…humans, animals, etc. had not been formed yet. But when God said **"Let there be light…"** and subsequently formed the latter, it was for the expressed purpose of forgiving us and our redemption.

Although God created Adam and Eve in His Image of Light with His embedded Holy Spirit, He knew they would fall when confronted by Satan, hence the planting of the two trees in the Garden, more later. Therefore, Earth is not just a school whereby you learn the Basic Instructions Before Leaving Earth, as many say the acronym of the word **"B.I.B.L.E."** represents. Earth is where you must **repent** and make your eternal choice regarding Jesus Christ before your demise. Life is solely to make your amends with your Heavenly Father or not and live a lifestyle that reflects your choice… eternal life or eternal death, according to **Deuteronomy 30:19**. Your lifestyle reflects your choice, but it is wise to let your choice reflect upon Jesus. Again, you are here, on Earth, to pay your sin debt with your life or the Natural Death of your body, for your sins that you committed against God in Heaven.

The "Evidence" of Your Betrayal And Rebellion Against God While You Lived In Heaven

"I will cleanse them [you] from all the sin they [you] have committed against me [God] and will forgive all their [your] sins of rebellion against me"
~ Jeremiah 33:8

When we fell or were cast out of Heaven, instead of God banishing us away from Him for all eternity, which is the definition of Eternal Death, God's overwhelming, devout love, mercy, and grace for each of us, prompted Him to put off Eternal Death (now called The Second Death) to allow us **"Time"** to **repent**, be forgiven; and to save ourselves from Eternal Death. However, our redemption is based on freedom of choice and the history of our lifestyle while living on the Earth; then our lives end with death, and our lifestyle is judged against God's Truth.

Instead, the Lord God chose to use Earth as the venue where our redemption would take place. He forgave us, saying: *"I will cleanse them [you] from all the sin they [you] have committed against me and will forgive all their [your] sins of rebellion against me" (Jeremiah 33:8)*. This scripture is God confirming both your sinful betrayal AND your rebellious behavior against Him. Recall the rebellion that you participated in against Him: *"And war broke out in heaven: Michael and his angels fought with the dragon [Satan]; and the dragon and his angels [us] fought but they did not prevail, nor was a place found for them in heaven any longer.*

So, the great dragon was cast out, that serpent of old, called the Devil and Satan, who deceives the whole world; he [Satan] was cast to the earth, and his angels [you and me] were cast out with him." (Revelation 12:7-9). I will explain why we do not remember this war later, but it is the result of this war that your **"Shadow"** displays to you everywhere you go. Your shadow is cast down to the ground, like mine, right?

God is giving us "Time," on Earth to ask for forgiveness and **repent** of our sins: *"You have abandoned your first love [your Heavenly Father]. Therefore, keep in mind how far you have fallen. <u>Repent</u> and perform the deeds you did at first [when you were first created in Heaven]" (Revelation 2:4-5).* If we have done nothing wrong, why does God's Word tell us many times to **REPENT**? **Repentance** through belief in Jesus Christ is our only way back home: *"Unless you repent, you too will all perish" (Luke 13:3).* And since *"the life of the body is in the blood" (Leviticus 17:11),* God's redemption plan called for the pure and Holy Blood of Jesus Christ to be shed to redeem our fallen Spirits and Bodies from all of our evil behavior. And fire is used for our purification **(Zechariah 13:9).** Now, that is absolute love, beyond anything we could ever imagine or know. This is the truth being revealed that many of us have never really heard of or know… **WOW!**

After receiving this evidence, directly from the Word of God, you should feel compelled to apologize to Him. I know that I can't apologize enough, I can't tell you how sorry I am for what I have done to betray His Truth and Love… I believed Satan's lie; he had me thinking that I could be like God: *"…You will not surely die. 5For God knows that in the day you eat of it your eyes will be opened, and you will be like God, knowing good and evil." (Genesis 3:4-5).* God's Word reveals the purity of truth to you, relative to your sinful nature and actions. His Word defines His mercy that He has extended to you.

Therefore, I employ you to take a moment, right here… right now, to reflect on the above. Read this section over again and perhaps, turn to your Bible and read the scriptures for yourself, then, if you so choose, humbly make your amends with Christ before you leave this earth. Please understand that your eternal life is extremely serious. Life is short, we are living in the end times and last days, or close to the end of His redemption plan, so you must decide now. Please accept this Book as a "last call" to hear your Creator's Holy Word so you can make an informed decision about your eternal future.

After God revealed the above to me, I cried out, ***"Lord, I am so...very sorry that I turned away from your Holiness, Love, Truth, and Righteousness to believe or fall for a lie. I did not have a clear idea of what I had done to hurt you."*** I **repented**, specifically, for my acts of transgression and rebellion in Heaven; and for my sins on Earth. "I confess that Jesus is Lord, please forgive me, Lord. I know I don't deserve your mercy or forgiveness, oh Lord, but you died to give it to me anyway." I am also overjoyed that redemption is available daily to each one of you, so that ALL may have eternal life! Oh, how I praise, worship, and thank God for His sacrifice to give us His Indwelling Holy Spirit through Christ, which is within me. I hope that you realize that our Creator has gone to great lengths to give Himself back to you and me.

Question: "Has anyone ever asked you if you are saved?" And you, being a believer in Jesus Christ, emphatically reply, yes! But you really don't know or understand exactly what you are supposed to be saved from. You know that you are not saved from dying because you see that everyone dies, no matter what. However, I hope that, from now on, you can answer this question with confidence in knowing that Jesus died to save you from all your sins and The Second Death, which is eternal. And for those who remain alive, when Christ comes in the clouds to Rapture His Church, remember, we will be saved from both Natural Death and the Second Death!! The Rapture truly is our "Blessed Hope" in Christ.

While the Lord's redemption plan is still available, in the Earth, the Rapture creates and implements a means for our sin-filled Eternal Spirits (you and me) to be forgiven and not have to pay the price for our sins with our lives for the sins that we committed in Heaven. Although **Romans 6:23** says, *"For the wages of sin is death,"* for believers, the Rapture... our Blessed Hope, voids Natural Death, if you are alive when it occurs, because your body is taken away to Heaven; therefore, your body never enters the grave. And if you are dead, when the Rapture occurs, it voids The Second Death because you are away to Heaven, so you will not experience the eternal Second Death.

However, during these end times, many ministers are saying that there will be a great revival in the church, but Bible Prophecy begs to differ, because *2 Thessalonians 2:3-4* says that there will be a great falling away, also called "The Great Apostasy." This means that many will turn away from the Lord, *"Let no one deceive you by any means; for that Day [The Day of the Lord's wrath] will not come unless the falling away comes first..."* after which the Antichrist will be revealed, verse four (4) continues, *"who opposes and exalts himself above all that is called God or that is worshiped, so that he sits as God in the temple of God, showing himself that he is God.*

When the New Third Temple is built (*Temple = House of Life*) in Jerusalem, it will require cleansing with a solution that consists of the ashes of a sacrificed pure "Red Heifer" (cow). The Red Heifer's hair must not have even one blemish or strand of any other hair color. Its hair must be completely red from head to toe. So, here again, let's take a closer look at life and death, as the ashes of the Red Heifer represent death, and the other cleansing ingredient in the cleansing solution is water, which represents life. The ashes and water are mixed together for the purification of the Holy Temple. One sign that the fulfillment of Biblical Prophecy is near is the fact that five pure red heifers were recently sent from Texas, USA, and have arrived in Jerusalem.

This Third Temple, unlike the only two Temples ever built in

Jerusalem, where God's Holy Spirit did reside in the innermost chamber, behind the veil, in an area called the Holy of Holies, this coming new Temple will be built for the Messiah that the Jews have been expecting since they rejected Jesus Christ. But recall that when you reject Christ, you get the opposite… the Antichrist. The secret is that the Spirit of God does not need a physical temple building to dwell in anymore because, through Jesus Christ, He gave us back His Indwelling Holy Spirit to dwell within us, so that our Souls are His Temple: *"… your bodies are temples of the Holy Spirit, who [reside within the Souls of all believers in Christ]" (1 Corinthians 6:19, NIV)*.

We have established that as we await our turn to die, we are offered the free gift of Eternal Life. However, to accomplish this great feat, recall that God's Holy Spirit came to Earth, concealed within the flesh of Jesus (Matthew 17:2), so that His Holy Spirit could be released, upon His death, to enter Hell; like everyone else's Spirit that left Earth and entered Hell before Jesus made the ultimate sacrifice. It was purposed for God to display the defeat of death before us by effectuating Jesus' resurrection to announce to us that Heaven is now open to the fallen (**repentant**) Spirits.

But remember that your redemption is based on your belief system, your belief in what Jesus Christ did on the cross for you, or not. God laid down His Holy Spirit for you in the body of Jesus, so please don't allow your PRIDE to keep you from accepting your Creator's forgiveness. But it's up to you to make a conscious decision to follow Christ, just like you made a conscious decision to believe Satan's lie and rebel against God in Heaven.

The Lord has a well-designed and perfect plan whereby death has already been defeated to give you Eternal Life back with Him. Still, you must declare Christ as Lord of your life, prayerfully confess your sins with your mouth, ask for forgiveness, and believe in Christ's finished work on the cross… pray Romans 10:9-10. I hope that you will begin to see how your sin has changed the course of your Eternal History, and that God indeed has a redemption plan in place to save you from the consequences of your sins, which is eternal death and the punishment of the Lake of Fire.

Our Spirit Energy transfers between the infinite realms of Heaven and Hell, to the finite realm of Earth, for the purpose of redemption. Now, let's revisit **Ecclesiastes 12:7**, which states that our Spirits transfer back to *"God who gave it,"* upon our demise from the Earth. Recall that Scientists have confirmed this fact in the First Law of Thermodynamics and the Law of Conservation of Energy, which states, ***"Energy [Spirit] can neither be created nor destroyed; energy can only be transferred or changed from one form [state] to another."*** Therefore, upon your death, your Eternal Spirit Energy can only change states **(infinite/finite)** between realms. Still, your Spirit never dies or is never destroyed, but is tormented day and night, forever.

Although the subject matter in this book may appear to be religious, it is not because neither life nor death nor the principles that govern them are religion. On Earth, religion is centered around man's concept of the worship and teachings (or strategic mis-teachings) of God. However, no matter what **Religious Denomination** you are affiliated with, including Christianity, none of them can impact your birth **(life),** and none can prevent your certain Natural Death from coming. Therefore, in the simplest terms, this book series is centered around our Creator, who has lost one-third of His Creation (you and me), who are now living separated from Him, captive to certain death due to our sins committed in our Spirit and body. Therefore, God has extended His grace and mercy to design a plan to forgive us and give Himself to those who receive Jesus Christ…His Indwelling Holy Spirit, which is Eternal Life!

So, although we may not all agree on Creation, the existence of

God, Angels, Satan, Hell, Jesus Christ, Religion, or various theories: The Theory of Evolution or the Big Bang Theory, we can all agree on the fact that we do all fall down and succumb to death **(as evident by our shadow).** Therefore, religion and artificial manmade theories only seek to divide and distract us from our true, common enemy, which is death, and more specifically, Eternal Death, now called The Second Death according to God's Divine Redemption Plan. Thus, we must realize that we need a Savior.

Eternal Death or The Second Death is permanent separation from the Presence of God, which is the true definition of death, and what we deserved when we disobeyed and rebelled against our Heavenly Father. We have a second chance now to choose to believe in Christ or to experience the default of eternal death in the Lake of Fire and Brimstone. This is our heavenly, judicially settled, eternal punishment according to our death sentence.

The Lake of Fire was first prepared for Satan, who sinned first, but after we...his angels decided to join him, all unbelievers in Christ will experience this same fate. Your eternal punishment will be executed at some point in your eternal future if you do not accept Jesus Christ as your Savior. Natural Death, that we experience on Earth, is just a shadow of our forever, permanent death, called The Second Death, which is sure to come. According to ***Psalms 23:4,*** *"Yea, though I walk through the valley [Earth/Natural Death] of the shadow of death [The Second Death (Revelation 20:14)], I will fear no evil."*

Therefore, Natural Death is the temporary shadow representative of our Eternal Second Death because Eternal Death is the "real thing" or our permanent separation from God, our forever death, according to God's plan of redemption. Our shadow also reflects this fact as it represents our fallen Spirit contained within our fallen body that was created from the darkness of Earth's surface, whereby our body will return to the ground where our

Spirit was cast down. Therefore, your shadow follows you everywhere as a constant reminder of our Eternal History. Now, you should understand that we face not one death, but two deaths… Natural Death of the body, and Eternal Death of the Spirit and Body, each with their respective punishments: Hell, which includes The Lake of Fire and Brimstone, that burneth forever.

We have already been separated from the Lord, in the Spirit, when we sinned and were cast out of Heaven **(death #1),** and as well in the body, when Adam and Eve sinned and were cast out of the Garden of Eden **(death #2),** as *Death = Separation from God's Holy Spirit... His Presence* and His Word, which is His Truth. Based on man's composition of Spirit and Flesh, our sinful nature was demonstrated in our Spirit, in Heaven; therefore, our body had to fall to the same mindset (Satan's lie), thinking that we could "like God." God desired to create Man with a Body to house our Spirit, on Earth, to give us a second chance through the composition of Man's Body. Therefore, the complete man (Spirit and Body) had to fall in order to carry out God's new plan regarding our redemption, which includes death, judgment, and punishment.

Our fall is evident, in both realms, by the mere fact that our Eternal Spirit Energy now lives away from the Lord, on Earth, instead of in Heaven. And we are living in a fallen state, meaning that everything perishes or will perish someday and return to the lower Abyss of Hell. Our shadow reflects this fact as it is a continuous reminder, as we await our deaths and penalties.

Your Consequences

*"For the mindset of the flesh is **DEATH**, but the mindset of the Spirit is **LIFE** and peace"*
*~ **Romans 8:6 LSB***

"Freedom of Choice" has always existed, both in Heaven and on Earth, which means that the foundations for each choice, *light, and darkness = good and evil,* etc., have always existed, even though we lived in Heaven with our Heavenly Father. However, before darkness and evil came into existence, all that we ever knew and dwelt in was the incomprehensible love and the glorious Holy Light of God's Truth. Hell had never existed as a place for us to live eternal life. Although we were living our eternal life in Heaven, in the light, love, goodness, and truth of God, the choice to sin was always an option. There was no place in Heaven where darkness could exist except by virtue of our freedom of choice, to individually decide to sin and turn against God. Again, this freedom is extended to all of us, in Heaven and on Earth.

However, as long as there was no eternal thought, decision, choice, or act to sin, there was no reason for God to withdraw His Light from us. Where the Lord's Light is, there is, absolutely, no darkness, not even a shadow: **"God is light and in Him is no darkness at all" (1 John 1:5).** Hence, the definition of darkness is the absence of God's Holy, Divine Light. Some question, "If God created all things, doesn't this mean that He created Hell? The following analogy will help answer this question: For instance, if you were in the military and had traveled and lived in multiple locations throughout the world, but you have never traveled to or been stationed in Africa, it doesn't mean that Africa doesn't exist; it simply means that you have never been there. Therefore, you have never visited or lived in any part of your life there… period, so you have no stories to tell about your being there… no memories to share, therefore, you have had absolutely no history living life there or affiliation with the continent of Africa, whatsoever. Well, the same is true regarding Hell.

Hell was created as a result of an individual Spirit's eternal action with eternal implications. For with every eternal action there is an eternal reaction with results that follow. Consequently, if there is no eternal action, there is no eternal reaction. As you know, Satan took an eternal action against God's Sovereignty; therefore, the eternal reaction caused his eternal darkness or his eternal death, which is eternal separation from God's Holy Spirit of Light. Just as if you had never lived or had any existence in Africa, so it is that, in Heaven, we never lived or had a history of living life in eternal darkness. Darkness had never existed before Satan's contempt that created our current state of being, called the chaos of Hell. In the body, you can pretend, but in the Spirit, you are what you think and do; this is why if you die without accepting Christ as your Savior, you will become eternal death, now called The Eternal Second Death.

Consequently, you become eternally dead or nonexistent as far as living eternal life with your Heavenly Father, which makes you nonexistent; this is the definition of what it means to **"exist no more,"** and also is defined as destroyed or annihilated. Death means the end of you; you are destroyed, annihilated, unalived, or removed from the Eternal Presence of the Lord. Thus, you are removed from the eternal memory of God and all believers in Christ, as you burn forever in the Lake of Fire and Brimstone, kindled with sulfur.

Therefore, according to ***Romans 8:6 LSB***, *"...**the mindset of the flesh is DEATH, but the mindset of the Spirit is LIFE and peace.**"* So, your consequences are *Heaven = Life, or Hell = Eternal Death* by default. It's your choice.

TO UNDERSTAND LIFE, ONE MUST FIRST UNDERSTAND DEATH!

Our Separation From God's Holy Light... Who Created The Darkness Of Hell?

"God is light, and in him is no darkness at all"
~ 1 John 1:5

Genesis 1:1 says, **"In the beginning God created the heavens and the earth."** Now, notice that it does not refer to His creation of Hell. This is because God did not create the darkness of Hell; the former Light Bearer created the darkness of Hell. For God alone **"...is light and IN HIM THERE IS NO DARKNESS AT ALL" (1 John 1:5),** like our Sun, there is no darkness in it at all, its light so shines on the just and the unjust from sun up to sundown, never failing. The only shadow that it casts is yours on the ground that follows you around everywhere to remind you of a very significant event from your eternity past.

Hell came along later when Lucifer harbored the first darkness of a sinful thought and acted out in sin. He acted upon his thought that he could be like God and formed and led a rebellion against our Creator. Since he desired to be like God, he was granted his wish within God's Divine Redemption Plan to establish his ungodly government on Earth, to be his natural evil self, to establish the foundation of our choice to be and do evil, do wrong, and to be a liar. He is the foundation of our choice to live any way that we want... *selfishness = unrighteousness = Satan's mindset.*

When Lucifer was cast down from Heaven, He became the essence of eternal living darkness of his own making, in every form of his existence. Everywhere darkness is...the darkness of the Abyss, the darkness of the night, the darkness of the grave, the darkness of outer space, and the darkness of the human mind, etc., this is the darkness that Lucifer created to begin an Eternal Life History of living and having our being in the depths of darkness in the Abyss of Hell. The darkness of **"thought flow"** manifests within the duality of the human mind to establish our two choices in life. The former Light Bearer created and established living eternal life in complete darkness, or without the Light of the Holy Spirit of God. This dense darkness affects Hell's inhabitants mentally **(spiritually)** and physically, in the surroundings of the Abyss, whereby we are all void of truth. The two realms of Heaven and Hell sustain our freedom of choice, thus providing us with two choices in life that interconnect all things in the Universe. These two choices were availed to us, on Earth, when God came down into our darkness and said, "Let there be light," with the spotlight on the two trees that He planted in the midst of the Garden of Eden, representing the eternal choice that our redemption is based upon.

The former Light Bearer created the definition of **"Eternal Death,"** which is eternal separation from God. Lucifer chose to take pride in himself and thus decided to go to war with God to attempt to exalt himself above His Sovereignty so that he could be worshipped. He defines and embodies darkness, sin, evil, chaos, death, Hell, and the grave. He lives and breathes death, as exhibits everything that his evil Spirit-mind thinks and everything evil that he says and does.

Satan's light energy transformed into darkness, and it projects through negative energy waves that penetrate through our thoughts, speech, and actions of those who succumb to his mindset. He is the author of lies, hate, fear, destruction… every evil, and death. He exists in every hideous form, like in movies or television, hideous-looking and evil characters represent Satan. He is the father of every form of evil behavior reported in the news (and otherwise), whereby you witness him in action, within people who have his mindset.

Satan's role in God's Divine Redemption Plan is to be his natural evil self. Again, he is the foundation of your reality to live your life unholy, unrighteously, or live any way that you want so that you will NOT regain your eternal life with God. So, the question becomes: What will you do about it? You can choose to remain deceived; it is your choice, or get yourself right with God while there is still time.

The Lord issued Lucifer an eternal death sentence because he committed the first sin and formed a rebellion against Him, so he became the definition of "spiritually dead" the moment that his Spirit transgressed. Therefore, God's Holy Spirit was no longer within him and will never be again. But let me be very clear: Although Satan is powerful in our world, due to his Spirit abilities from his former heavenly rank, just know that there is, absolutely, NO competition...between Satan and His Creator... **NONE!** Satan is simply playing his assigned role within God's redemption plan so that you have the choice to be damned to eternal death, just like him.

God's plan encompasses living your life in transition to all three realms: Heaven, Hell, and Earth. However, while we live on Earth, in mental darkness, *John 8:12* says, *"Jesus spoke to them [the people] again, saying, 'I am the light of the world. He who follows Me shall not walk in darkness, but have the light of life.'" "For you were once darkness [when you were cast out of Heaven into the Abyss], but now [because of my redemption plan to save you from eternal death], you [believers in Christ] are light in the Lord. Walk as children of light" (Ephesians 5:8).* Keep reading as we explore the design details of God's Divine Redemption Plan to save us, in greater detail throughout this book series.

Since God has a Divine Redemption Plan to restore us to eternal life with Him, it became Satan's top priority to know His plan...God's written word, so that he can counter God's every move to mount a defense to keep you from regaining your eternal life. First, he gets you to depend on *yourself* = *selfishness* = *pride* = *Satan,* and he gives you a burning desire to live any way you want. He will cause you to commit all sorts of sins… break all of God's Ten Commandments, and promise you the world. He will take your Soul by any means necessary!

Sheol is the name of Hell as a whole. It is in the center of Earth's core (Ephesians 4:9) where the Hellfire of Gehenna and Paradise **(punishment #1)** exist, and the Hellfire of the Lake of Fire and Brimstone **(punishment #2)** are our certain consequences for sin and rebellion against God **(see diagram in the index).** However, because of redemption through Jesus Christ, we can now avoid both punishments…you decide. The Word of God says this regarding our eternal burn: ***"In a similar way, Sodom and Gomorrah and the surrounding towns gave themselves up to sexual immorality and perversion. They serve as an example of those who suffer the punishment of eternal fire" (Jude 1:7, NIV).*** This scripture demonstrates the extremes of the duality of our mindset that leads us towards *righteousness = Life and unrighteousness = Death:* ***"For the mindset of the flesh is DEATH, but the mindset of the Spirit is LIFE and peace" (Romans 8:6, LSB).***

And regarding Sodom and Gomorrah, God further said, ***"As I overthrew Sodom and Gomorrah along with their neighboring towns," declares the LORD, "so no one will live there; no people will dwell in it [ever again]" (Jeremiah 50:40).*** Sodom and Gomorrah and its surrounding cities are on world maps, over by the Dead Sea (interesting). You can witness this truth for yourself by booking a trip through your travel agent today to visit the site that is covered in thick, hardened salt and brimstone from Heaven, never to be inhabited by any human being ever again. Some say that you can still see Lot's wife, who disobeyed God by looking back to see her birthplace burn… Hmm.

Some say that if God does not do anything to America for the same behavior, He will have to apologize for Sodom and Gomorrah. It is also said that ***"PRIDE leads to destruction, and*** *arrogance to downfall" (Proverbs 16:18, GNT).* Not my words. I am just saying, God loves all of us, but there are certain boundaries that should never be crossed. He has never destroyed a city or nation for adultery, murder, or the breaking of His Ten Commandments, but the defiance of what He created you to be at birth angers Him to no end, with the destruction of Sodom and Gomorrah being our example. Although our earthly societies are complicit with this behavior by saying it's ok, take heed that it is definitely not ok with your Creator. Therefore, due to the law allowing the pride and arrogance of same-sex marriage… the ultimate rebelliousness, expect the fall of America. Later, in Bible prophecy, it is not a global superpower.

Natural Death is a temporary state because it serves as the shadow of our coming permanent death, or **The Second Death**. Natural Death is designed to allow us to see and experience how real, devastating, and permanent The Second Death will be. Natural Death is our example of The Second Death whereby you will be blotted out of remembrance as if you never existed (Psalm 69:8). Natural Death and the Gehenna part of Hell are temporary because God's redemption plan calls for all men to be resurrected; Jesus Christ is our example. Because we will ALL be resurrected, He tells us to take comfort in knowing that we will see our deceased loved ones again: **"...*there shall be a resurrection of the dead, both of the just and unjust" (Acts 24:15).***

The righteous shall be resurrected to reward; subsequently, the remainder of the dead will be raised to judgment to determine who will be condemned to The Second Death. ***Revelation 14:11*** describes God's consequence of the Eternal Second Death created for those who live a life of ungodliness and disbelief in Christ: **"*And the smoke of their torment ascended forever and ever: and they have no rest day nor night…"***

Therefore, Christ is **"the way,"** meaning that He is the only way for us to avoid Hell, eternal death, and punishment and regain our eternal life with God: *"I am the way, the truth, and the life. No one comes to the Father except through Me" (John 14:6).* By virtue of Christ's resurrection, He can proclaim: *"I am He who lives, and was dead, and behold, I [Jesus] am alive forevermore. Amen. And I have the keys of Hades [the grave] and of Death [Natural Death and The Second Death]" (Revelation 1:18).* Please know that **without repentance** and your confessed belief in Jesus Christ, you will experience Hell that leads to the permanent Eternal Second Death, in the forever realm. But you don't have to, since Jesus Christ rose with the keys to Hell.

You do not have to fear death because we are redeemed through Natural Death; thus, you don't have to go through Hell's door that will never be opened again once you are on the other side of it. Recall that your life or Spirit Energy cannot be destroyed; it can only transfer from the infinite realms of Heaven and Hell to the finite realm of Earth, as confirmed by Scientists in the Law of Conservation of Energy and the First Law of Thermodynamics. As a result, your burn in Hell is continuous and never-ending. On Earth, fires consume nouns (people, places, and things) until they are destroyed or don't exist anymore, but in the eternal realm, you burn, but you never completely burn up. This is very similar to a woman who experiences a hot flash, but of course, Hell is exponentially and incomprehensibly worse.

In my opinion, a hot flash is a reminder of what God says about hellfire because it is truly a harrowing internal experience of feeling like you are literally burning up!!! At the onset, you will do anything to get air to quickly extinguish your burning. You are in a mad dash to remove clothing, open windows or doors, or go outside to get air. Nothing else matters to you; your mind is consumed with finding a solution to stop you from feeling this way. However, **in Hell, there is no way to quench the burning memories of your**

sinful life, which burnth like fire. Therefore, you may want to consider accepting Jesus Christ before you end up there.

Hot flashes are a horrible experience, yet they are oh so real…as real as Hell. I can't imagine feeling that way, or even worse, in the forever realm of eternity. However, because of my redemption due to the confession of my sins, and my belief in the finished work of Jesus Christ on the cross that paid the price for my sins, I don't have to worry about experiencing Hell or a second and eternal death. I have my Eternal Life back with the Lord; do you have yours?

Hell was made to be the temporary holding place for the Eternal Spirits of departed humans who are allowed to be born on Earth to participate in God's redemption process. According to the plan, as recorded in **Hebrews 9:27**, we must die to be redeemed because: *"it is appointed unto men once to die, but after this the judgment"* and **Romans 6:23**, states: *"For the wages of sin is death,"* whereby both scriptures apply to our sins committed in both our Spirits in Heaven and in our Bodies on Earth. Our sin and our rebellious behavior, in Heaven, are why we come to Earth to die a Natural Death, while also being offered our Eternal Life back with God.

I am stating this truth in as many different ways as I possibly can to drill this information into your mind, in hopes that you will understand and acknowledge the seriousness of your life, death, and eternal future. Is it finally sinking in yet, or do you still believe in the man-made theories that you were taught in school? Although we face death with each breath, neither The Theory of Evolution, the Big Bang Theory, nor any other man-made theory or hypothesis defines or addresses the subject of death, why? But yet Scientists can explain how our lives came into existence billions of years although none of them lived back then to observe and witness their own theorized event… smh… really?

Through Jesus Christ, we have received deliverance from Hellfire, which includes Eternal Death (permanent separation from the Lord). Again, the penalties of Hellfire, including the everlasting Lake of Fire and Brimstone, are designed specifically for Satan and all unbelievers. The former Light Bearer was the first to wage a direct attack against God's Sovereignty. Therefore, he lost God's Holy Spirit, which was his eternal life, forever. However, since we sinned by persuasion and chose to follow Satan, The Eternal Second Death has also become our penalty, as well, unless we choose to believe in Jesus Christ.

Nevertheless, we will experience two death sentences and two death penalties, not just one. Remember that the punishment of Fire and Brimstone is designed to accommodate the burning of your Body, Spirit, and Bones because the whole of man's composition is what effectuates God's redemption process, which includes death, judgment, and punishment for sins committed in the Spirit, in Heaven, and in the flesh, on Earth.

Our two death sentences (two separations from God…in Heaven, and on Earth) and the two respective punishments resulting from the only two death sentences that God has ever issued to His Creation. So, we can all agree that we are born on Earth, with nothing but our Spirit **(mind),** Body, and our word to confess our belief unto righteousness or unrighteousness. And we leave Earth with nothing but our word, which will be judged against God's Truth, *1 Timothy 6:7* confirms, *"For we brought nothing into this world, and it is certain we can carry nothing out."* Nevertheless, take care to keep your word and do not use your words to sell your Soul to gain money, prestige, fame, or material possessions that the former Light Bearer may offer you. To "Sell Your Soul" means to deny the Indwelling Holy Spirit (Christ) for material gain.

I hope you can grasp and understand the seriousness of your sins and rebellious behavior towards God, and as a result, you are now aware of the consequences that you face; again, you truly do face the death of your body and two death penalties, not just one. That is, unless you accept Jesus Christ as your Savior, who has delivered you from the Eternal Second Death. So, please allow this to sink in as you continue to explore the truth about your eternal existence. It is only because of God's Divine Redemption Plan to save us from eternal death that we have the opportunity, right now, to **repent** and accept Christ so that we can regain the eternal life that we once had with the Lord.

I will reiterate that ***Romans 10:9-10 (NKJ)*** explains how you can accept Christ as your savior: ***"If you confess with your mouth the Lord Jesus and believe in your heart that God has raised Him from the dead, you will be saved. One believes unto righteousness with the heart, and confession [of your sins with your mouth] is made unto salvation."*** However, you must **repent**; the choice is completely up to you, but of course, the way you live your life will make this choice for you if you never confess your allegiance to Christ. Your non-confession is also an answer of disbelief. If you desire to be forgiven for your mistakes, guilt, iniquities, or sins, forever, please pray **Romans 10:9-10.**

We have established that without God's Holy Spirit within you, you are in a state of waiting to die so that you can transition to Hell, which leads to Eternal Death. However, death and punishment go hand in hand, meaning you can't have one without the other; they go together. So, it is easy to forget to drill down and differentiate between the two separations from God (two deaths), which resulted in two respective punishments that are distinct and separate in their purpose, application, and timing. Therefore, when we say death, we are also saying Hell or various places within Hell and its punishment.

By now, I hope you have a deeper understanding of the truth regarding your existence as a Spirit, whether in the body or outside of your body, when it comes to your Natural Death and your Second

Death to come. Perhaps you have realized that your eternal life is still at stake, God loves you enough to save you from being eternally separated from Him, and that you need a Savior. However, if you still do not clearly understand your consequences… two deaths and two penalties, let's take a closer look at the truth about Natural Death and **The Second Death** by using this one last approach.

My goal is to ensure that you know and understand the truth about life (light) and death (darkness) from God's perspective, especially the Second Death, which many are unaware of, before your certain demise. You have undoubtedly seen many Obituary programs; therefore, the following exercise is designed to bring about a sense of reality to you, utilizing what you already know and experience relating to death, an Obituary, and more specifically, your own **Obituary:**

A CLOSER LOOK AT LIFE AND DEATH

Homegoing Celebration

FOR

Sunrise
My Birthday

Sunset
Coming

ME
(PHOTO)

MY NAME

DATE & TIME OF SERVICE

TBA

NAME OF LOCATION

ADDRESS

NAME OF PERSON OFFICIATING

ABOUT ME

[Your Name] was born to
[parents]_____.

He/She was... or worked for..._____

_____.

He/She (circle one below mentally or with pen/pencil)

>Accepted Jesus Christ as my Savior or
>Did NOT Accept Jesus Christ as my Savior

If You <u>Chose</u> NOT to Accept Jesus Christ, continue to your 2nd Obituary

---

Interment

Burial Cemetery Name

Address

After reading your obituary on the previous pages, if you circled your acceptance of Jesus Christ, then this exercise is complete. However, for those who did not choose to accept Christ, perhaps now that you know that God's Word is the reason why you attend these ceremonies, you may desire to re-evaluate your thinking regarding your eternal past, present, and future. Your Spirit will indeed live on in one of the two eternal realms: *"For [upon death] man goes to his eternal home [Heaven or Hell]" (Ecclesiastes 12:5).* Therefore, you must decide which one.

However, please know that it is perfectly fine if you DID NOT accept Jesus Christ as your personal Savior from a Second Death or Eternal Death; it really doesn't matter if you believe God's Word or not, because both of your deaths and penalties are certain. Recall that Jesus died to make this choice completely up to you. But if you have denied Christ, you have another Obituary to review…The Obituary of your Second Death is exponentially worse than Gehenna **(Hell)** because **Revelation 20:10** says that Death and Hell are cast into it: *"And death and hell were cast into the lake of fire. This is the second death."*

Your Second Obituary...
Acceptance Of Your Second Death

*"...they were judged every man according to their work And death and hell were cast into the lake of fire **This is the second death**"*
~ Revelation 20:13-14

At this juncture, you will have experienced **"The Last Judgment,"** *Revelation 20:11-15: "And I saw a great white throne, and him that sat on it, from whose face the earth and the heaven fled away; and there was found no place for them. And I saw the dead, small and great, stand before God; and the books were opened: and another book was opened, which is the book of life: and the dead were judged out of those things written in the books, according to their works. And the sea gave up the dead which were in it; and death and hell delivered up the dead which were in them; they were judged every man according to their works.*

And death and hell were cast into the lake of fire. This is the second death. And whosoever was not found written in the book of life was cast into the lake of fire." This is an extremely serious scripture that has absolutely nothing to do with your church or religious affiliation. God is your Creator, and you must answer to Him regarding your choice to have a personal relationship with Jesus Christ or not. Your belief in Christ is the determining factor regarding where you will spend eternity, and it is upon this freedom that your choice is based.

The Last Judgment is your last face-to-face appearance before the Lord, which will lead to your second death and your second **(2nd)** Obituary. God's plan clearly explains that we must die once because *"the wages of sin is death"* for both Angelic Spirits and Human Beings: *"...it is appointed unto men once to die [a Natural*

Death], but after this the judgment [and The Second Death]" (Hebrews 9:27).

Jesus tells us that at the Last Judgment, some will hear these words: *"Not everyone who says to Me, 'Lord, Lord,' shall enter the kingdom of heaven, but he who does the will of My Father in heaven. Many will say to Me in that day, 'Lord, Lord, have we not prophesied in Your name, cast out demons in Your name, and done many wonders in Your name?' And then I will declare to them, 'I never knew you; depart from Me, you who practice lawlessness (Matthew 7:21-22)!'"*

However, since you have chosen to deny Christ, at this juncture, you will be transferred from Gehenna to the general resurrection, where **"all men"** will be judged and condemned to the Lake of Fire and Brimstone. *I [Jesus] am He who searches the minds and hearts [of Spirits/Man]. And I will give to each one of you [Heaven or Hell] according to your works"* (Revelation 2:23).

Therefore, you fully acknowledge your sinful ways and works, your betrayal, and your rebellious behavior against God. You refuse to **repent** or change your ways. You have made **YOUR OWN CHOICE TO DENY "the way, the truth, and the life"** or God's Word that was sent to materialize before man's eyes as Jesus Christ... our Savior. You hereby accept and acknowledge your choice to die a second and permanent death, which is hereby recorded in the heavenly books to eternity; now, please review your second and **Final Obituary:**

A CLOSER LOOK AT LIFE AND DEATH

Homegoing Celebration

FOR

Sunrise
N/A

Sunset
N/A

NO PHOTO
OF ME EXIST

MY EXISTENCE
HAS BEEN ERASED
OR BLOTTED OUT
FROM MEMORY

"Let them be before the
LORD continually,
that he may cut off the
memory of them from
the earth"

PSALMS 109:15

N/A
MY NAME
"BLOTTED OUT" OF EXISTENCE

DATE AND TIME OF SERVICE
"ETERNITY"

LOCATION
"THE LAKE OF FIRE AND BRIMSTONE"
Revelation 20:10

NAME OF PERSON OFFICIATING
"GOD"

Therefore, ***"Let them [their sins] be before the Lord continually, That He may cut off [or blot out] their memory from the earth" (Psalms 109:15).*** You **(your name)** will never be remembered by anyone in God's Universe ever again; you are blotted out of Eternal History forevermore. However, if you choose to believe in Christ, you do not have to be blotted out of eternal memory by experiencing The Second Death, which will occur at God's appointed time. God is JUST; therefore, He must have a plan in place that separates the righteous from the unrighteous based on each individual's choice according to **Deuteronomy 30:19**. Nevertheless, we all must stand before the Lord; He will ensure that all of Creation will understand all things, especially the reason why The Second Death is your fate. God will officiate over The Second Death, the consequence of the lifestyle that you, specifically, chose or received by default.

Please ensure that your family affairs are in order in preparation for your certain meeting(s) with the Lord upon your death. **So, again I ask you, "How can you believe that 'death' exists, but you say that you do NOT believe in the one true Creator-God, who issued your death sentence to you for what you, individually, did to Him in Heaven?" Yet, He chose to forgive you and came to Earth to die for your sins?** Go figure that out.

Satan Has Always Communicated With Man... He Drives Man And Technology To Meet His Desires

"Away from Me, Satan!" Jesus declared. "For it is written: 'WORSHIP THE LORD YOUR GOD AND SERVE HIM ONLY'"
~ Matthew 4:10

God, just as Satan, has always communicated with each other and with humanity. Matthew 4:10 confirms that Jesus, as a man, spoke with Satan. Just as God communicates with Spirits and Man, so do we. For us, communication with eternal Spirits has always been continuous because we are eternal Spirits, and thought is spiritual. Jesus walked the Earth as a Man (Immortal and of fallen flesh), and He spoke and interacted with humanity and the former Light Bearer. There are many instances in the Bible where Jesus, Adam, Eve, and others had direct and indirect communication with Satan, so why would it be any different for you and me in the present day?

You and Satan are and will always remain Spirits and in communication due to the **"Duality of Thought"** which is spiritual, however, the above scripture regarding communication has not dawned on you, even though God's Word plainly states: ***"For we do not wrestle against flesh and blood [the human body], but against principalities, against powers, against the rulers of the of this age, against spiritual hosts [Satan's Spirit who reside in the Souls of men] darkness of wickedness in the heavenly places" (Ephesians 6:12).*** From this scripture, it is very clear that we continuously struggle and strive with the Spirits of others, not their human. The body is the host or incubator of your Spirit. Recall that our Spirit contains our mind... thoughts, eternal memory, and character.

However, since we only see the physical body of someone, we forget that it is their Spirit that we really wrestle with, based on whether their Spirit is righteous or unrighteous. Recall that God tells us to *"...test the spirits, [to determine] whether they are of God" (1 John 4:1).* Please keep this in mind, or you can allow the distractions of your daily life to consume you because you do not believe that Satan exists, which is exactly what he wants you to believe, so that you will die and go to Hell by default.

For the sake of our redemption, the Garden of Eden purposefully took the spotlight along with the two trees, **"The Tree of Life"** and **"The Tree of the Knowledge Good and Evil,"** that stand out as all the other trees fade into the background in this beautiful Paradise, to reveal this fact. These two trees are the place of testing or the place of proving loyalty to our Creator or to Satan and his quest for dominion over all Creation in Heaven and on Earth, so that he exalts himself above God. However, since man is made of both Spirit (from Heaven) and Flesh (from the dirt of the Earth), representing the fall of the complete **"Man."** Our composition subjects both our Spirit and Body to interaction and communication with Satan, and it holds us captive to death, Hell, and the grave. So again, our body is the vehicle that carries or transitions us to and through death, judgment, and Hellfire punishment upon our death.

Now, let's take a closer look at the inconceivable beauty of God's Paradise, in Eden, filled with His Immortal Holiness and Glorious Divine Light, as well as the light of our Spirit and immortal fleshly bodies, in His likeness. Now, imagine this incredible scene before you, the glory of this heavenly landscape flowing with the purity of God's living waters... the fountain of eternal life, the indescribable radiance of the trees bearing brightly colored fruit that shine like glass. As we make our way to the center of this incomprehensible scene amidst the two trees that represent our only two choices in the Universe: eternal life and eternal death

(Deuteronomy 30:19). Hence, the latter equates to right/wrong, truth/lies, etc., that we previously established. These two trees are the foundation for our redemption.

First, we arrive at God's Tree, **"The Tree of Life,"** full of the fruit that sustains Eternal Life, exuding the truth of His Divine Knowledge, which flows from the Divine Mind of the Lord. Jesus is our eternal food and drink. He fuels the minds of believers in Christ with His Divine Knowledge…Food for thought? He shared this fact with His disciples at the **"Last Supper:"** *"…[Jesus] took bread; and when He had given thanks, He broke it and said, "Take, eat; this is My body which is broken for you; do this in remembrance [thought] of Me." In the same manner He also took the cup after supper, saying, "This cup is the new covenant in My blood. This do, as often as you drink it, in remembrance [thought] of Me" (1 Corinthians 11:24-25).*

Now, as we turn around, we arrive at Satan's Tree, **"The Tree of The Knowledge of Good and Evil,"** full of the fruit of his knowledge **(Science and Technology),** laced with the beguiling mixture of truth and lies that flow from Satan's demented mindset, which leads to unbelief in *God = Jesus,* destruction, and death. Satan's tree represents the good and evil that he intertwines to deceive us and leads its partakers to death, Hell, and the grave. Adam and Eve's fruit consumption in the Garden provides us with a first glimpse of DNA manipulation (more later).

Gehenna, or the temporary section of Hell, and the permanent section of Hell is called The Second Death…The Lake of Fire and Brimstone. The fruit from Satan's tree fuels our daily lives with chaos… mental darkness, **lack of control**, surrounded by tribulation, murder, destruction, violence, lies, deceit, graves, and death. Therefore, it is painfully obvious that we chose Satan's tree; you can tell by our fruit… our Spirit of unrighteousness, therefore, we do surely die!

The former Light Bearer's communication with us began as Spirit to Spirit, in Heaven, but on Earth, communication is with Spirit **(Satan is a Spirit)** to Humans, yet communication is still Spirit to Spirit, by virtue of the fact that our Spirit is held within our body. When God repurposed the Earth for our redemption, where He created the vessel of Man as the means to take us through Hellfire **(those who do not accept Jesus Christ),** humans, by virtue of their Spirit, remained in direct discourse with Satan. And direct discourse started with the conversation that took place in the midst of the two trees in the Garden of Eden. And it continued to occur after they were cast out of the Garden (more later in the book series).

Communication between fallen man and fallen angels, in the likeness of Satan, has always been a constant part of life on Earth, and has never stopped. Recall that in Noah's day, fallen angels taught humanity idolatry, witchcraft, magic, the use of makeup, the use of portals, other hidden knowledge, dark arts, and technology. According to the Oxford Dictionary, the word **"Technology"** is derived from the Greek term **Tekhne**, or techne, **technê (τέχνη)**, meaning art, craft, technique, or skill. And it is through Satan's communication with man that he passes his techniques, crafts, and skills to humanity. The former Light Bearer offers humanity his knowledge, based on our "tree selection" in the Garden, that is disguised as high intellect used for our advancement, which comes with the pride of ego. Satan's knowledge is always geared towards the detriment of man…destruction, death, Hell, and the grave. When are you going to **wake up**?

Communication between Satan and humanity was apparent when Jesus came to Earth. There are numerous occasions when Jesus and Satan had direct discourse:

Luke 4:3-4 "And the devil [Satan] said to Him [Jesus], "If You are the Son of God, command this stone to become bread." But

Jesus answered him, saying, "It is written, 'Man shall not live by bread alone, but by every word of God."

Mark 8:33 "And Jesus answered and said to him [Satan], "Get behind Me, Satan! For it is written, 'You shall worship the Lord your God, and Him only you shall serve."

Mark 1:13 "And he [Jesus] was there in the wilderness forty days, tempted of Satan; and was with the wild beasts; and the angels ministered unto him."

The above scriptures reveal that this same direct communication with Satan continues in the Earth today, but it is reserved as a secret amongst his elite and his agents throughout the world. However, after the flood, communication became more indirect because the fallen angels were destroyed, while others are chained in Earth's realm: *"...the sixth angel who had the trumpet, "Release the four angels who are bound at the great river Euphrates" (Revelation 9:14)*. The four fallen angels at the Euphrates River and the Nephilim offspring begotten when fallen angels mated with human women and yielded a breed of Giants called the Nephilim (the elite have kept hidden the artifacts of giants from us). After the flood, the Giants no longer roamed the Earth.

Satan has compelled man to create methods of communication with the unseen world of antimatter or dark demonic energy by using UFO Technology. However, due to the high visibility that propels curiosity, these visits became problematic and disruptive, so the powers that be and their militaries sought to keep these visits secret. Consequently, Satan guided man to create a less visible method of communication with the unseen realm with the innovation of Computer Technology.

As you know, UFOs **(Unidentified Flying Objects),** or their new term Unidentified Aerial Phenomenon **(UAP),** have been hidden from society because they reveal the elite's communication with the former Light Bearer and the continuous knowledge that they receive from his so-called Aliens **(Fallen Angels)**. The evidence of the relationship between Man and Satan's Alien Beings yields top-secret information, and this direct communication has been closely guarded by the Vatican, Secret Societies, Governments, and their Military. However, under the guise of Science, Scientists have taken credit for knowledge obtained from Satan's tree or Satan himself. Satan cloaks his work in secrecy, but have you noticed that suddenly, the United States Government and the Vatican have recently acknowledged the existence and belief in **UFOs** and **Aliens**?

After many decades of covering up UFOs or UAPs, in May 2021, CNN and other media outlets reported that President Obama came out publicly stating that *"footage and records of objects in the skies, that we don't know exactly what they are. We can't explain how they moved, their trajectory"* is in keeping with a broader acknowledgment by official arms of the government – after decades of denial! – **UFOs are real**." The article below states that the U.S. Navy has confirmed videos from among its ranks: https://www.nbcnews.com/science/weird-science/obama-ufo-videos-dont-know-exactly-are-rcna963

Space Force: The Rise Of Drone Technology And Strong Delusion

"The coming of the lawless one is according to the working of Satan, with all power, signs, and lying wonders"
[even in the Sky]
~ 2 Thessalonians 2:9

And verses **10-12 continue: "and with all unrighteous deception among those who perish [unbelievers], because they did not receive the love of the truth, that they might be saved [from The Second Death]. And for this reason, God will send them <u>strong delusion</u>, that they should believe the lie, [so] that they all may be condemned who did not believe the truth but had pleasure in unrighteousness."** In November 2019, the United States launched a new military division: the U.S. Space Force. Officially, Space Force is the space service branch of the U.S. Armed Forces—one of the eight uniformed services and the world's first and only independent space force.

The stated mission is to ensure space security, project combat power, enhance space mobility and logistics, facilitate information mobility, and maintain space domain awareness. However, this may not be the true mission. Throughout history, the elite have concealed the truth, revealing it only when absolutely necessary. The truth lies beyond their official narrative, so it remains shrouded in secrecy.

U.S. Space Force is a branch of the government's Armed Forces, designed not only to advance military operations in space but also to create, develop, and implement chaos and a "strong delusion" to manipulate the minds of the masses. By disrupting societal norms, they pave the way for subversion, making global control easier to achieve.

Their tactics are openly displayed in the Obama-produced film Leave the World Behind, which serves as a chilling revelation of the elite's plan. The movie depicts orchestrated isolation and synchronized chaos leading to a staged **Coup d'État,** a sudden and violent overthrow of a government by a small, powerful group. I urge you to see through this **covert conspiracy**, now unfolding before the public's eyes.

Even though Satan is the father of lies, he MUST speak and reveal truth in the Presence of the Lord, for instance when he confessed to Jesus, *"...I know who You are—the Holy One of God!" (Luke 4:34),* just as you will certainly bow down to the Lord and confess who He is because, once again, *Romans 14:11* states *"...Every knee [your knee, my knee, Satan's knee and every knee in Heaven, on Earth and under the Earth] shall bow to Me, and every tongue shall confess to God."* Therefore, ready or not, you will stand before God and confess. If you are not ready, I urge you to get ready. However, before that day comes, understand that Satan must reveal his true intentions, for even he is bound by divine law. He does this through Hollywood, Bollywood, or the entertainment industry, which serves as his tool of deception.

While disguising truth as fiction, it conditions the masses and manipulates reality, while hiding in plain sight. movies and production within. Later in the book series, you will discover that Satan had to come clean or tell the truth about himself in the presence of Adam, Eve, and the Lord after they were expelled from the Garden. I say this to say that Satan's lies to you will eventually run out, and then you will see the truth, but it will be too late; you will stand before a Holy God, where it will be revealed that you obeyed and followed Satan rather than the Lord's truth. And of course, **Hellfire awaits you**. The Earth was designed to be the place where God's Truth will be seen as triumphant over Satan's lies and every evil like it was shown at Christ's resurrection.

ALL Truth will be revealed before the Holiness of God, which is where truth originates from and where only truth resides in its Glory. Those who do not accept God's truth through Jesus Christ will default to encountering His wrath and Eternal Hellfire. This is the bottom line of what God, through His Word, Jesus Christ, came to reveal to us.

The elite, who have long relied on Satan's blueprints to develop advanced technology, are on the verge of having their agendas exposed. What has occurred to compel the military, world leaders, the Pope, and other powerful figures to publicly acknowledge the existence of **UFOs** (UAPs) and extraterrestrial beings? It appears they have encountered an obstacle in their communication with the unseen realm, leaving them with no alternative but to disclose their connection with Satan, his fallen angels, or so-called aliens.

What could have led to this unprecedented revelation? A military insider with access to highly classified information has confirmed the elite's reliance on satanic knowledge. He disclosed details about two secret projects he worked on years ago: Project Stargate and Project Looking Glass. Through Project Looking Glass, researchers established computer-based communication with fallen angels (aliens), posing questions, much like artificial intelligence (**ChatGPT**) systems today, regarding forecasts and predicting future events that will shape their policies, laws, and plans.

Computer-based systems would generate various outcomes and timelines, enabling the elite to manipulate global affairs accordingly. High-level strategy meetings, planning committees, and geopolitical agendas were then formulated based on these computer-generated predictions, all under the guidance of the former Light Bearer himself. However, the project eventually reached an unprecedented turning point. The once-divergent possibilities and timelines suddenly converged into a single, definitive outcome—one that the elite were entirely unprepared to face. This revelation further supports the argument that computer technology has become a gateway for communication with the unseen realm, a concept explored in the following section. However, he said that the project came to a juncture, unlike any other time in history, when all their computer-based "scenarios of possibilities" and timelines converged into one answer that they were unprepared to receive.

At this juncture, every question they fed into the computer to analyze through what he referred to as "The Looking Glass" produced the same outcome, causing panic among the elite. Alarmed by this revelation, the military insider was assigned to investigate further. What he discovered only reinforced the validity of the computer's response: every scenario and timeline pointed to an inevitable, world-altering event, one that had been biblically foretold. He called this event "The Awakening," a moment when the truth of God's divine plan would be undeniably revealed. It confirmed that the Rapture of believers in Jesus Christ is real, imminent, and completely beyond human control. There is nothing mankind can do to stop it, alter it, or prevent it.

How can the elite prepare for this massively disruptive event, where millions will vanish as they are Raptured from the Earth? For nearly 6,000 years, the elite have placed their hope and trust in Satan's deception, but their reliance on his lies came to an abrupt end when the military officer turned whistleblower delivered the stunning revelation of God's end-times plan.

God's supreme will always prevails over the plans of His created beings, whether spiritual or human, throughout the universe. When Satan and his followers hit an impassable roadblock, as exposed by the whistleblower, they had no choice but to acknowledge their interaction with Satan, fallen angels, and so-called aliens. In response, they began developing new strategies and counter-

A CLOSER LOOK AT LIFE AND DEATH

narratives to explain away the Rapture before it occurs. The elite are fully aware of what time it is; they know that we are living in the final moments of the end times, approaching the last days of God's Divine Grace, which will usher in the Rapture of the Church, the outpouring of God's wrath, and ultimately, the final battle that began in Heaven will end with the War of Armageddon.

This is why, over the past few years, he has been revealing his plans through Hollywood films such as **"*Avengers: Infinity War,*"** **"*Spider-Man: No Way Home*"** (A not-so-subtle message—Satan has no way home to Heaven, but you do). Satan is not in control of anything except for sin, evil, chaos, tribulation, death, Hell, and the grave, but even that control was stripped away from Him at the resurrection of Jesus Christ.

Rather than acknowledging the next major event on God's prophetic timeline as the Rapture, the elite, under Satan's directive, have instead rebranded it as **"The Great Reset,"** The Awakening, or anything but the Rapture. Yet, regardless of what they choose to call it, the fact remains: we are at the very threshold of this divine event, as confirmed by military insiders. Knowing they cannot stop the Rapture, the elite devised a deception to obscure the truth. They plan to convince the masses through media, propaganda, and controlled narratives that the sudden disappearance of millions of believers will be due to UFOs (UAPs), or alien abductions. The whistleblower's revelations sent shockwaves through their ranks, leaving them scrambling to deal with the inescapable reality of biblical prophecy coming to pass.

In their desperation, they resorted to delays and disinformation, constructing an intricate web of lies to keep the truth hidden. But as time ran out, they were forced to disclose their secrets, slowly admitting to their longstanding knowledge of UFOs, UAPs, and extraterrestrial life. The whistleblower also warned that once the truth is fully revealed, there will be no denying the depths of their deception.

In response to this impending exposure, the government has recently acknowledged the existence of UFOs and UAPs, while initiatives such as President Trump's launch of the Space Force, Project Blue Beam, CERN, and other covert operations serve as tools to manage public perception. Whether they call it The Awakening, The Great Reset, or any other fabricated term, their true objective remains clear—to conceal the undeniable fulfillment of God's Word and mislead the world regarding the Rapture of the Church.

The following are recent news reports that have spurred speculation regarding Aliens. It is reported that **NASA** has hired Priests to prepare humanity for contact with aliens (fallen angels), "NASA used religious experts to predict how humans may react to aliens; two dozen theologians were recruited by a NASA-funded program to assess societal implications for the agency's astro-biological and search for life efforts." -thehill.com| (Dec. 28, 2021). "British priest to advise NASA on what to do if alien life is discovered on another planet." – mirror.co.uk You can be certain that the elite would never have disclosed the truth about UFOs and extraterrestrial beings unless they were forced to do so. Fallen angels are an essential part of their plan to establish a totalitarian one-world government and enforce the public worship of Satan.

As communication between Satan and the elite increasingly manifested through UFO encounters, these disturbances became too frequent and too visible to keep hidden from the public. To counter this exposure, Satan devised an alternative method to maintain his connection with humanity and the darkness of his unseen realm, one that would integrate seamlessly into modern society: Computer technology and programming. Computer hardware was deliberately designed as an input device, enabling humans to interact with the unseen world through coding and programming. By entering commands, formulas, and complex algorithms, users unknowingly translate their inquiries into a form that can be processed within the spiritual realm. This system, though perceived as a mere technological advancement, serves as a gateway for continued communication with the forces of darkness.

The software operating within a computer's architecture compiles human language and translates it into numeric machine code, known as binary code, the universal language of energy. In this system, bits are grouped into sets of zeros and ones to form larger data sets called bytes; in Quantum Computers, they are called Qubits:

1 represents Positive Polarity, **On**, and Light

0 represents Negative Polarity, **Off**, and Darkness

In essence, computer software processes our words, instructions, and requests by taking the input we type, compiling it through a compiler, and then assembling it into binary code (0s and 1s) via assembly language. This breakdown further converts into machine code (bits and bytes) for analysis and processing, ultimately generating the desired output or response. Interestingly, consider the symbolism associated with Apple Computers:

- The company's logo, a bitten apple, mirrors Eve's bite of the fruit from **"The Tree of the Knowledge of Good and Evil."**

- In Apple's computer terminology: Bit = Bite = Byte = Qubits.

- Apple's first computer, the Apple I, was originally priced at $666.66 in July 1976... Coincidence? Or something more?

I remember that my Electrical Engineering curriculum required that I take computer programming, where I learned how to write Computer Binary Code, Machine Code, and Computer Language, commonly called Computer Programs. I also learned how to compile my programs, run them, and analyze the output results. I was taught Assembly Language (early 1980s), and according to

Wikipedia, it is a programming language where "there is a very strong correspondence between the instructions in the language and the architecture's machine code instructions." Notice the definition states "very strong correspondence!"

The words **"Correspondence"** and **"Language"** indicate communication between two or more, and in the case of Computer Technology, communication occurs with the unseen realm through the exchange of letters, numbers, instructions, formulas, etc. that are converted into computer code or machine language so that the data is understood by someone or an entity on the other end; they respond back in like manner. The receiver of the machine code reads it, carries out our instructions, compiles and assembles the data, and returns it to us in words, numbers, formulas, etc., as our answers. This hidden, yet at our fingertips, manner of communication is so subtle that no one realizes what is happening.

To visualize the results of our communication, computer monitors or backlit screens, or LED backlit displays were developed. Because we exist in the darkness of the Abyss, light is required for us to see. Backlight, a form of illumination used in liquid-crystal displays (LCDs), was introduced. LCDs do not produce light on their own; instead, they require an external light source, either from ambient lighting or an integrated backlight, to create a visible image. This illumination, positioned behind or along the sides of the display panel, enables us to perceive digital content. Backlights are now a fundamental component of smartphones, computer monitors, and LCD televisions (Backlight, Wikipedia.org).

Satan has imparted knowledge to humanity regarding how to build computers that enable communication with him and his unseen realm. Since antimatter or dark matter thrives in light wave energy, in this fallen world, it manifests as electrical energy (current), as well as ocean waves that move in oscillating patterns.

Ocean wave energy is naturally harnessed and stored in high capacity within sand on ocean shores. As a result, the former Light Bearer has guided mankind to develop computer components using sand, specifically beach sand, which is refined to produce silicon. The process involves heating sand with a carbon-reducing agent, generating carbon monoxide and pure silicon. This silicon is then used to manufacture semiconductor chips that form the foundation of computer hardware, such as motherboards and other electronic components.

In the late 20th century, modern computer technology emerged, eventually leading to the rise of Silicon Valley, a region in Northern California, near San Francisco Bay, that serves as a global hub for advanced technology. Ironically named after silicon itself, this area has become home to Big Tech giants like Apple, Google, and Cisco, along with numerous tech startups and leading corporations.

We unknowingly invite Satan into our world through computing, particularly through software programming languages that bear symbolic connections to the serpent. For example, Python, a high-level, object-oriented programming language introduced in 1991, enables programmers to write concise and logical code, resembling natural human language. For decades, the elite have utilized computing operations to send and receive information from the dark side in secrecy. Eventually, this technology was made available for individual use, allowing for a more advanced form of communication. Today, this communication manifests as search engines, **ChatGPT**, and **OpenAI**, where users can type or use voice commands to search, request, and receive answers instantly.

Programming, in the age of Artificial Intelligence Systems, programs are technically called Algorithms. However, the word "Algorithm," more specifically, is a term used by robotic computer programmers when they don't want to explain what they are doing, meaning they don't want to reveal their ability to communicate with the darkness of the unseen realm. According to the Merriam-Webster Dictionary, the word Algorithm is defined as: *"The current term of choice for a problem-solving procedure, algorithm, is commonly used nowadays for the set of rules a machine (and especially a computer) follows to achieve a particular goal. It does not always apply to computer-mediated activity."* Think of it as step-by-step programming, like following a recipe.

As an Electrical Engineer and NASA Fellow at Lewis Research Center in Cleveland, Ohio (renamed NASA John H. Glenn Research Center at Lewis Field in 1999), I had the opportunity to research and test aircraft engines in huge wind tunnels. My computer tasks were performed on the Cray-1 Supercomputer. This was the first, fastest, and most successful mainframe supercomputer of its era. Developed by Cray Research, the Cray-1 was a 64-bit processor operating at 80 MHz and was introduced in 1975. It utilized a vector-based processing system, designed to handle high-level mathematical operations on large data sets.

However, in pursuit of God's omnipotence and omnipresence capabilities, Satan seeks to obtain, store, and process data on the entire global population. This data is gathered through surveillance systems, cashless currency transactions, and other tracking mechanisms, enabling monitoring and control over Earth's population. The former Light Bearer has influenced humanity to develop large-scale databases through companies like Oracle, which specialize in the collection and storage of massive data sets. As the global population grows, so does the demand for data collection, processing power, memory, and storage capabilities. This necessity has driven the advancement of computing technology.

Now that we have entered the era of Artificial Intelligence (AI) and Quantum Computing, which enable high-level, nano-based technology for devices, such as cell phones that now operate on 5G network infrastructure, with ongoing advancements leading to 6G technology. These developments are paving the way for Artificial Super Intelligence (ASI), a level of machine intelligence that could surpass human intelligence and extend beyond the limitations of fallen humanity.

6G networks will harvest AI energy to support infrastructure that will sustain high-tech Smart Cities with enhanced surveillance technology, autonomous driving or self-driving vehicles, Cloud and Edge Computing, Drone Technology, 3D Virtual Reality (Metaverse Technology), Holographic Technology, Drone Technology, Mind Control Technology, AI Energy, and "The Internet of Things" which are key to total population control. The goal is to have everything, and every BODY embedded with a chip or vaccine administered metallic technology in order to alter their DNA and enable connection and subjection of the entire population to the Antichrist's all-knowing Beast System Computer Matrix. For those who have chosen not to believe in Jesus Christ, it is "…for this cause [reason] God shall send them [unbeliever] strong delusion, that they should believe a lie:" (2 Thessalonians 2:11), which makes it easier to capture the minds of the masses as they are led into total population control.

In China, the **dragon** serves as the proving ground for Satan's **Totalitarian Technology**, which will eventually be deployed worldwide. The country dominates in Drone Technology, a tool that will play a critical role in **global deception**. The elite will leverage **drones**, in combination with **Project Blue Beam** and **Artificial Intelligence Technology,** to transform the **sky into a vast theatrical backdrop**. This sophisticated system will be used to create staged events, deceiving the masses with lying signs and wonders: *"The coming of the lawless one is according to the working of Satan, with all power, signs, and lying wonders, and with all unrighteous deception among those who perish, because* *they did not receive the love of the truth, that they might be saved. And for this reason God will send them strong delusion, that they should believe the lie, that they all may be condemned who did not believe the truth but had pleasure in unrighteousness" (2 Thessalonians 2:9-12).*

Breaking News: Social Media is all a buzz surrounding the report that Jesus Christ has been sighted in the sky over the United States, in Alabama. This is Project Blue Beam in action to bring **STRONG DELUSION** to the masses. Per the videos circulating, it is reported that on July 12, 2025, a Jesus-shaped light could be seen in Alabama's sky after extreme thunderstorms. Google it or see this video: https://www.facebook.com/share/v/19FdqegtuN/.

Let's not forget that not long ago, an extreme number of drones were reported in the skies across many US states and abroad. However, government officials disregarded it, lied, or failed to explain the phenomenon; now you know. Do not be surprised if this technology is used to introduce the Antichrist, fabricate an alien invasion, promote global worship of Satan, or even stage a false Rapture event. Remember that the Lord does not want you to be deceived!

On New Year's Eve 2023, China deployed drones to project an AI-generated image of the **"God of Technology (AI),"** a chilling parallel of the Image of the Beast, in the night sky. And to mark the arrival of 2025, over 10,000 drones were used to create a massive depiction of a dragon, with a portal opening above it. The event was fittingly called **"The Year of the Dragon."** The elite are making their intentions clear. So, when will you **wake up** and stop risking your eternal future?

As of late, there have been many drone sightings reportedly hovering over many American cities, as well as in various countries around the world, for weeks and months. Some, they say, appeared to be spraying chemicals, and in New Jersey, many residents have reportedly taken ill. Therefore, it causes me to wonder about the titles of several movies that foretold this technology, dating back decades, and some recent ones like *"Avengers: End Game"* and *"The Matrix Resurrection."* Also, other movies feature drones, but *"Drone"* is not in the title. Furthermore, there are interactive drone games for gaming platforms, like *"FPV Drone Kamikaze," "Drone Tactics,* etc. As I said, Satan tells us what he is up to, but we don't pay attention.

We know that Satan's ultimate goal, through his AI computer-generated image, is to be worshipped for all of the knowledge and technological advancement that he has provided to mankind, ever since **Eve (humanity)** chose to eat from Satan's tree, **"The Tree of the Knowledge of Good and Evil,"** instead of God's **"The Tree of Life.**

Although in the Book of Redemption… the Holy Bible, God reveals the increasing rise of **STRONG DELUSION** during the end times and last days, He makes certain to warn those of us with ears to hear Him and eyes to read His Holy Word so that we are prepared for what is to come and we can, *"Watch out that no one deceives you!" Matthew 24:4*

Real Intelligence

God = Real = Truth = Nature = Natural = Godly Beings

RI

vs.

AI

Artificial Intelligence

Satan = Fake = Lies = Artificial = Unnatural = Ungodly Beings

    First and foremost, there is no comparison or competition between God, the Creator's infinite **"Real Intelligence,"** and the finite **"Artificial Intelligence"** system that Satan, a created being, has guided humanity to create. A created being will never be even remotely equal to our Creator. Now, consider this question: *Is artificial sugar real sugar?* Of course not. The same applies to Satan's Beast System, which is powered by Artificial Intelligence, a counterfeit of God's Divine Eternal Intelligence, reflecting his own deceptive nature and dark mindset that is designed to fuel the ultimate deceptions during the end times and last days when strong delusion will be rampant.

    Satan makes his intentions clear, even the name itself, Artificial Intelligence, whereas it is self-explanatory that this is his own technology and is counterfeit or not of God. While AI technology can be used for both good and evil, it is the mindset and intent of the creator of this technology that is the real concern; his intent and goals for its use render it sinister and ungodly. Everything God has made reflects His Divine Design and His Divine Order. In contrast, Satan, the ultimate copycat, seeks to create his own beings for his purposes, outside of God's will. But he knows one undeniable truth: God will never allow him to create real human life in His own image.

So, the question becomes, *"What defines 'real' and 'fake' or artificial?"* The answer lies in whether the *"object of creation"* is created with the mindset of God or not: *"We [the Apostles and those who teach God's word] are from God [energized by the Holy Spirit], and whoever knows God [through personal experience] listens to us [to have a deeper understanding of Him]. Whoever is not of God does not listen to us [or have His Divine mindset] By this we know [without any doubt] the spirit of truth [motivated by God] and the spirit of error [lies, falsehoods, or fakeness is] motivated by Satan" (1 John 4:6 AB).* Everything in the Universe is centered on and around the one and only true Creator-God, who by His Holy Word, Jesus, was sent forth to create everything that was made *(John 1:3)*.

God = Real = Truth = Nature = Natural = Godly Angelic Beings = Godly Human Beings

God is the sole Creator of "Life" and that which is real and defines our reality in Heaven and Earth... Spirit Beings, Human Beings with Spirit within, Mammals, Birds, Vegetation, all that is Nature; Natural. The Holy Spirit of Truth does not lend Himself or His Divine Knowledge to create anything *fake = Artificial = AI = Artificial Intelligence* created by the mindset of the former Light Bearer. We know that food grown in a lab or that is Genetically Modified Organisms **(GMO) food** is altered or exists in an unnatural state, not created in its entirety from God's Nature or comes from His Natural Earth; therefore, GMO food is fake or artificial. Recall that the source of our knowledge and mental intent is defined by our **"Tree"** selection in the Garden of Eden, unless you are born again in Christ Jesus.

Who controls Reality? My answer is: The only one who created the reality of Heaven and Earth, each having their own respective "Realities." Since we are created in the Holy Image of God, we also have the ability to create our own reality by virtue of our thoughts. **"Thought"** is energy that constantly directs outward into the universe; thus, your energy within your mind is used for the preponderance of thought that includes data analysis as we send and receive eternal spiritual energy, make observations, and evaluations that support your decision-making process to derive your mental content. During the course of thinking, your mind subconsciously and consciously focuses and concentrates on various things that lead to your lifestyle choices and actions.

Reality is formed by the oscillating flow of negative and positive thought energy, which equates to: $R = I \times C$ or REALITY = the INTENSITY of what you are thinking, times (multiplied by) the CONTENT of the thoughts you choose to focus on. Your thoughts, words, and *emotions = energy in motion*, act as seeds of energy sown into the fertile ground of your life to create and affect your reality for good or evil. For instance, if you are passionate about buying a house, it creates INTENSE concentration and effort to save up for the purchase and requires searching for and eventually buying the house. This endeavor takes up a lot of your thoughts, time, and emotions as you complete the steps to make your thoughts of homeownership a reality for you. These thoughts are considered mentally dominant CONTENT that consumes your mind until you fulfill the objective that will manifest your new REALITY of homeownership achievement, in which case, Congratulations are warranted.

On the contrary, if you are having problems that cause you to worry, and thus worry intensifies in your thoughts and becomes the focus of your mental content, you create an adverse reality of a negative attitude, depression, and anxiety that may lead you to unrighteousness. Thus, your REALITY (R) = (I) INTENSE Worry X (C) 75% ± MENTAL CONTENT of Worrisome, Negative Thoughts or Mind Content Consumption = Unfavorable outcomes for you. Therefore, be mindful, pay attention to what your mind consumes or focuses on the most, and "…take captive every thought to make it obedient to Christ" (2 Corinthians 10:5) so that your REALITY will reflect Christ Jesus from the inside and out.

Real Knowledge is divine light within our minds. The Knowledge of Truth and Righteousness, in all things, comes only from the LORD alone. The pathway of knowledge from Heaven to Earth is in His Garden and within His Tree… **"The Tree of Life."** As well, artificial knowledge emanates from Satan's tree, "The Tree of the Knowledge of Good and Evil," or the fruits of unrighteousness, evilness; the wickedness that beguiles the darkness of our minds so that we cannot see, think, hear, or know the truth of God. Yet, according to the name of this tree, which includes the words **"good"** and **"evil,"** meaning that the duality of God's goodness is always present within a lie; therefore, wherever evil is, the truth of God was there first. There was truth long before a lie was ever confessed before the Lord; truth is always first and present… before our Reality became Duality.

Satan = Fake = Artificial = Lies = Unnatural = Ungodly Beings = Demonic Beings = Alien Beings = Clones = Robots = Hybrids = Infants Born from Artificial (Lab) Wombs

Ironically, it takes the truth to be present first, then the truth is distorted or twisted; things are added to the truth to make it seemingly not true. For instance, when the serpent approached Eve, she quickly told the serpent exactly what God said to her: *"We may eat the fruit of the trees of the garden; but of the fruit of the tree which is in the midst of the garden, God has said, 'You shall not eat it, nor shall you touch it, lest you [surely] die" (Genesis 3:2-3).* Then in *Genesis 3:4,* the former Light Bearer, beguiling (deceptively lying) to Eve, said: *"Then the serpent said to the woman, "You will not surely die. For God knows that in the day you eat of it your eyes will be opened, and you will be like God, knowing good and evil "Freedom of Choice" exists relative to His Divine Redemption Plan to save you and me from The Eternal Second Death". (Genesis 3:4-5).*

Satan told Eve, *"You will not surely die."* He added the word **"not"** into his sentence to twist the truth so that God's truth would become a lie. I am sure Eve was rattled by the encounter, which caused her to second-guess what God had said to her, nevertheless, she knew exactly what God said. It is the manipulation of God's Truth that creates the artificiality of lies.

We can tell the difference between these two trees, spotlighted within the midst of the Garden, by the fruits that they yield in your life, towards righteousness or unrighteousness. Jesus Christ is now **"The Tree of Life,"** which all born-again believers can eat from daily to produce the fruits of God's Glory in their lives. Take a moment to assess your fruits of righteousness from God's Tree through Christ that yield love, peace, positivity, or fruitful outcomes in your situations and circumstances, versus your life filled with the fruits that yield anger, hate, fear, confusion, frustration, death, Hell, and the grave. Your mind is racing, constantly processing negative thoughts that create chaos as your tongue spews foul language and violent rhetoric while yielding to your eccentric emotions that produce evil acts and behavior; thus, revealing your lack of self-control. But again, this is personal because it is your choice, alone, as to which fruits your lifestyle will bear… Think about it.

During the End Times and *"in the last days perilous times will come: For men will be lovers of themselves, lovers of money, boasters, proud, blasphemers, disobedient to parents, unthankful, unholy, unloving, unforgiving, slanderers, without self-control, brutal, despisers of good, traitors, headstrong, haughty, lovers of pleasure rather than lovers of God, having a form of godliness [going to church, serving in church, carrying or reading the*

Bible] but denying its power [unbelievers are] led away by various lusts, always learning [gaining intelligence] and never able to come to the knowledge of the truth" (2Timothy 3:1-3). This scripture says that unbelievers seek and gain knowledge to become intelligent in science, technology, etc., but never learn God's truth. Wow! Let that sink in. Therefore, the intelligence that unbelievers gain from the former Light Bearer is Artificial Intelligence, which leads to death, Hell, and the grave.

The Last Days will usher in the worship of Satan; this will no longer occur in secret as it has for thousands of years. There will be public worship of him as he exerts his global control over humanity by utilizing computer technology that communicates with the unseen realm or Aliens, under the guise of science and advanced technology. This technology offers man convenience, super abilities, and hidden knowledge that will lead man to destruction. Again, Satan tries to copy God's Creation of Humans as he attempts to create His own **"Beings,"** human clones and robots that can be programmed and/or inhabited by demonic Spirits as well. He will use artificial limbs or prostheses made to conjoin with the human body, various metallic implants, etc.

Daniel 2:41-43 foretold of this technology: *"Whereas you saw the feet and toes, partly of potter's clay [flesh created from the dirt or clay of the Earth] and partly of iron [metal prosthetics, etc.], the kingdom shall be divided; yet the strength of the iron shall be in it, just as you saw the iron mixed with ceramic clay. And as the toes of the feet were partly of iron and partly of clay, so the kingdom shall be partly strong and partly fragile.*

As you saw iron [metal prosthetics, etc.] mixed with ceramic clay [flesh created from the dirt or clay from the Earth], they will mingle with the seed of men; but they will not adhere to one another, just as iron does not mix with clay." This means that Satan will try to integrate or mix the two kingdoms together, having the strength of God as represented by humanity along with the weakness of the kingdom of darkness; however, the two will never be one, only co-mingled. This scripture confirms that Satan's ability to create is extremely limited compared to God's supreme power. He has never and will never be able to create a real human being or match God's intelligence regarding the ability to create life. The Lord designed human beings with an inner temple whereby Christ, through the indwelling Holy Spirit, can reside.

The former Light Bearer is incapable of creating human beings designed for a personal relationship with their Creator, beings with the ability to express love, truth, and righteousness according to God's commands. For God alone is the source of love, truth, and righteousness. Satan can only manipulate external elements, mixing machines with human flesh, but he will never have access to the spiritual essence of mankind or the divine connection between humanity and its Creator. Separation from God happens by choice, choosing an unholy, worldly life aligned with Satan or choosing a holy, Christ-centered life aligned with Heaven. The decision is yours, and no one can make it for you.

[Exercise]: Seek the REAL Intelligence that is within "You!" RI is the fiber of our being; it is a part of our real DNA that God created within our body as our divine connection to Him. Now, find a quiet place to reflect and pray while looking upwards unto Jesus Christ, the name above all names. Call upon His peace as you begin to examine the source of your belief in the artificial or lies that you continue to fall for, instead of depending on the truth of God. Reflect on everything within yourself that is opposite to righteousness.

These days, people are so angry, hateful, frustrated, saying foul words, filled with violence, unforgiveness, pride, etc., therefore, ask God the following: "Why am I so quick to get angry and curse people out or even become violent? And although I later realize that

I was wrong, I can't bring myself to go back to them and apologize... Why? Lord, why can't I forgive others like you have forgiven me? Or why am I so jealous-hearted and judgmental, or think that I know it all? Who am I around that may influence my behavior?" Begin to investigate, analyze, and deal with yourself from the inside out. Talk to God, go inward to Him seeking to bring His **"Peace"** within you, ***the peace of God, which passeth all understanding" (Philippians 4:6).***

Step into the "Eternal Mind of Christ" where Real Intelligence (RI) resides. Call upon His Holy Light to lighten the pathways within your mind, which elevates the vibrations of your thoughts unto eternal things. Pray His Light and Peace over your thought life, your tongue, actions, and your behavior; immerse your reactions and your interactions with others, your situations or circumstances in the peace of Christ. Sincerely, humble yourself and surrender ALL of your thoughts, emotions, anger, hatred, fears, jealousy, foul words/tongue, negativity, depression, anxiety, stress, behavior, selfishness, sexual improprieties, pride, or whatever ails you; give it over to your Heavenly Father, consistently. Read and pray Proverbs 3:5-6 again, look upwards towards the direction of the Good of Heaven, the source from which His divine light and your help cometh.

"I Surrender ALL to Christ" is the most transformative change to your mind, body, and Soul (where the Indwelling Holy Spirit dwells per your invitation). Surrendering ALL is the best spiritual move that I ever made because it relieved the weight of burdens and the act of trying to figure out my life because I know that my life is Christ's life and He is in control, He directs my path as only He can do: ***"Thus says the LORD, your Redeemer, The Holy One of Israel: "I am the LORD your God, Who teaches you to profit, Who leads you by the way you should go" (Isaiah 48:17).*** However, surrendering ALL is a process as you remember to surrender new things to the Lord, the big and the small things and it lasts until all things are laid bare before Him so that worry doesn't exist anymore. And please remember to surrender your bed and/or your bedroom activities, your sex life, unto the Father.

Also, take time to forgive yourself and allow God's Peace to rush in the comfort you, then work towards forgiving others; even if you cannot physically face someone to tell them that you are sorry, or that you forgive them, practice telling them or say it out loud with your mouth until you can actually go before them if you are so lead too. Allow the Holy Spirit to lead you as you ***"lean not on your own understanding" (Proverbs 3:5).*** When I surrendered all, I stopped trying to figure out my life. I learned to talk to Christ first, rather than as a last result, meaning not after I have called my family and friends to get their opinion; they can't do a darn thing to help me because my help cometh from the Lord, above, read Psalms 121:2. Internalize everything, realizing that your issues are internal to your being and that they must be addressed between you and your Creator-God who sent His Son to save you.

Lastly, learn the power of the **"Silence"** within you, where God resides and speaks to you. Turn within yourself to ask Him for the answers that you seek instead of turning to family and friends. Learn to just shut up sometimes, instead of lashing out at others or acting out of the character of Christ because you cannot deal with your inner self where He resides (if you invited Him in). Silence is a true virtue! Sit in your quiet place and relax your mind and body. Clear your mind and just be, then notice what comes through your mind while in the silence. Reject negative thoughts, past worries, and thoughts about the future because all you have is today, the current moment, to enjoy the silence within the Holy Spirit.

When you continue to surrender, practice forgiveness and silence, it brings patience, you will notice a change…a renewing of your mind (read Romans 12:2), you will gain mental clarity (1 Peter

A CLOSER LOOK AT LIFE AND DEATH

4:6-8), strengthen your faith (Hebrew 11:1) and harness a deeper trust in God (Proverbs 3:5). Be careful as to what you allow into your Spirit, what you read, listen to or watch to avoid being led towards the artificial or the fakeness of lies, negativity, and unholiness.

And guard your heart by letting ***"NOT your heart be troubled," John 14:1*** offers you a choice… read it. I say that you can choose to allow or not to allow your heart or yourself to be troubled by situations and circumstances; it's best to choose not to. Think upon eternal or fruitful things. The Holy Spirit will direct your path to all truth and righteousness and will guide you to everything that you need, as well as guide you to those whom you need in your life.

Again, you must deal with your own internal self by monitoring and catching your thoughts before you act to lash out with anger and foul language. Notice the feelings that come upon you just before you react out of your old habits and take back your self-control; pay attention to yourself. STOP allowing others to push your buttons to make you fall into your old "out of control" ways. Deal with yourself first, from within, then watch how your outward behavior changes to reflect your humbleness unto the Lord within. This leads to peace and leadership in Christ Jesus and is a true blessing to others. Turn inwards to your Temple within where Christ dwells, however, if you haven't invited Him in, consider doing so today because your issues, that need your immediate attention are within you, and they must be addressed in a personal relationship between you and your Heavenly Father; in your quiet place so that you can hear Him and learn His voice, Amen. **[end]**

Now, as I was saying, God is real, and by His Word, He created the Earth, vegetation, animals, humans… the reality of nature as we know it: ***"Then God said, "Let the earth bring forth grass, the herb that yields seed, and the fruit tree that yields fruit according to its kind, whose seed is in itself, on the earth"; and it was so.***

A CLOSER LOOK AT LIFE AND DEATH

And the earth brought forth grass, the herb that yields seed according to its kind, and the tree that yields fruit, whose seed is in itself according to its kind. And God saw that it was good" (Genesis 1:11-12). Nevertheless, everything that God created is called natural, and everything that Satan has created is called "Man-Made." Again, food grown in a lab is not natural because it does not come from God's soil, so it is deemed fake or man-made.

The End Times and Last Days will usher in the public worship of Satan so that it will no longer occur in secret as he exerts his global control over all humanity by utilizing Computer Technology that communicates with the unseen darkness of the Spirit realm or Aliens, under the guise of science and advanced technology. This technology offers man convenience, super abilities, and supported hidden knowledge that will ultimately lead man to destruction.

As of late, we have begun to hear about stories like a Florida mother's lawsuit against a tech company alleging that an AI chatbot, called Character.AI, pushed her 14-year-old son to kill himself, AP News (Oct 25, 2024). And allegedly the same chatbot, Character. AI is the source responsible for a second, more recent teen suicide. What does this tell you about anything with the word "Artificial" in it? If you cannot see the darkness of Satan's intent and motives for mankind, which is to steal, kill, and destroy *Man = You,* according to *John 10:9-10, "I [Jesus] am the door [of your mind and heart]. If anyone enters by Me, he will be saved, and will go in and out and find pasture [safety]. The thief [Satan] does not come except to steal, and to kill, and to destroy [you]. I have come that they [you] may have life, and that they [you] may have it more abundantly."*

The Lord wants you to know His voice, but you choose to be distracted by your cell phone, social media, television, movies, work, entrenched in business or deal making, interacting with friends, family, or playing video games, partying, or being entertained; you are reading and studying every book but the Holy Word of God. You always have something captivating your mind's attention, and therefore, you cannot know or hear God. If you cannot see Satan's secret agendas to distract you and to steal, kill, and destroy YOU, then I don't know what else to say except… **Wake the Hell up because Hell certainly awaits you!**

You are now witnessing Bible Prophecy unfold before your eyes, in the news. You see globalization and the ushering in of a One-World Government (on the back of the US Dollar) and a One-World Religious System. Satan's elite are following his lead by funding his advanced technology, funding both sides of wars, the climate change agenda, and biomedical health plagues disguised to lock us down as they implement their Totalitarian AI Beast System. We see increased population surveillance, a forthcoming cashless society, gender distortion, prosperity preaching that replaces Hell with greed, and bartering for blessings. Furthermore, cannibalism, mass killings, violence, corruption, depopulation, and all of the evil and sinister things that God warned us of in His Holy Bible or Book of Redemption.

A CLOSER LOOK AT LIFE AND DEATH

CHAPTER 2

Life Is Governance

Kingdom = Government = Empire = Superpower = Reign = Supreme Being = King = Realm = Power = Beast System = Ruler = Antichrist = Global Ruler

I AM [that I AM] God [over all], and there is no other" (Isaiah 45:22). "I am Alpha and Omega, the beginning and the end, the first and the last" (Revelation 22:13), thus saith the Lord. *"[God] alone is immortal and dwells [above the Kingdom of Heaven] in unapproachable light. No one has ever seen Him, nor can anyone see Him. To Him be honor and eternal dominion! Amen" (1 Timothy 6:15).*

"Since what may be known about God is plain to them [us, the inhabitants of Earth], because God has made it plain to them [us]. For since the creation of the world God's invisible qualities—his eternal power and divine nature—have been clearly seen [the sky, stars, planets, the oceans, weather, air, fire, wind, nature, animals, Spirit, humans, etc.], being understood from what has been made [by His Word (Jesus) or Command], so that people [you and me] are without excuse [regarding the knowledge of who God is]" (Romans 1:19-20, NIV).

A CLOSER LOOK AT LIFE AND DEATH

[SIDE NOTE]: God, through Jesus Christ (in His Human Form), said in **Revelation 22:13, "I AM ALPHA [the beginning of all = Spirits and nouns that exist] AND OMEGA [the end of all = Spirits and nouns that exist]."** Google and NASA collaborated to create the most pristine, highest level of Quantum Computing using Qubit topology data for handling computations with the largest number of data sets on the planet. The goal is to perfect the integration of Quantum Computing with Artificial Intelligence using Google's AI Willow Chip Processor.

This is the highest level of computation of this era, which will produce endless problem-solving, calculations, and scenario possibilities, as well as continue the search for answers they could never find on their own. And of course, just as with the invention and launch of the James Webb Telescope to search for the unknown, this collaboration also seeks to soothe their curiosity of God's ways, means, and methods of creating Earth, time, matter, humans, consciousness, search for life on other planets, etc., and Satan's way into Heaven to challenge God.

The marriage of Quantum Computing with AI will unleash unparalleled capabilities of computing and analyzing multiple and varied data sets regarding real-life circumstances. This will enable the revelation of high-level answers to the elite for planning and navigating humanity into the future. This will further satisfy their insatiable quest for knowledge, intelligence, and dominance, which would propel us to and through the next generations and beyond.

In 2023, NASA and Google mysteriously shut down their collaborative efforts without explanation. However, it was recently reported that the reason they ended their quest to obtain knowledge, so that they can be like God, based on the "Tree" selection in the Garden of Eden, is because God sent them a message. This divine message was something engineers and scientists couldn't understand or register in their brains. I am sure they thought, "We were doing so well... How could this be?" All of their hard work and efforts failed to resolve the issue, and thus led them to shut down operations... Hmm.

So, what did God reveal that was so devastating to these very high intellect, highly trained, advanced degree individuals who chose to fall for Satan's lie by eating the forbidden fruit from **"The Knowledge of the Tree of Good and Evil,"** *and thus receive their knowledge and intellect from Satan, thinking that they could be like God?* In the Garden, Satan said to Eve (humanity): **"For God knows that in the day you eat of it your eyes will be opened, and you will be like God..." (Genesis 3:5).** And she believed and fell for Satan's lie; then she offered the fruit to her husband, and he too fell. Keep reading, we will answer the question above later. [**end**]

Now, back to the original subject matter: The Lord's Divine mind and ways are Supreme above ALL in His Eternal Universe: **"For as the heavens are higher than the earth, so are my ways higher than your ways, and my thoughts [are higher] than your thoughts" (Isaiah 55:9).** Heaven is the Headquarters of God's Sovereign Government as indicated by His Throne which is affixed in Heaven's Capital which is called Jerusalem. Ironically, Jerusalem is the only city in the Universe that exists in both Heaven and Earth. The Word of God explains the following regarding Jerusalem, in Heaven: **"The city has no need of the sun or of the moon to shine in it, for the glory of God illuminate it" (Revelation 21:23).** And regarding Jerusalem on Earth, the Lord says: **"...I have chosen Jerusalem, [so] that my name might be there forever" (2 Chronicles 33:7).**

The Lord reminds us that **"...our citizenship is in heaven, from which we also eagerly wait for the Savior, the Lord Jesus Christ, who will transform our lowly body that it may be conformed to His glorious body, according to the working by which He is able**

A CLOSER LOOK AT LIFE AND DEATH

even to subdue all things to Himself" (Philippians 3:20-21). God's Holy Divine Word establishes Universal Law that is everlasting: *"Your word, Lord, is eternal; it stands firm in the heavens. Your faithfulness continues through all generations; you established the earth, and it endures. Your laws endure to this day, for all things serve you" (Psalms 118:89-91 NIV).* On Earth, His written Holy Word is given to us because: *"All Scripture is given by inspiration of God, and is profitable for doctrine [foundation], for reproof [scolding], for correction [in your life and], for instruction in righteousness" (2 Timothy 3:16). "I am the LORD, I do not change..." (Malachi 3:6).*

After God's Word became flesh, in the body of Jesus, to dwell amongst us, in the Earth, He eventually died for our sins and was resurrected. He ascended into Heaven, whereby His Human Body was glorified in the unapproachable Divine Light of the Father, which established His Divine Human Immortal form, the same as it existed in the Garden of Eden. He is the risen Christ as King of Kings: *"And He [Jesus] has on His robe and on His thigh a name written: KING OF KINGS AND LORD OF LORDS" (Revelation 19:16). "Jesus Christ [who is God, is] the same yesterday, and today, and forever" (Hebrew 13:8).* Jesus Christ, in human form, made of Immortal Holy Spirit and Glorified Human Flesh... A Divine Man who has all power and dominion OVER ALL things and beings...Spirit Beings, as well as those Spirits who reside within a Human Body.

However, God's ultimate plan and desire is to live and dwell with "Man," on Earth, forever: *"Behold, the tabernacle [dwelling place] of God is with men, and He will dwell with them [like in the Garden of Eden as an Immortal Divine Man made of both Spirit and Flesh], and they shall be His people. God Himself will be with them and be their God" (Revelation 21:3),* thus, once again confirming that *God = Emmanuel = means Read Matt 1:13 = Jesus*

Christ. He will dwell with us forever in the likeness of His **Masterpiece… "Man,"** made of both Spirit and Immortal Flesh.

God's Holy Word is Universal Law, and therefore, the Universe is governed by the laws commanded directly from His Lips. His Holy Word creates, establishes, and defines all words and laws in the Universe. Recall that in order for God to interact with us… His Creation, He clothed or covered the brilliance of His Divine Light in a Spirit-looking human form; thus, originally, our Spirits were created to live an eternal existence within God's family, under His perfect rule of government. It is in Heaven that the Lord God established and defined the word **"family,"** which is structured for all of us to dwell together in His Divine Holy Spirit, exhibiting love.

As above, so it is below; therefore, on Earth, we pattern this same family concept in single units within the collective family of God. Family is the nucleus of society, whereby the father is the head (ruler through love) and a protector over all those in his household. The mother and children complete the family unit that operates as one united spirit under the father. We also refer to each other as "brothers" and "sisters" in Christ because our Spirits were created and established to live together as a family in Heaven as we perpetuate and share truth, goodness, and love.

God is the Sovereign Creator or King over all things associated with living life. Therefore, He gives us instructions regarding how to live and what we are to do. He created Heaven and Earth; He established and defined the boundaries of all realms in His Universe. This was made clear as the Lord revealed His Omnipotence during a conversation with Job: *"Where were you when I laid the foundations of the earth? Tell Me [Job], if you have understanding. Who determined its measurements? Surely you know! Or who stretched the line upon it?*

To what were its foundations fastened? Or who laid its cornerstone, When the morning stars [Light Bearers] sang together, And all the sons of God [all of us in Heaven] shouted for joy? "Or who shut in the sea with doors, When it burst forth and issued from the womb; When I made the clouds its garment, And thick darkness its swaddling band; When I fixed My limit for it, And set bars and doors; When I said, 'This far you may come, but no farther, And here your proud waves must stop!' (Job 38:4-11)"

And the Lord tells us... NO! He, vividly and physically, shows us by example that we need His Breath of Life, or oxygen, in order to breathe and live. The Lord also defined His Creation, on Earth, as a man and a woman who are created in His Holy Image: **"He created them male and female and blessed them..." (Genesis 5:2)**, so that there is no confusion or no reason to challenge God regarding your sexual orientation at birth, again our Holy Divine Creator did not create any birth defects, such as brings... non-binary, queer, transgender, etc., as these are of the mindset of Satan or man-made.

God does not create anything that goes against His Divine Order because it leads to chaos and disorder, which leads to disputes and lawsuits related to gender-based restrooms, gender roles in sports, etc. Your gender is God's Law, and therefore, your life is governed by the sexual orientation that God assigned and created you at birth. This means that you must play your male or female role, or your position on the playing field of life, throughout the entirety of your life, as you encounter daily situations and circumstances.

Although God gave "Man" authority and governance, on the Earth, when they fell to sin based on Adam and Eve's **"Tree"** selection, **"The Tree of the Knowledge of Good and Evil,"** they passed spiritual authority over their lives over to Satan and became captive to him through death; recall Earth Rule One (1), before Christ's resurrection, everyone who died from the Earth, their Spirit went down into Hell and their body went into the grave. And as well, their tree choice means that they choose to receive their knowledge from Satan instead of from God, represented by the Tree of Life.

Adam and Eve's "Tree" choice subjected humanity to tribulation, judgment, death, and Hellfire punishment because we lost our spiritual dominance over Satan, but we have regained our dominance over him through Christ's resurrection, thus *"...all things are possible [for those who believe in Him]" (Matthew 19:26).* Yet and still, it remains that Adam is the headship over his family which holds, the men directly accountable to The Father. Men must understand this godly concept; women are supposed to marry so that they will have the covering of a man who is directly accountable to God, but this is not taught. Men must be serious-minded about their life and future and of sound mind to be the leader over their wives and children; however, they have fallen to lust, sex, and perversion, which greatly hinders their walk and favor with God. This is exactly why the Prince of the Airways... Satan uses the media to program man towards lust, but the Lord says: *"He who finds a wife finds a good thing, and obtains favor from the Lord" (Proverbs 18:22).*

God also created and defined the institution of marriage to reproduce children of light to populate the Earth, which also represents our union with Him at the Rapture. He defined the woman (Eve) as Adam's wife/bride and helpmate, and Adam as the husband/groom, and He blessed them (us) with the pleasure of sex and told them (us), according to His Divine Law, to *"...Be fruitful and multiply..."* His Image throughout the Earth, as recorded in *Genesis 1:22.*

Since God, through His Word (Jesus), created everything that was made, He dictates to us the instructions for living on His Earth. And for His purpose alone, He determines your sex at birth. He establishes who should mate with whom within the animal and

A CLOSER LOOK AT LIFE AND DEATH

mammal (human) kingdoms. Therefore, you DO NOT get to define your sexual orientation or tell God what "you want or how you feel" or "who you want to be" …a lesbian female, a gay male, bi-sexual, transgender, queer, plus others, or LGBTQ+ (intersex, pansexual, etc.), again, creating chaos and confusion, especially amongst young children. Neither can you choose whom you want to mate with.

The same is true when humans invent and create things, like God, who gave us instructions in His Holy Word… The Bible, He created a male for a female for the purpose of procreation. When we create things for a specific purpose, we provide usage instructions and criteria to the end user. However, utilizing the object or device outside of the provided parameters of instruction can cause adverse conditions, danger, or even death. Therefore, you do not get to dictate your will or your feelings to the maker or manufacturer.

Consequently, if something goes wrong, a court of law will deny your liability claim, and your case will be deemed "Dead on Arrival" (DOA). Therefore, the same is true with God's Creation of us: any deviation from the righteous ways of His instructions relinquishes your claim to His Eternal Life, which renders you dead… DOA in the fires of Hell. Living life opposite to that which God has created for you means that you are living in defiance and in accordance with Lucifer's sinful, wicked, and rebellious mindset, which leads to death. Therefore, God will turn you over to your heart's desire and completely remove Himself… His Holy Spirit, from you and leave you to your fate of choice… Hell.

The Lord will not see you (you are nonexistent to Him), and He will not hear your prayers, according to *Isaiah 1:15, "When you spread out your hands [to pray], I will hide My eyes from you; Even though you make many prayers, I will not hear,"* unless you turn from your sinful ways. These are not my words… these are the Words of your Creator. So, don't take my word for it; I employ you to look up this scripture right now for yourself. Consequently, you don't have to remain in a lifestyle where God does not acknowledge you or your prayers, which leads to a punishment of eternal death in unquenchable Hellfire. But you can choose to **repent** of your sins and invite Christ (the Indwelling Holy Spirit) into your heart.

Therefore, surrender your thoughts, feelings, and desires for this lifestyle to Christ, and sincerely allow Him to lead you and show you how to change your ways, today; while there is still time…tomorrow is not promised: *"…you who say, "Today or tomorrow we will go to such and such a city, spend a year there, buy and sell, and make a profit"; whereas you do not know what will happen tomorrow. For what is your life? It is even a vapor that appears for a little time and then vanishes away [according to Genesis 2:17, which defines your death to come]" (James 4:13-15).*

Now, while you can call upon the name of Jesus, sincerely **repent** by confessing your sins, and be governed by Romans 10:9-10, you will then be saved from eternal damnation. Based on the above, is there a valid definition for a *"Gay Christian"* = *Christ-like*? Biblically speaking, the answer is NO because your defiance is your **"Pride"** in the LGBT+ lifestyle, which is strictly a choice, not a "Birth Defect" created by your Creator. However, Jesus Christ died for you because He loves you, and to also make your lifestyle choice completely up to you. We must know and understand that *"To fear the LORD is to hate evil; I hate arrogant PRIDE, evil conduct, and perverse speech [of anger, curse words, and words and behavior that coerce the LGBTQ+ lifestyle or any lifestyle that is outside of God's Holy Order] (Proverbs 8:13, BSB).* God, and we as believers in Christ, love the sinner, but we cannot celebrate the sin.

God dearly loves each one of us more than we can ever comprehend, because He created us; however, there are boundaries and consequences for our actions that are eternal. Therefore, we are to love Jesus Christ and each other and follow His righteousness alone to be saved. As believers in Christ, we must love the behavior that the Lord loves and hate the behavior or lifestyle choices that He hates. Again, although He truly loves you as His child, He hates it when you choose a lifestyle that leads you to be eternally separated from Him, forever, which is called Eternal Death. Life has consequences that God has firmly established… *Heaven = Light = Eternal Life and Hell = Darkness = Eternal Death* (**Deuteronomy 30:19**).

Therefore, **FEAR the LORD**, for His wrath is coming and it is inconceivably mighty, fierce, and everlasting. Don't allow your PRIDE to cause you to neglect God's forgiveness of your sins. When you know better, choose to do better towards righteousness. We are living near the end of God's Divine Redemption Plan whereby He is offering you Eternal Life, in Heaven, and on Earth, through **repentance** and belief in Jesus Christ; however, the default is Hell… you decide.

We neither created, defined, established, nor continually sustain life, so who are we to defy God? The choice to challenge your assigned sex at birth is defiant, sinful, rebellious behavior, the same kind of behavior that got us put out of Heaven, along with Lucifer, in the first place. [**Side Note**]: Although our sin and rebelliousness led to our expulsion from Heaven, it had nothing to do with sexual orientation but everything to do with selfishness and **PRIDE!** Keep reading to find out the details of this truth. [**end**]

Let's recap with a few facts or clues that reveal that you were cast out of Heaven: The first clue is the fact that you are no longer there before His Throne in Heaven, so that you can see His Holy Face. Consequently, since you are currently separated from Him (spiritually dead), and awaiting the second clue: your coming death and punishment in Hellfire upon the death of your body. Thirdly, recall that the Lord said, *"Before I formed you in the womb, I knew you…" (Jeremiah 1:5).* Lastly, your shadow continually reveals that you are cast down, and this truth follows you everywhere you go. The only time that you cannot see your shadow is when you lie down in the "cast down" position… Hmm.

Jeremiah 1:5 causes me to disbelieve those who have had near-death experiences and say that we get to choose our parents because God says "I" formed you in your mother's womb. I cannot refute God; can you? This scripture reveals that God knew you in Heaven before your birth on Earth. However, since your Spirit rebelled and is now dead unless you believe in Jesus Christ, you are currently awaiting the death of your body on Earth. As explained earlier, this is because the composition of our Spirit and Body means that both fell, and the body became the vessel that holds your Spirit and Bones for their transition through the grave and Hellfire punishment. This is the same pathway that every human followed before Christ's resurrection, including Jesus, which is how He ended up in Hell. Consequently, Jesus went to Hell, but according to the design of God's redemption plan, He did not remain there… **Glory!**

As a sinner myself, I am certainly not qualified to judge anyone; however, your lifestyle will judge you against God's Truth upon your death. The goal is to point out the truth of God's Word so that you might know the seriousness of your plight, before the truth that God spoke to Adam and Eve, finds you when it is your turn to return to the ground: *"Of every tree of the garden thou mayest freely eat: But of the tree of the knowledge of good and evil, thou shalt not eat of it: for in the day that thou eatest thereof thou shalt surely die" (Genesis 2:16-17).* And again, to our surprise, we do surely die! This truth, which defines the certainty of your death, was spoken into our reality. Therefore, you are awaiting your turn to die, right now, right?

However, for some reason, God's Truth offends the unrighteous just like truth offended the former Light Bearer when Jesus Christ was resurrected from the dead. So, since we cannot deny God's Truth which is evident by the fact that we do die, again, we DO NOT get to dictate anything to our Creator, i.e., we do not get to tell Him what we want or what we want to change because of our "feelings," including your sexual orientation that He established at your birth.

This kind of thinking and/or physical transformation from what God has created you to be is a war within yourself, whereby you have chosen to align yourself with the opposer of God while knowing full well the sex that the Lord created you to be at birth. However, if you choose to defy God, don't hate on those who believe and cling to His righteousness; accept the consequences of your living, which leads to not one but two death penalties… Natural Death and The Second Death… the Lake of Fire and Brimstone. The Good News is that redemption is still being offered to you through Christ, so you can choose to **repent** and change your ways when you discover God's truth. You can be forgiven of all your sins, forever.

Lucifer: The High-Ranked Cherubim Angel

"You were the anointed cherub who covers; I established you, You were on the holy mountain of God; You walked Back and forth in the midst of fiery stones[army]. You were perfect in your ways from the day you were created, till iniquity was found in you"
~ Ezekiel 28:14

In the Kingdom of Heaven, we were created to perform uses for the Lord in various capacities within His government and as citizens. Life is always a governed state of existence; in Heaven, it is governed by the Lord; consequently, in Hell and on Earth, it is governed by God's adversarial opposer, Lucifer. He is a former eminence of beauty and a high-ranking Cherubim Angel. His name, "Light Bearer," means bringer of the Light of the Lord. He brings God's Light to all, in the Heavens and on Earth, as directed.

He was stationed above God's Throne as a covering over His Divine Throne (see diagram in the index). This is where he carried out his divine duties. He was called the *"morning star, son of the dawn!" (Isaiah 14:12, NIV),* which reveals another aspect of his duties as a Light Bearer or bringer of God's Light, not his own light, because God alone is Light. Cherubim Angels cover God, as depicted in the design of the **"Ark of the Covenant,"** therefore, Cherubim Angels are extremely close to God and privileged to the highest level of His knowledge. Lucifer's responsibilities also included providing and orchestrating the praise music of Heaven.

As you discovered, Lucifer created and produced music in the heavenly realm. The source of Lucifer's music comes from God's Light that is broken down using a Prism to produce visible spectra of Light Waves that manifest as colors, sound waves, tidal waves, etc. His Light produces sound waves measured in units of frequency to yield musical notes. When Lucifer sinned, God told him: *"All your pomp [public show-off of your magnificence;*

ceremony and splendid display] has been brought down to the grave [Pit of Hell], along with the noise [music] of your harps;" (Isaiah 14:11).

Again, Satan's name means God's accuser and opposition: *"And the great Dragon...that old Serpent, called the Devil, and Satan" (Revelation 12:9).* Lucifer's name was later changed to Satan to reflect the change in his character, motives, behavior, and actions. Names have meaning; find out what your name reflects about you.

Devil = Lived (spelled backward), Satan lived in Heaven but is now the devil who is expelled; Mad = dam(ned) = Mad about your Redemption that he will never have & Damned to Eternal Fire; Greeting: Hello = Hell is Low; Evil = Live Eternal Life Fire & Brimstone; Satan = Santa (more later)

Lucifer waged a direct assault against God's Sovereignty and the sanctity of our Eternal Life. Therefore, God calls him a murderer, *"He was a murderer from the beginning [where His Spirit was created in Heaven], and does not stand in the truth..."* **(John 8:44 NKJV).** Consequently, he lost his Eternal Life! He lost God's Presence or His Holy Spirit, which is Eternal Life and the Truth of God's Word that was within him. And like Lucifer, we too lost God's Holy Spirit within us when we decided to align with the former Light Bearer. God's Holy Spirit will always be missing if you do not invite Christ into your heart. If not, you will experience the Eternal Lake of Fire and Brimstone.

Lucifer remains a Spirit with His same exact character from the moment that he sinned. On Earth, Satan never received a body to participate in God's redemption plan; therefore, he is dead to God and all Creation. He is the creator of Death and Hell, he is the ruler of the fallen Earth, the embodiment of Death, and the overseer of Hell. When our spirit leaves Earth, we report directly to Him and live in his domain, that is, until the resurrection of Jesus Christ. Satan was cast out of Heaven into the Abyss of Earth, which was

A CLOSER LOOK AT LIFE AND DEATH

void, without form, and in darkness (Gen 1:2). According to ***Revelation 12:9, "He was cast out into the earth, and his angels (you and I) were cast out with him."*** We know and acknowledge that Hell is below Heaven every time we greet each other... **Hello, which means "Hell is Low."** [Side Note]: Although Satan was initially cast out of Heaven, he did still have access to God (Job 2:2) due to his role in God's redemption plan, until later when he lost access. [end]

At the conclusion of God's redemption plan, *"...the devil, who deceived them [God's Holy Angels], was thrown into the lake of burning sulfur, where the beast [Antichrist] and the false prophet had been thrown. They will be tormented day and night forever"* **(Revelation 20:10).** God's plan demands judgment, which is death for sins committed against Him. The Last Judgment will be the very last chance for you to face your Creator to determine if you will join Satan in The Second Death or The Lake of Fire.

Again, recall that all graves will be opened and all men shall be resurrected: *"And I saw the dead, great and small, standing before the throne, and books were opened. Another book was opened, which is the book of life. The dead were judged according to what they had done as recorded in the books. The sea gave up the dead in it, and death and Hades [the grave] gave up the dead in them, and each person was judged according to what they had done. Then death and Hades were thrown into the lake of fire. The lake of fire is the second death. Anyone whose name was not found written in the book of life was thrown into the lake of fire"* **(Revelation 20:12-15).** Enough said!

It is God's Indwelling Holy Spirit that Jesus Christ sent to us so that we might have His Truth and Divine Light, which is Eternal Life if we so believe that Jesus died for our sins and that God raised Him from the dead, and we **repent** of our sins. However, Lucifer's primary goal is to ensure that you don't! Your belief system is a target of your enemy, which is why you must determine if your beliefs align with Christ or Satan. If you do not take time to figure it out or don't care to believe in Christ's finished work on the cross and His resurrection, then by default, your **"I don't care"** choice aligns with Satan by default. Therefore, Hellfire and eternal Hellfire with Brimstone await you.

Lucifer's betrayal and turning away from God and rebellion produced the dark energy associated with words like pride and self-dependence or independence from God. Lucifer is the epitome of the Spirit of **PRIDE** in his **SELFISHNESS** and dependence on himself alone. Instead of obeying and depending on God, he chose to disobey, which resulted in an eternal death sentence with an eternal punishment of the Lake of Fire and Brimstone, which, per the redemption plan, is now called The Second Death (Revelation 20:10).

Therefore, *"Those [Satan and all unbelievers] who are dominated by the [their] sinful nature think [in their mind] about sinful things, but those who are controlled by the Holy Spirit think [in their mind] about things that please the Spirit. So, letting your sinful nature control your mind leads to death. But letting the Spirit control your mind leads to life and peace. For the sinful nature is always hostile to God. It never did obey God's laws, and it never will. That's why those [Satan and all unbelievers] who are still under the control of their sinful nature can never please God"* (Romans 8:5-8).

Lucifer's selfishness and pride are what I call the **"I" Syndrome**. He took his focus and desire off His Heavenly Father, the I AM THAT I AM, and put his focus on himself… "I" … his own glory, and what he wants and desires for himself. He certainly doesn't care about you. The former Light Bearer's "I" syndrome resulted in: "I" want to be like God. "I" want to exalt myself over God and be worshiped like God, so he rebelled; however, you see how that turned out. This is why **Psalms 23:1** teaches us to pray, **"The Lord is my shepherd; I SHALL NOT WANT,"** thus placing our dependence back on Him instead of ourselves. We will then want for nothing. Many of us have the *"I" Syndrome = selfie generation*, so we must learn to surrender those thoughts, our ego, and place our focus on Christ alone. The Lord provides us with His wholeness so that there is no reason to "want" for anything.

Remember that Satan is a Spirit, which means he can simultaneously affect his body of followers so that they move and live in concert with his consuming dark mindset. Pride is a common, prevailing Spirit that the former Light Bearer mentally exerts over all unbelievers to varying degrees. You are unknowingly led by his mental darkness as your heart turns cold to God's Truth, Goodness, and Love; these no longer resonate in your being anymore.

Your first impulse and reaction to others is now from a dark place of anger and rage that draws the darkness of depression, anxiety, mental illness, disease, etc. Then you turn to drowning your sorrows with alcohol and drugs. Your life then spirals out of control, but you don't understand why. You have become a different person, so under that pretext, you live any way that you want in defiance of God.

At this point, no one can tell you anything; you have tuned everyone out. These are symptoms of not knowing the Truth of God and His Divine plan. Remember He said, **"My people are destroyed for lack of knowledge" (Hosea 4:6).** Therefore, you must know God's redemption plan, which means knowing His promises, prophecies, supernatural events, and Satan's countermeasures through laws, technology, Aliens, UFOs, etc. that will bring Bible prophecies into our reality. Your knowledge must come from the Word of the Lord, not television or Satan's social media, which seeks to sow seeds of disinformation and confusion, whereby he is the prince of the airways: *"...the prince of the power of the air, the spirit who now works in the sons of disobedience" (Ephesians 2:2).*

The former Light Bearer uses subtle tactics so that you do not realize his covert actions that are disguised as life's comforts, conveniences, and pleasures that keep your mind in a trans or in the illusion that you can live any way that you want without any repercussions. However, God makes it very clear that if you live your life without dependence on Jesus Christ, Hell awaits you by default. We have come to enjoy and depend on television, movies, video games, music/radio, sports, competition, entertainment, partying, sex, alcohol, drugs, gambling, cell phones or electronic devices, the media, and social media, etc., or things that purposefully lead us away from God's truth. Satan guides us into the love of money, seduction, and materialism with the insatiable desire to want more. These desires are evidence that you have succumbed to Satan's mindset of sexual indulgence, perversion, violence, greed, and ungodly behavior through the subtlety of his broadcasting through the airways.

The latter scripture, *Ephesians 2:2*, calls him *"the prince of the power of the air [broadcasting/broadband],"* meaning that Satan was given power and authority over our airways according to his role in God's redemption plan. As a result, we have television, radio, and now social media broadcast programming designed to detrimentally affect our minds. The *"NEWS"* = *Broadly Casting "Satan's Spells"* of lust, sex, and promiscuity, or the Spirit of his mindset to the masses of the people, in all directions: **North (N), East I, West (W), South (S)** = *NEWS*; this is not simply a coincidence, nothing in this life is a mere coincidence.

We do the actions of what we see and hear through his media, broadband and broadcasting airways. And we must deal with the fallout, we fall for his enticement that leads to fornication, adultery, disease, boring babies born out of wedlock, along with the economic depression due to child support. God did not intend for His children to live part-time at their mom's house and part-time at their dad's house per a court order. This is not the family structure that God created. Sex is reduced to a good feeling, a closeness that we desire for a fleeting moment. It is more of a good feeling or a lustful desire instead of being that which God created to be sacred and holy, for the purpose of multiplying "Children of Light" throughout the Earth within the sanctity of Holy Matrimony.

However, as we embrace the sexual messages from the prince of the airways, our "BED" has become our biggest obstacle and distraction that causes most of us to fall. What happens in the bedroom between a married couple was designed to occur **"behind the veil"** which relates to the innermost part of God's Temple or King Solomon's Temple, also referred to as the second Temple —a physical building that was built by King Solomon for the Holy Spirit of the Lord to come to and dwell therein, on the Earth: *"Then he (King Solomon) built the twenty-cubit room at the rear of the temple, from floor to ceiling, with cedar boards; he built it inside as the inner sanctuary, as the Most Holy Place" (1 Kings 6:14).*

As per the first Temple in Jerusalem, the Holy Spirit of God did come and dwell in King Solomon's Temple: *"Then the glory of the Lord went up from the cherub, and paused over the threshold of the temple; and the house was filled with the cloud, and the court was full of the brightness of the Lord's glory. And the sound of the wings of the cherubim was heard even in the outer court" (Ezekiel 10:4-5).* Can you imagine witnessing the Glory of God? However, when King Solomon began to worship idols and chose to bring an idol into the Temple, the Glory of God left the Earth: *"Then the glory of the Lord departed from the threshold of the temple and stood over the cherubim. And the cherubim lifted their wings and mounted up from the earth in my sight" (Ezekiel 10:18-*

19) ... WOW!

The innermost part of the Temple, commonly called "The Holy of Holies," is where the Lord dwelt, which was closed off by a curtain veil, and called behind the veil. However, the only person allowed to enter once a year was the High Priest, for the purpose of atoning for the sins of the people. This Divine Holy space is also referred to as **"behind the veil,"** and the sacredness of the Temple coincides with the sanctity of the marital bed of the couple, which is an extremely private worship experience ordained by God. In reference to marriage, this is the state of secrecy that the marital bedroom and the **purity of the marriage bed** hold.

The bond of love shared between a husband and a wife, in worship before God within the "Bond of Holy Matrimony," was created to be holy and not for the public to see, therefore, Satan's counter move created the ungodliness of sex that separates you from the Holiness of God, hence his agenda is to cause us to defile ourselves before God through fornication, adultery, and pornography brought that which is sacred and should take place **"behind the veil"** into the mainstream via television, movies, music, social media, and games. Your marital bed is not to be defiled with others through fornication and adultery, and even if you are single, your bed must maintain its purity and holiness.

Also, you should regard your body…your Temple within your body, as holy unto God, and it should only be given to someone who, equally, respects God's principles and who embraces the holiness of their body. Abstinence and conversations with the Holy Spirit (Prayer) regarding your sex life are a recognition of your accountability unto the Lord's virtue and essence of Holiness. What is the state of your holiness as to your body (Temple of God) and the sanctity of your **"bed,"** right now?

The defilement of our **"BED"** has reached epidemic proportions, correction, it is the largest pandemic in the world!!!

A CLOSER LOOK AT LIFE AND DEATH

Don't you see Satan's vicious, lust-filled attack on your mind through his media conglomerates, which glorify lust because of the "sex sells" mentality? You must take control of your thoughts and be careful of what you think about because *"...the LORD says to the people...I know every thought that comes into your minds" (Ezekiel 11:5);* thoughts whereby you will be judged accordingly. *"We [must] tear down arguments and every presumption set up against the knowledge of God; and we take captive [pay attention to our] every thought to make it obedient to Christ" (2 Corinthians 10:5, BSB).*

[**Exercise**]: Take a closer look at your body and your bed/bedroom standards, and honestly evaluate your respect for your body and its holiness unto God, as well as your bedroom ethics. Then pray and talk to God about it, and do as you are led by the Holy Spirit to make the necessary changes. Commit and submit to God's holiness. Also, confront your thought life relative to the bombardment of lust-filled programming via radio, TV, movies, and video games. Evaluate your mindset and your desire for more sex or fornication, whether it is with the same person or different people or even multiple people, heterosexual or homosexual, which are all outside of God's standards. Ask yourself, why do I behave in this way?

If you are single or committing adultery, commit to taking a month off from having sex, pray, meditate, and call on the Lord for help and guidance; the Holy Spirit will lead you towards holiness and accountability. Analyze your lifestyle and STOP the vicious, ungodly cycle of your lust and sexual desires that are the result of broadcast programming to your mind through the media, especially music and music videos with scantily dressed women doing seductive bedroom acts with someone who is not their spouse, for the public to see. They do this for the public to see. This is Satan's Jezebel Seduction Spirit (Revelation 2:20). STOP IT… **Don't go**

to Hell by default!

Satan is using you to defile yourself (and your children) before God... **WAKE UP!** Women, cover your bodies in holiness unto God alone. Realize your perversion against a Holy God. Take action now by paying attention to how you dress. Is it pleasing to the Lord? Notice the sexual nature of music lyrics and how movies and soap operas portray adultery and fornication to entice you to do the same. The next time you look at TV or movies or hear songs about sex, think about what Satan is subtly projecting to your mind or your Spirit and the minds of your children... parents, pay attention! The little ones know every word, and they sing right along, and before long, a baby is delivered to a thirteen-year-old's parents. Teach them what God says about the holiness of their body, it is the **"Temple of God"** where He dwells within...STOP **the madness!** Create a standard of holiness for your body and your bed. Pray and invite God's holiness into your life. [**end**]

All of the above is designed to distract us from God's truth and it's working, some of you are so distracted that God or reading the Bible never crosses your mind but you are interested in reading Harry Potter or wizardry and secular books and movies or you choose to experiment with a Ouija board or drink alcohol; doing these things bring demonic Spirits into your life (alcohol is called Spirit for a reason...you do the research as to why). You are thus following Satan's plan for your life very well, never mind Christ Jesus' plan for your life. When you fail to consult God about the truth of any matter, it means that you reject His Truth, which lights your mental pathway towards doing what is right.

Therefore, you will fall prey to lies, destruction, death, or the darkness of relying on yourself... your "feelings," or whatever fads or trends that Satan is peddling to you at the time. You are not in tune with God's ways, promises, and warnings. So, when you reject God's warnings and choose your own way, you unleash the darkness of chaos, confusion, addiction, depression, etc., into your life, which spirals downwards towards the Hell of your own creation.

However, by choice, you don't have to concern yourself with God's truth, but surely **Genesis 2:17** will certainly find you when it is time for your date with death; but it will be too late for you to turn your self-dependent, pride-filled life around. Nevertheless, you will have been tricked out of your eternal life with the Lord. Another fact is for certain; you did accomplish one thing... living life your own way. And you will continue to live **"your own way"** in the eternal consequences of Hellfire. Instead, you believe in your government **(Satan's government),** Politicians, and Scientists rather than the Word of God.

Since you now control your own life, instead of relying on your Heavenly Father, you should know what to expect upon your death. Before you reach the Lake of Fire, you will have experienced the Hellfire of Gehenna, then upon the resurrection of your body from your grave, it will conjoin back with your spirit whereby you will stand before God at the Last Judgment (Revelation 20:12). After which the living of your life, on Earth, will testify to what you love to do...evil! Therefore, you will be thrown into the flames, along with Satan, the Antichrist, and the False Prophet, kindled with sulfur, and both your Spirit and Body will burn forever.

As you live forever in the Lake of Fire, you will be the same Spirit, with your same human body, bones, mind, memory, and senses. And every sin that you have committed, in Heaven, and on Earth, will eternally burn through your thoughts as you repeatedly relive them in the agony of torture. Your body will feel the intensity of every flame, which will be far worse than the Hellfire torture in Gehenna, which only temporarily held your Spirit, not your flesh, because your flesh entered the grave.

The Bible mentions Hell over 200 times, with 162 references in the New Testament alone, and over 70 times were referenced by the Lord Jesus Christ! This is because God wants us to know the truth about what will happen to us so that we can make informed decisions about our eternal future. Remember, Bible Prophecy is what makes God…God because He is the only one who knows everything. However, Satan's punishment…The Second Death is only mentioned four times in the book of Revelation. But I forgot, you don't have time to study God's Word because finding out what God says really doesn't matter when compared to all the other things you have going on in your daily life. Therefore, I am reminding you now, so that you will not go to Hell by default.

The Bible gives explicit examples from those who have experienced Hell in order to warn others not to go there, for instance, ***Luke 16:22, "…The rich man also died and was buried. In Hades [Hell], where he was in torment, he looked up and saw Abraham far away [separated from him by a fixed Gulf or fixed surface], with Lazarus by his side. So, he called to him, 'Father Abraham [who was in the "Paradise" section of Hell, see diagram the appendix], have pity on me and send Lazarus to dip the tip of his finger in water and cool my tongue, because I am in agony in this fire.' And Mark 9:23, "If your hand causes you to sin, cut it off. You should enter life maimed, rather than having two hands, to go to hell, into the fire that shall never be quenched."***

The Lord allows people to have near-death experiences so that those who experience Heaven and Hell can warn you. Again, your eternal future is very serious, so take it that way. Please heed these warnings of truths that are as true as the scripture that defines your death (Genesis 2:17), which is sure to come.

Beware of prideful ministers who tell their congregations the fallacy that they are little "gods." And, in their greed, they teach prosperity, whereby you will prosper or acquire big fine homes, cars, airplanes, etc., like the minister, if you give 10% (or more) of your income to the church, and it's working. However, God does not barter money for blessings. Also, some ministers tell you that you will be saved if you pray the **"Sinner's Prayer,"** which is a false sense of assurance because they don't tell you that you must do something in order to be forgiven, and that is to **repent** of your sins. If a pastor tells you that you are forgiven without repentance, then there is something wrong with that picture. *Warning! "Woe be unto the pastors that destroy and scatter the sheep of my pasture! Saith the LORD" (Jeremiah 23:1).*

The Sinner's Prayer is not comparable to ***Romans 10:9-10: "If you confess with your mouth, 'Jesus is Lord,' and believe in your heart that God raised Him out from the dead, you will be saved. For in the heart is belief unto righteousness, and confession [of your sins] unto salvation in [using] the mouth..."*** If a pastor does not tell you that you must **repent** or ask Jesus Christ for forgiveness, naming your sins, then something is wrong with that picture. Therefore, please re-evaluate if you are saved according to God's Word or if you have fallen victim to religious false doctrine. If you determine that you are a victim, please pray Romans 10:910, whereby you MUST confess your sins with your mouth, out loud, believe that "Jesus is Lord", and believe that God raised Jesus from the dead. Pray from your heart, in your secret place, confessing your wrongdoings by incident, and invite Christ to live within you. Then accept that you have been forgiven and that you are now saved.

The former Light Bearer's earthly government thrives on the energy of evil... fear, hate, destruction, deceit, death, Hell, and the grave. Lucifer's opposition to God led to the formation of two separate Eternal Spirit Energies in Heaven and the entire universe: the opposer and his angels (you and me) were expelled, which resulted in two separate governments:

1. The Kingdom of God in Heaven and its righteousness. The embodiment of Truth, Goodness, and Love.

2. The Kingdom of Satan is on Earth, which includes death and Hellfire. We have established that per God's redemption plan, Satan is given authority by God to assume his true, evil nature and to establish his Kingdom on Earth. His government is based on: ***"The rich ruleth over the poor, and the borrower is servant to the lender" (Proverbs 22:7)***, fear, hatred, corruption, and every evil. He is the foundation of our choice to live unrighteously or any way that we want.

His government is established upon the death of God's created human beings, mind control, exploitation, lies, deception, magic, theft from his citizens, and submerging us in debt: ***"The rich ruleth over the poor, and the borrower is servant to the lender" (Proverbs 22:7).*** He thrives on creating fear, hatred, corruption, and every evil. He is the foundation of our choice to live unrighteously or any way that we want.

Again, according to the redemption plan, God is the foundation of our choice to live righteously, and Satan is the foundation to choose to live any way that we want to live, doing every evil or all that is opposite to the Lord's righteousness. Satan has established his dark, sinful government over fallen humanity through deception, perversion, hate, fear, tribulation, death, Hell, and the grave. By design, these two spiritual forces are the foundation of our thought process, whereby good and evil thoughts flow through us for preponderance within our minds.

This means that with every breath…second by second of every moment of our day, we are, individually, in a position of decision, to choose between our two spiritual thought waves of light and darkness, good and evil, truth and lies, or right and wrong. However, only you can experience or play your position in life, and only you will give an account of your choices and actions before God. Therefore, the summation of your life's history of thoughts, choices, decisions, and actions will determine where you will spend eternity upon your demise if you do not confess belief in Christ with your mind, a **repentant heart**, and the confession of your sins to Him with your mouth (more on this as the book series progresses).

Due to our separation from God, which created duality, I asked a friend: How many government leaders are there in the world? He said there are thousands. I replied, realistically, there are only two… righteous ones, and the other, unrighteous. So, no matter how many leaders exist on Earth, they align with one of the above two categories. Ultimately, everything in life can be reduced to two because our Universe only has the two choices of Heaven and Hell, which ties all things together through duality.

A CLOSER LOOK AT LIFE AND DEATH

The Art of Deception And Satan's Countermeasures

*De-cep-tion: The act of causing someone to accept as true or valid what is false or invalid; **a lie***
~ Merriam-Webster Dictionary

Satan is the father of lies, but he takes you deeper into his evilness with his art of deception. Deception takes lying to the next level as a succession of lies and secrecy takes on a life of its own to shape the darkness of our minds so that we are manipulated to believe what Satan's world leaders and his agents want us to believe. It is a devious cycle of deceit that can last for years, generations, and centuries. For instance, under the deception of Science and Technology, Scientists contend that Dinosaurs are giant creatures that roamed the Earth millions and billions of years ago. Scientists also contend that they have created Carbon Dating Technology, whereby fossils, artifacts, discoveries, etc., and our Universe have been analyzed and dated back millions and billions of years. These bogus astronomical numbers only serve to support their false doctrine of the **Theory of Evolution** and the **Big Bang Theory**.

Does the Bible mention **Dinosaurs**? No! According to newspring.com, "The Bible does not specifically address Dinosaurs regarding when they existed, or how they became extinct. The closest examples of dinosaur-like creatures are translated in most Bibles as **"Serpent," "Dragon," "Leviathan," "Behemoth,"** and **"Sea Monster" (see Job 3:8, Job 40:15-24, Isaiah 27:1, Ezekiel 29:3, etc.).**" And in regard to the age of the Earth, Scientists utilize Carbon Dating equipment to substantiate their lies. According to the University of Chicago, visit: https://news.uchicago.edu/explainer/what-is-carbon-14-dating.

Carbon Dating was developed in 1940. This radiocarbon dating, or carbon-14 dating, is a scientific method that can accurately determine the age of organic materials as old as approximately

60,000 years. However, 60,000 years is a huge stretch based on the Bible's genealogy of the age of the Earth, but notice that the university does not state that Carbon Dating has the ability to date artifacts millions and billions of years.

According to Don Stewart, "Today the earth is assumed to be approximately 4.6 billion years old, while the universe is believed to be at least 10 to 15 billion years of age. For the theory of evolution to be true, it is necessary that the Earth be very old. For life to spontaneously develop from an original single cell [The Big Bang Theory] to our present complex universe, billions of years are needed(https://www.blueletterbible.org/faq/don_stewart/don_stewart_613.cfm)." Logically thinking, if God created humanity in the Garden for the purpose of redemption, do you reasonably think that He would allow these giant creatures to exist and roam the Earth and kill them so that the offering of Eternal Life could not be possible for us? No! So, how do Scientists, who were not there and never lived millions and billions of years ago, come up with the design and implementation of equipment that supposedly calculates **"Time"** in a manner that is contradictory to the Word of God?

According to God's redemption plan, He likened the period for man's redemption to a week (7 days). Hence, there are 7 days in a week, as defined by God, no more, no less…it has never changed. According to *2 Peter 3:8, 1-Day = 1,000-Years: "with the Lord one day is as a thousand years, and a thousand years as one day."* Therefore, since Man was created on the sixth day, he is given 6,000 years to participate in the redemption process, i.e., to choose or deny Jesus Christ. However, remember that **Matthew 24:14** is the determining factor relative to when this age will end: *"And this gospel of the kingdom shall be preached in all the world for a witness unto all nations; and then shall the end come."*

The seventh day of the week, Saturday, is the biblical Sabbath, a day of rest ordained by God. From sundown to sundown, it is a time dedicated to worship and reflection, symbolizing both God's rest after creation and Christ's coming 1,000-year reign on Earth. The final millennial reign will complete God's 7,000-year plan for salvation and the restoration of the Earth and humanity.

Historically, early Christians, particularly those influenced by the Roman Catholic Church, shifted the day of worship to Sunday, the first day of the week, in honor of Christ's resurrection. However, this change also aligned with pagan traditions, as Sunday was historically dedicated to the worship of the Sun God in various cultures, particularly in Rome. This transition played a significant role in shaping modern Christian worship, yet many still observe the original Sabbath as commanded in the Ten Commandments. The Sabbath remains a sign of God's covenant with His people, emphasizing obedience, rest, and spiritual renewal.

To analyze and **trace human life on Earth**, the truth regarding the age of the Earth, is found in the Bible, in which the details of the family lineage or genealogy from Adam to Abraham is listed in **1 Chronicles 1** and from Abraham to Jesus, see **Matthew 1:2-16 and Luke 3:23-38**, and from Jesus to now, as this is detailed in the Bible. God purposefully and precisely laid out the genealogy of "Man" in His Holy Word from Adam and Eve to Jesus so that you will not be fooled by hyperbole. The land mass of Earth is the beginning of humanity, which is approximately 6,000 years old.

Since, according to the Word of God, it was only 6,000 years ago since God said let there be light and formed land that we walk on, thus the question becomes: *"What land mass did the dinosaurs roam upon billions of years ago?"* And *"How can man-made Dinosaurs and the use Carbon Dating Technology that put the age of Earth and the Universe at millions and billions of years old?"*

Ironically, we visit museums to view the huge archeological structures of various Dinosaur species that they have "supposedly"

A CLOSER LOOK AT LIFE AND DEATH

unearthed. However, we know that the Bible confirms that Giants existed, so why don't scientists have Giants from around the world in museums instead of Dinosaurs that don't exist? I believe it is so that the Bible will not be proven true; therefore, Giant artifacts have always remained hidden from us. Also, we spend millions at the box office going to see Dinosaur movies: *"Age of the Dinosaurs," "The Lost World," "Jurassic Park,"* etc. And we also spend billions buying Dinosaur toys for our children. Have we been duped? You decide.

Recall that I said that Satan knows God's Word…The Bible, and God's redemption plan better than any of us so that he can mount his countermeasures against God. Satan knows that the Rapture is the next big event on God's calendar and that, as prophesied, several events are converging at once, globally, to infer that it is very near time for the Rapture to occur. For instance, the prophetic Matthew Chapter 24 equates the intensifying tribulations to that of the birth pains of a woman in labor, as well as the fig tree parable in relation to Israel. And he knows God's 7,000-year redemption plan, that the Earth is fast approaching 6,000 years old, and the prophecy that states that the generation (approximately 80 years) that saw Israel become a nation in 1948 will not pass away before He returns.

In addition, Israel has just turned 70 years old, and in 2017, President Donald Trump, prophetically, acknowledged and declared Jerusalem the capital of Israel. This was a prophetic moment because, according to Revelation 3:12 and 21:2, the Capital City of God or New Jerusalem will come down out of Heaven to Earth, to rest at the landmark that is acknowledged as the capital of Israel… Jerusalem, on Earth.

Also, the fact that the Euphrates River is, reportedly, drying up to pave the way for the army of the king of the East to come to compete in Earth's final war, the War of Armageddon. This river is also where the Bible says that there are four Angels chained but will be unleashed during the last days to wreak destruction upon the Earth (Revelation 7:2). There are reportedly horrible sounds from caves that are now uncovered due to the loss of water.

The war that began in Heaven, while we existed in the Spirit, and must be fought to its finality, in the Body, made of flesh, to complete the whole of Man's composition (Spirit and flesh). This war will encompass the globe. During these end times, there is a war going on at Israel's northern border, in Syria (which began in 2011 with Russia, and the United States eventually intervened), and more specifically, it involves the prophecy of Damascus, Syria (the oldest modern city on Earth). The destruction of Damascus is an end-time prophecy soon to be fulfilled (Isaiah 17:1).

And as well, there is the 400-year slave trade prophecy against America, the offspring of Britain, who are responsible for enslaving Africans with no remorse or reciprocity, *"Then the LORD said to Abram, 'Know for certain that your descendants [Black People of Jesus descent, The Tribe of Judah] will be strangers in a land [Britian/America] that is not their own, and they will be enslaved and mistreated four hundred years. But I will judge the nation they serve as slaves, and afterward they [Black People of Jesus descent, The Tribe of Judah] will depart with many possessions…'" (Genesis 15:13-14).* This scripture confirms that there will be another exodus movement in Earth's History, or as Moses declared to Pharaoh, "Let my people go!" Recently, more end-time prophecies have become a reality since the printing of the Book's first volume (November 2022).

Iran, which supplies its proxies with military weaponry through Damascus Airport and road routes, has suffered more extensive bombing by Israel; hence, the city fell in one day, on December 7-8, 2024, while the President, Bashar al-Assad, fled to Russia. However, there remains more prophecy regarding Damascus yet to come, according to *Isaiah Chapter 17:* *"See, Damascus will no longer be a city but will become a heap of ruins... In that day their strong cities, which they left because of the Israelites, will be like places abandoned to thickets and undergrowth. And all will be desolation...In that day their strong cities, which they left because of the Israelites, will be like places abandoned to thickets and undergrowth. And all will be desolation. You have forgotten God your Savior..."*

Israel is God's chosen land, and his chosen people, the Jews, will always be Satan's number one target, which is why His land and His people are always at the center of attention, consistently in the news. God refers to the inhabitants of Israel as *"His people,"* according to *Deuteronomy 7:6,* and *"His land,"* according to *Zechariah 2:8,* which refers to **Israel** as *"the apple of his eye."* God handpicked this plot of land and set its boundaries (yet to be reached) for His people to dwell. This is why **Israel** is the most attacked country on Earth. It has been attacked 52 times, captured 44 times, and has been completely destroyed twice. Persia, modern-day Iran, has vowed to wipe Israel off the map, which propels their nuclear weapon agenda. However, God said in *Zechariah 14:2-4* that He will destroy all nations that come against Jerusalem: *"For I will gather all nations against Jerusalem to battle... Then shall the LORD go forth, and fight against those nations, as when he fought in the day of battle. And his feet shall stand in that day upon the mount of Olives, which is before Jerusalem on the east, and the mount of Olives...and you shall flee..."*

Now, can't you see that the focus on Israel and the Jews is about fighting against God? It is not politics. It is the continuance of the same war that began in Heaven. It repeats itself over and over again in the Spirit (the mind of man, the duality of thought) and in the Flesh (every war that happens on battlefields and all opposition in relationships). It will continue until it culminates at the Battle of

Armageddon, at **"The Second Coming of Jesus Christ." Wake up!**

[Side Note]: The Jews were chosen, not because they are better than any other race, but because these are the people whom God set aside to teach them His Holiness, His mission, His Commandments, His Feast Days, and His customs or ways and methods, etc. For it is through God's land and His people, that His people, that He will show His Divine Love and His Supreme Might to defend and protect Israel from its enemies to the rest of the world. The Lord said: *"For you are a holy people to the Lord your God; the Lord your God has chosen you to be a people for Himself, a special treasure above all the peoples on the face of the earth. The Lord did not set His love on you nor choose you because you were more in number than any other people, for you were the least of all peoples; but because the Lord loves you, and because He would keep the oath which He swore to your fathers..."* (Deuteronomy 7:6-7).

However, countries like Iran and its proxies desire to wipe Israel off the face of the Earth. On June 21, 2025, Israel and the U.S. bombed Iran's nuclear sites and others to eliminate that threat. Also, it appears that the Western World (Rome, Britain, and more specifically, America has purposely set out to teach its citizens the total opposite of the ways of God. The elite, within world governments, and the Catholic Church know God's Laws, the Ten Commandments, whereby Saturday is the seventh day of the week, a day that He set aside for us to rest and worship Him, was changed to Sunday worship. The Bible speaks of this in **Daniel 7:25, "[they will] think to change times and laws..."** As well, they know of God's Feast Days (Passover, Pentecost, the Feast of Trumpets, and the Day of Atonement) that He taught the Jews to observe, but they intentionally do not honor God's eternal instructions. [end]

Furthermore, according to prophecy, there have been signs in the

Heavens or skies: Blood Moons indicate warnings to Israel and eclipses signify warnings to the Gentiles As well **CERN** (whose logo is 666), the European Organization for Nuclear Research states that they are looking for the "God Particle" (the juncture in Genesis 1:2, when God's Light first entered our darkness where we were cast down to from Heaven…the darkness of the Abyss of Hell). However, Scientists are using CERN to facilitate a darker, deceptive, hidden, more sinister objective that seeks to open portals, and more specifically, the portal to the bottomless pit (Revelation 9:2).

The goal is to usher in demon Spirits (dark matter or antimatter) from the unseen realm into our world. The Large Hadron Collider (LHC) is a physics laboratory that is networked with over 10,000 scientists and hundreds of universities and is defined as a particle accelerator and is the largest machine on Earth, as it is a 17-mile ring-shaped circular tubal system that is used to collide protons and neutrons together at the speed of light. The facility is reportedly built between Switzerland and France, 300 miles underground, over the Temple of Apollyon, a name of Satan that means destroyer. It is also reported that if you draw a line from CERN at a 666-degree angle, the line passes through New York, where 9/11 occurred, and New Orleans, where Hurricane Katrina made landfall…could it be a coincidence?

Ironically, the symbolism of the bottomless pit is eerily on display at the World Trade Center Memorial in New York City, where the Twin Towers were attacked and brought down by airplanes. I visited this site and as I looked down into a black, seemingly endless hole with black marble surrounding the top edge, which displays the names of those who lost their lives. However, I wondered why the memorial is a big black hole opening with water flowing downward into the darkness of the Earth, or an endless pit. Then the question came to my mind, *"How does looking down into a big black hole represent the lives lost on 9/11 in an uplifting manner?"* I later traced the date of 9/11 to the actual scripture that coincides with the Book of ***Revelation, Chapter 9, verse 11:*** *"And they had a king over them, which is the angel of the bottomless pit, whose name in the Hebrew tongue is Abaddon, but in the Greek tongue hath his name Apollyon."*

After reading this scripture, I was stunned at the correlation, in that the memorial depicts a similar deep, dark bottomless pit, just as the scripture Revelation 9:11 describes…WOW. This monument and the fact that CERN is opening a portal(s) and its specific location that is associated with a temple of Satan (Apollyon, the destroyer), which is reportedly over the pit mentioned in Revelation 9:11, is chilling. Who sought out and found this location and decided to build such a structure related to opening the pit or this demonic portal? This truly aligns technology with biblical fulfillment. Could CERN's location be the location of the bottomless pit of Revelation 9:11? Years ago, we could have never figured out the reality of certain things or events mentioned in the Book of Daniel and in the Book of Revelation, but now, the truth is unfolding and is staring us in our face!

CERN is also where Satan's World Wide Web was created, establishing the infrastructure of his coming Beast System. Interestingly, the Hebrew number **"6"** equates to the English letter "W," nevertheless, ***www = 666***, so when I type the name of my website in a browser…www.FaceEternity.org, I am essentially typing **666.FaceEternity.org… Hmm**. The goal of CERN is to collide atomic particles at the speed of light and then cause the particles to collide in order to collect smaller particles and antimatter or dark subatomic matter. Reportedly, antimatter brings out the dark side of people; their behavior becomes bizarre, violent, etc., like what we see happening with people in the news today. Scientists are seeking to open portals and to release the Spirits of

A CLOSER LOOK AT LIFE AND DEATH

the Nephilim, or half-human and half-fallen angels that resulted when the Sons of God came down from Heaven to mate with beautiful women on Earth. This union gave birth to giants (Genesis 6:4), men of renown. We will revisit that era and discuss the prophesied return of Nephilim through the technology at **CERN.**

Another end-time convergence of global significance is World War III (WWIII). It is an increasing threat as alliances between nations have recently begun to form as prophesied in Ezekiel 38-39; more later. Satan and his elite know what **"Time"** it is! He knows, although you may not care to know, it is time for you to **WAKE UP!** The Bible warns of all these events occurring simultaneously and that it is **"a sign" of Christ's return.** This is the reason why Satan's elite are coming forth, at this particular time, to reveal that UFOs and Aliens are real, as they prepare us for their defensive narrative to explain away the missing people from the Earth after the Rapture. And, also to prepare those who are left for interaction with Aliens.

Although those who will be left behind after the Rapture will have witnessed an undeniable, auditable, and very visible heavenly event that proves that Jesus Christ is the Messiah and that God's Word is always precise and true, there will still be those who choose not to believe. Their minds will remain in utter darkness with their hearts waxed cold. Their only focus will be to do Satan's bidding until their eternal punishment occurs; many will be the Nephilim.

Satan deceptively parades himself as an Angel of light, or he comes to you as a friend or peacemaker, only to deceive you. In this way, he will deceive the Jews into signing a 7-year agreement that will divide Israel, which is contrary to God's Word. It is also why the contention to divide Israel has been in the news for decades now, with the United States at the forefront of talks. On July 29, 2029, the United Nations convened to renew the Israel-Palestinian two-state solution. God says: **"... *I will also gather all nations,***

And bring them down to the Valley of Jehoshaphat; And I will enter into judgment with them there. On account of My people, My heritage Israel, Whom they have scattered among the nations; They have also divided up My land [per the 7-year agreement that the Antichrist will sign with Israel]" (Joel 3:2). Could Pope Francis' 7-year plan (Laudato Si') also be a part of their 7-year plan with the Antichrist? This plan is designed to unite the world through Climate Change; he signed this agreement with world political leaders and with world religious leaders.

Satan fills his followers with the pride of his scientific and technological knowledge (remember his "Tree of the Knowledge of Good and Evil" that we chose in the Garden); therefore, we each chose to receive our knowledge from Him rather than from God. So, he gives us the knowledge to yield the technology that meets his ends, which we now depend on under the guise of convenience. He gives us his knowledge to make us "think" that we know so much or are so intelligent; however, we will never obtain enough knowledge or be intelligent enough to save ourselves from death... Hmm.

The former Light Bearer will never be able to do anything to change the fact that you, I, and he will die. But he certainly has many fooled regarding his power; even some help him spread his wickedness, as you blindly follow his mindset and worship him. Pay attention and wake the Hell up because Hell certainly awaits you! Lucifer and all unbelievers will be thrown into the eternal Lake of Fire and Brimstone, which is called The Second Death.

I know that UFOs, **Nephilim**, the opening of portals, etc., sound like a sci-fi movie, but it is the Truth of God's Word. Just in case, you have never read His book... the Bible (Book of Redemption), please check it out, now. Our movies portray the good and evil characters that represent our daily lives. These movies reflect the opposition forces that mirror our heavenly rebellion, which sets the universal definition of the word **"War."** However, if you choose to continue to fall for Satan's lies, it will be too late to change your mind when you find yourself being cast into the Lake of Fire. But just know that it will be the last lie that you will catch Satan in, as you follow him into the Lake of Fire, right behind him... sorry.

The former Light Bearer tries to copy God's ability to heal the sick, raise the dead, or perform miracles by using witchcraft. Witchcraft is his supernatural power to cast spells to control people through manipulation, intimidation, deceit, and trickery so that they will do what he wants them to do by using any Spirit **(person)** that is not of the Holy Spirit. He uses trickery through deception to promise and afford you material gain through his earthly elites and agents. They use the results of magic to deceive and encourage blind followers to follow Satan. You think you are reaping rewards from his **"enlightenment"** and his knowledge, but you are enlightened by the darkness of tricks, lies, and his agenda to use you to gain his desires. The dragon will ensure that your behavior will defile you in the sight of God. His goal and his gain are to deceitfully lead you to destruction, death, and Hell.

Satan causes his followers to believe that his artificial light is the Light of God, the same as he had us believing his lies while in Heaven and on Earth, that we could be God. However, the truth is that Satan's light extinguished itself into utter darkness the moment he sinned; he was subsequently expelled. Consequently, his name was changed to Satan to reflect the character he had become, the opposer of God. However, he still has his Light Bearer attributes that manifest in the Earth to deceive us.

Since living life creates and forms our mind's Eternal History, which establishes our eternal memory, it is plausible to conclude that if you live a sin-filled life, you will only create a life history of sin-filled memories resulting from your thoughts, speech, and actions. And so, this history and your established memories will torture you in your own private Hell when you leave this Earth. You will continue to be consumed and tortured by your evil lifestyle in Hell, and you will continue to do the evil things that you love to do.

Lucifer's sin, rebelliousness, deception, and vile evil behavior made this lifestyle available to you when he took away both his eternal life and yours in Heaven. For that, he received an unforgivable Eternal Death Sentence and the penalty of permanent eternal punishment. We all witnessed his sentencing, as well as our own… Natural Death, on Earth, and Eternal Death, which are to come. However, I continue to remind you that the good news is that you can avoid the eternal Second Death, which is still on your horizon if you choose to believe in Jesus Christ.

Satan has received and experienced his death sentence or permanent separation from God's Presence when he sinned. This is evident because he is no longer in Heaven; therefore, he is awaiting the Lake of Fire and Brimstone that was made especially for him. On the other hand, we received God's mercy through Christ to return to God so that we will avoid Hell, permanent separation, and its punishments. Recall **Matthew 8:29 NIV**, where Satan asked Jesus, *"Have you come here to torture us before the appointed time?"* This scripture confirms that Satan knows that his time for punishment is coming and that it will be at God's appointed time alone. By his question, Satan acknowledges who Jesus is and that Jesus has the power to punish him, although he makes certain that you do not know so that you will continue to fall for his lies. Haven't you fallen enough?

Therefore, the former Light Bearer's eternal punishment… The Lake of Fire and Brimstone **(Revelation 20:10)** has NOT occurred yet because his punishment was put off until the redemption process, which includes Natural Death, is complete. We decide by choice, and/or our lifestyles will determine if we will join him in the Lake of Fire. Therefore, Satan and all unbelievers in Christ, who die from the Earth, will all experience it together. As a result, unbelievers in Christ still face the death of their bodies and two punishments. Christ's resurrection from the dead was prophesied thousands of years before His birth to announce the pivotal point of the redemption plan to defeat death. Again, Bible Prophecy is what makes God... God! No one can predict what will happen on Earth with 100% accuracy, but our Creator can.

Jesus' death on the cross and His resurrection were purposely made visible for all the inhabitants of Heaven and Earth to see that He arose from the grave after three days, with His Body and Spirit intact. It was important to let us (the fallen) know, by using God's Word (Jesus), that Heaven is now open to us again so that we can regain our eternal life. This monumental event was witnessed by His disciples, and many others, as well as those who were also resurrected from the grave along with Jesus on that day: ***"And the graves were opened; and many bodies of the saints which slept arose, and came out of the graves after his resurrection, and went into the holy city, and appeared unto many" (Matthew 27:50-53).*** This verse serves as our example because, according to God's Divine Redemption Plan, ALL graves will open. **[Side Note]:** Their bodies slept, but their Spirits never sleep because they are in constant motion in one of two eternal realms.

Please know that to depend on yourself, extricate God from your life. Satan drives governments to expel God from society. In America, he used the formation of its government to separate church and state, which has allowed us to sink further into sin. His **"Cancel Culture"** excludes God's laws in our life, government, corporations, and school systems, as well as spreading hate throughout the societies of the world. He unleashes all sorts of corruption, perversion, and violence that lead to destruction. So, since you have taken control of your life like the former Light Bearer thought that he could when he sinned and rebelled, but you

A CLOSER LOOK AT LIFE AND DEATH

see how that turned out. How do you think it will end for you? You and Satan can indeed accomplish everything under the sun, except to save yourselves from death. Since you can control your own life, why can't you and Satan control or prevent your deaths? [**end**].

The Former Light Bearer is powerful enough to give you Eternal Life based on our **"Tree"** selection in the Garden, but it will be eternal life in the Lake of Fire, kindled with sulfur, which is Eternal Death or **The Second Death**. There, your Body and Spirit will burn forever, according to Revelation 20:14. But do not take my word for it; do your own research and compare what Satan says and does, through man, versus what the Word of God says. Also, think back on the things you were led to believe in school, church, or other means. None of man's theories or hypotheses are authoritative or have been proven true, like the word of God. His word is the only source that addresses our life and death conclusively, relative to **Genesis 2:17, 3:3,** and **Ecclesiastes 12:5-7**.

[Exercise]: Read the latter three scriptures to determine the factual results relative to your life and death. Then compare the Theory of Evolution, whereby Charles Darwin, in his book, ***"The Descent of Man,"*** presented the idea that human beings and apes have a common ancestor; therefore, humans evolved from apes. Now, take a look at the Big Bang Theory, which contends that our Life began with an infinitely hot and dense single point in the universe that has inflated and stretched for over 13.7 billion years to the continuously expanding cosmos that exists today.

However, the Scientists who made up this hyperbole were not around to witness what happened billions of years ago, but they frown when we choose to believe what happened on the Cross at Calvary 2,000 years ago… go figure that out. Please Google these theories for a more in-depth study. Lastly, see the diagram in the index or visit www.FaceEternity.org and download the Animated Overview to study so that you can determine what you believe.

A CLOSER LOOK AT LIFE AND DEATH

These never-proven theories or lies were created to muddy your thoughts and distract you from the truth, but you decide based on your own research. See more exercises in the index. **[end]**

Neither Satan nor any man can change or reverse God's Words; for instance, in Genesis 3:3, whereby God told Adam and Eve: ***"You must not eat fruit from the tree that is in the middle of the garden, and you must not touch it, or you will die."*** As a result, you and I attend funeral and burial services, right? This is the reason why nothing has ever changed regarding this fact. However, it's your choice to continue to believe lies or the truth.

The former Light Bearer may have fooled you, but your certain death is the measure of this truth. Both ***Romans 6:23, "…the wage of sin is death,"*** and ***Hebrews 9:27, "it is appointed unto men once to die,"*** are God's Word that will forever hold true. The evidence of these scriptures is your certain death. AND consequently, your death, on Earth, is evidence of Satan's (and your) impending eternal death…The Second Death, the coming punishment of the Lake of Fire and Brimstone (this is your punishment too if you do not accept Christ as your Savior). Natural Death is only a shadow of the real definition of our real death… The Second Death, permanent separation from God. However, your punishments are fast approaching, so if you are still unsure where you will spend eternity, I encourage you to think about your life and death and make a definitive decision about your eternal future…choose to believe in Christ today.

Unfortunately, Satan will never deliver on reversing death because he is not God. He is a defeated foe, although he may still have fooled you into thinking that he is an angel of light, but deep down inside, you know this is not the truth. He thought he could exalt himself over God, but it was just a thought that would never come true. Although many of you do not believe in Hell, Satan, Heaven, Jesus, etc., it doesn't matter because your death is your evidence. There is no longer any fear of Hell because Satan has guided pastors away from preaching about it, so that the wildness of your living will blindly take you there. This was the stated agenda of many Pastors when they created the Mega Churches Agenda. Google it. It is Satan's determined will that you will be tricked out of your eternal life with the Lord.

Jesus Christ brought God's written Holy Word of Truth to Life, in Earth's atmosphere, as visible flesh, our prophesied Messiah. For approximately 2000 years before the birth of Jesus, various prophets proclaimed that He would come, but you have been programmed not to study God's Word, so you attend church and believe whatever the pastor tells you, right? He or she can tell you anything, and you will believe it because you don't have time to seek and learn the truth on your own. But you seek to learn everything else that you're interested in, on Google or YouTube, but your eternal future means nothing because Christ doesn't interest you.

Since you can't see Him, you choose not to believe in anything that you cannot see. You have no faith in God's Word, you don't believe the facts surrounding His virgin birth, death, and resurrection because you were not there to see it: ***"But without faith it is impossible to please him [God]: for he that cometh to God must believe that he is, and that he is a rewarder of them that diligently seek him" (Hebrews 11:6).*** Yet you believe that death is real because you see it happening all around you, but you don't believe in God, the Most High Judge who issued you, your death sentence... go figure that out. You would rather believe that Scientists were around billions of years ago to witness a big bang or apes evolving into humans... Hmm.

Nevertheless, you have to know that God, who is Jesus, exists to deny belief in their oneness, but now you have discovered their roles in the redemption plan, so that you have a better understanding. It stands to reason that if you don't know that someone exists, it means that you do not know their name or anything about them. Although you deny God, who is Jesus, in your unbelief, you do call their names to state that you do not believe they exist, and to say that you don't believe what God has done through Jesus. This means that you had to have heard something about them to express your disbelief in them. Again, go figure.

The bottom line is that God has a redemption plan in action for your life; it's not a game; it is as serious as attending memorial services and burying our dead while knowing that you may be next. However, Christ is the only meaningful way that God gave us to get back our eternal life with the Lord; without the existence of death, ever again! But the kicker is, it does not matter whether you believe in God or Jesus or not, because the fact of the evidence is your certain death from the Earth to come. You know that Natural Death is real; you see it, experience all the hurt, pain, and emotions that are associated with it, and you will, for certain, experience it for yourself one day.

Therefore, as sure as you are born into the Earth, you will certainly die out of it, as evidenced by our **"Tree"** selection in the Garden of Eden. Again, just as certain as you see the existence of Natural Death, you can be certain that The Second Death awaits you. But the good news is that you DO NOT have to die a Second and eternal Death if you believe in the finished work of Jesus Christ on the cross, whereby He defeated Eternal Death by His resurrection.

Life outside of the Presence of God's Holy Spirit subjects us to the former Light Bearer's rule. We are led by his Life outside of the Presence that we receive from **The Tree of the Knowledge of Good and Evil**... the good (Truth of God) or the lies of evil that Satan intertwines to deceive us. This is why he is depicted as a cunning serpent with a forked tongue that represents the mixing of

God's truth with his lies, and we fall for it. Additionally, as we gain knowledge from the father of lies, based on our **"Tree"** selection, *Ecclesiastes 1:18* tells us: *"For in much wisdom is much grief, And he who increases knowledge increases sorrow."*

And as foretold in *Daniel 12:4,* God edified to *"Daniel, shut up [keep secret] the words, and seal the book until the time of the end; [when] many shall run to and fro [Worldwide Air Travel and Outer Space Travel] and knowledge shall increase [by way of Computer Technology, and the World Wide Web…Facebook, YouTube, TikTok…all Social Media, Television and Radio Broadcasting Networks, Gaming Systems, Satellites, Cell Phone Communications, Language Translation, CERN, Artificial Intelligence, etc]."* The Holy Word of God foretells all technology that will befall our reality from the beginning to the end of time; it is mind-blowing that He chose me to reveal these things.

[**Side Note**]: While writing down the Holy Spirit's revelations, I feel like I have received the mantle from Daniel and John to reveal surprising End Time facts about our Eternal History, which includes naming agendas, methods, and modern-day technologies that reveal what the prophets were talking about. My first-volume book publisher told me, "Talking to you is like talking to John the Revelator." The Lord is providing us with His perspective of our behavior against Him, in Heaven, the Creation, and the purpose of the Earth relative to our redemption, our consequences, and so many other truths. He is highlighting your role in our Eternal History, simplifying what you and I must do to be saved; He is revealing that the solution for our common problem… death, is Jesus Christ. Additionally, He explains the purpose of eternal life and death as we discover how death fits into the mystery of our Eternal Life. [**end**]

Now that we are in the End Times and the Last Days…the Tribulation and Great Tribulation are fast approaching, it seems that God is utilizing me to fill in some of the pieces of the puzzle relative to the writings of Daniel and John, who were told to seal up or keep their writings secret until the End Times. *"The Little Book"* is a monumental work that has come along precisely during the end times to bring a simplistic, chronological overview of The Big Book… The Holy Bible. It specifies end-time human behavior, government and religious agendas, and modern-day technologies that bring God's latter-day prophecies to our realization. Furthermore, this book also reveals the most important choices that we must make prior to our demise… **repent**, and be forgiven, thus choosing eternal life through Christ, or automatically default to experience The Eternal Second Death.

Lastly, we must come to grips with death and make peace within ourselves about the reality of our eternal consequence of Hellfire, so that we might choose to get ourselves right with the Lord before we return to the ground.

Satan has guided Man… Scientists, Engineers, Mathematicians, Physicists, etc., to create the most diabolical military technologies on the planet… the Atomic Bomb, Missiles, Drones, Electromagnetic Pulse (EMP), Nuclear and Supersonic Technology, and Laser Weaponry, as well as the most destructive of them all is "Antimatter" that they are currently collecting at CERN. The former Light Bearer continues to wage the war that began in Heaven, and will eventually end here, on Earth. Nonetheless, who is it that engages in war combat on Earth? **"Human Beings,"** whom it is Satan's goal to kill and destroy…again, wake the Hell up because surely Hell awaits you! The former Light Bearer's knowledge, throughout Earth's History, brings about sin, fear, chaos, destruction, tribulation, grief, and death. However, again the Lord tells us, *"…do not fear those who kill the body but cannot kill the soul. But rather fear Him who is able to destroy both soul and body in hell"* (Matthew 10:28). **FEAR THE LORD THY GOD!** Amen and Amen.

Our death sentence for the sins we committed in the **"Spirit"** and our death sentence for sins committed in the **"Body"** constitute the fall of the whole man, made of both Spirit and Flesh, which unleashed the certainty of the execution of both Natural Death and The Second Death and their respective punishments. Although we know the reality of Natural Death and see the nature of its certainty, many of us do not realize our fate of a Second Death. The Second Death is the real reason for God's intervention into the Earth. His coming was the only way to defeat death and make eternal life available to us again.

Our plight prompted God to use the Earth to give us a second chance to **repent**, accept God's forgiveness, and receive the free gift of eternal life back unto righteousness. The Lord came to show us His death and resurrection so that we do not have to fear Satan and death ever again, *"For whoever wants to save their life will lose it, but whoever loses their life for me will find it" (Matthew 16:25).* You must be willing to die, or lose your life, in the same manner as God did through Jesus Christ in order to gain back your eternal life. **Do NOT FEAR DEATH**, but understand its purpose from God's perspective. And always remember to thank God for your Eternal Life.

Only a Divine Savior who loves you more than his own life would forgive you and offer a plan to save you…Hallelujah! However, just as we witnessed the eternal death sentence that was issued to Lucifer (and ourselves) in Heaven, we will certainly be present to witness the execution of his death penalty, according to ***Revelation 14:10, "…He [Satan] shall be tormented with fire and brimstone in the presence of the holy angels [us, believers who are now back living eternally in the Presence of God] and in the presence of the Lamb [Jesus Christ in human Form.]"*** Therefore, we will either witness or participate in his eternal death penalty of everlasting Fire and Brimstone. Again, you are probably reading this because God may be trying to tell you something. **Pay Attention!**

A CLOSER LOOK AT LIFE AND DEATH

A CLOSER LOOK AT LIFE AND DEATH

Our Life Is the Lord's Breath of Life

*"The Spirit of God has made me, And the **breath** of the Almighty gives me life"*
*~ **Job 33:4***

God = Creator = Holy Spirit = Heaven = Earth = Eternal Life = I AM THAT I AM = Alpha & Omega = The Beginning and The End = The Word = Supreme Being = Person = Jesus = A Man = Messiah = Lamb of God = Lion of Judah = Christ = Indwelling Holy Spirit Within the Fallen Human Body = Holy Spirit of Truth = Light = Order = Holy Image = Holy Ghost = Goodness = Love = Righteousness = Judge = Redeemer/ Defeated Death = Savior = Emanuel (God with us) = Divine Immortal Human = Perfect Son = Son of Man (Son of the Human Race) = Hope = Rapture = Divine Revelation = Bible Prophecy = Believer = Mental Light = Redemption = Resurrection Back to Eternal Life = Restored Earth = New Jerusalem = New Heaven & Earth

Since we are no longer living in the glory of Heaven's atmosphere, it is extremely difficult for sinful humans to relate to words akin to holiness and the purity of truth. So, let's focus a bit on our current Flesh-Spirit existence, or more specifically, when God created life on Earth, according to *Genesis 2:7* when He molded man from the dirt of the ground, ***"And the LORD God formed man of the dust of the ground and breathed into his nostrils the breath of life, and man became a living soul."*** When humanity was first formed out of the dirt of the Earth, Adam did not function or move a muscle; he just lay there, absent of energy (Spirit); he had no Life. It wasn't until the Lord blew His wind or Breath of Life (His Holy Spirit) into Adam's nostrils that caused him to become a vibrant human living Soul with a mind fit to live

Life on Earth. The word wind or breath is derived from the Hebrew word Ruach, which means **"wind," "breath,"** and **"Spirit."** Think about it, when we feel the wind blow, we are experiencing "Breath" or the feeling of Spirit

The Lord's Breath of Life flows as invisible energy throughout the realms of our Universe…Heaven, Hell, Earth. The Lord's Breath flows as wind and manifests in the Earth as oxygen within our respiratory system. His Breath of eternal, abundant life is freely given to both believers and unbelievers. I am sure we can all agree that we cannot live without taking our next wind or breath, right? We know that Genesis 2:7 states that God *"breathed into his [Adam] nostrils the breath of life,"* so how then will His Breath of Life be passed on to other Children of Light? From Adam and Eve onward, His Breath of Life is effectuated through the reproductive system within the mother's womb. God, masterfully, created the placenta to carry out this function. The placenta is an organ that develops within the uterus during pregnancy. This is the mechanism that carries vital nutrients to the baby, but most importantly, its task is to carry God's Breath of Life to the lungs of developing Children of Light.

His Breath or wind manifests within humans as oxygen, which flows into infant embryos before their heartbeat is detectable. It is the source of all bodily functions, like the blood system, which is designed to remove waste products from the baby as it carries oxygen throughout its body. This is God's handy work, not the result of a Big Bang or a make-believe fallacy that humans evolved from apes. However, you are free to believe as you wish, but just know that your death to come is proof that God's Word is true; man has no proof to provide you regarding life and death.

Again, *Jeremiah 1:5* confirms our former, heavenly, eternal existence: *"Before I formed you in the belly [of your mother's womb], I knew you."* This means that God knew us before we were ever implanted in our mother's womb for birth. How could this be? I was intrigued by this verse, and it inspired me to dig deeper into why eternal life no longer applies to you and me. It prompted me to explore the purpose of the Garden of Eden and humanity as they relate to life and death. This verse also casts a new light on the pro-abortion contention, neglecting that God created the reproductive system, its process, and its purpose.

Although we do not consider the spiritual implications behind the physical mechanism of the childbearing process, we desire to define or judge when "we think" an infant becomes a person. But we fail to realize that oxygen or God's Breath of Life is included in everything that happens within the body. Still, God says that He formed our earthly lives in our mother's womb, so only He can define the point of conception. God created the womb to be the setting whereby our Spirit merges with our developing human flesh or physical body so that we are fit for living on Earth. He designed and implemented this spiritual yet physical process within the womb during gestation.

The undeniable rule that governs infant conception is what I call **Earth Rule Two (2):** The seed that impregnates a woman always comes from the father to fertilize a woman's egg. This law that God has created and established will never change. Therefore, now you can begin to understand why the mother of Jesus... Mary, was required to be a virgin... pure, not having slept with any man. This is because the seed that impregnated her had to come directly from our Holy Heavenly Father, in Heaven, and not from any fallen man on Earth.

Thus, Mary carried the seed of God, which is His Divine Word made of flesh. To create a Perfect Son or a perfect one of us, God alone had to be the Father because we are all fallen, drowning in sin. Therefore, God's Divine Word would manifest on the Earth as the visible flesh of Jesus to save us from eternal death. This is because the only one who could save us had to exist outside our sinful circumstances. For instance, if you are drowning, someone else who is also drowning along with you cannot save you. It would take someone outside of the water (or circumstance) you are drowning in, to save you... a lifeguard, emergency services, family, or friend, etc.

God also equipped man with the respiration of the lungs, a pulse from a beating heart, limbs to act on thoughts, a belief system to drive our will, and a Soul that, by choice, can house God's Holy Spirit or the Spirit of the former Light Bearer. Our Soul, the internal part of our being, consists of our functioning mind to process the thoughts that we use to ponder our choices within our mind to navigate through daily situations and make daily decisions, which consists of our thought life. Since all of us *"fall short of the glory of God" (Romans 3:23),* again, it will take someone outside of the Earth, who is NOT living in sin, to rescue us from eternal death. For those of us who are drowning in the depths of sin and facing certain death, it will take someone outside of our stinking, sinful circumstances to save us.

Again, the Breath of God's Word flowing from His Lips is what is meant when people say God "sent" Jesus. However, most people think of Jesus as a "Person" who sits next to God in Heaven, but we know that Jesus was the Spirit of God...His Word; after His return from Earth, He remained in His Divine Human form while God the Father always exists as an intangible Spirit of exponentially Brilliant Bright Light that no one has seen but Jesus. So, when the Bible says that Jesus sits or is at the **"right hand" of the Father,"** righteousness is meant.

Also, recall that no human has ever entered Heaven because only the "Spirit" resides there. Like John and others who said that they were taken to Heaven, or were with the Lord, they ensure that they let us know that they are in the Spirit. Also, recall that the human body was formed from the dust of the Earth; our bodies were not created in Heaven, nor have our bodies ever been accepted into Heaven by God, the Father, until Jesus Christ's ascension. We have already established that before the creation of Earth and before the Son was born, Jesus *"was the Word, and the Word was with God, and the Word was God" (John 1:1)*. We have established that as the Word, Jesus Christ, exists as a Spirit, not flesh, therefore, no flesh had ever entered Heaven before Jesus Christ's death and ascension.

God's Word, directly from His Lips, cannot be seen by humans unless His Word materializes on the Earth, before our eyes. The Word, in Heaven, is a Spirit which we cannot see. Therefore, Jesus materialized in the flesh so that our five senses could realize His life, death, and resurrection…some saw Him, touched Him, smelled Him, heard Him speak, and some tasted the glory of His resurrection.

We are born only with our word to confess our beliefs and a body to perform actions that reflect whether we are living towards righteousness or unrighteousness. With Life and Death hanging in the balance, life is all we have, yet it is all that we stand to lose for all eternity at the close of God's redemption plan.

Who Are We?

"...the angels [Satan, you and me] which kept not their first estate [position assigned by God], but left their own habitation [in Heaven], he [God] hath [expelled and] reserved [us] in everlasting chains [confined us] under [mental] darkness unto the judgment [to determine who will experience The Second Death]"
~Jude 1:6

And Why Are We Born As Sinners?

"For all have sinned and fall short of the glory of God."
~ Romans 3:23

Well, please allow me to make it plain and clear to you because some of us seem to believe that we are born into the Earth as **"good people,"** meaning that we have done nothing wrong, so we (adults and children) should not have to endure suffering, tribulation, and death... WRONG! We are born into the Earth to be given a second chance because we did do something wrong... something unforgivable to God; yet He chose to forgive us and wants us (His Children) back to live with Him. As a result, He put off Eternal Death (now called The Second Death in His redemption plan) to allow us to be born into the Earth to participate in His redemption process whereby the following law applies: ***"For the wages of sin is death" (Romans 6:23).*** At our juncture in Genesis 1:1, we are in Heaven, whereby Satan has committed the first sin, and thus Romans 6:23 was first applied.

To recap, Satan became death, evil, and the father of lies, for which an eternal death sentence was issued, which is called The Second Death **(Revelation 20:10-14).** His penalty is eternal life in the Lake of Fire and Brimstone, which is the definition of the word destroy or annihilation, and it is still pending; this death sentence was also issued to those who believed his lies and decided to follow Satan, instead of Jesus Christ. Therefore, God created "the way" through Christ to avoid the Second Death. He put off Satan's eternal death penalty to give you and me "Time" to **repent** and be forgiven. Still, due to the sins that our Spirits committed in Heaven, we must die a Natural Death on Earth. But while we wait to die, we are offered the chance to avoid a Second Death, if we believe in Christ's finished work on the Cross. Therefore, again, we come to Earth to die because ***"...it is appointed unto men once to die [a Natural Death], but after this the judgment [to determine who will experience the second death]" (Hebrews 9:27).***

Since we betrayed God's Love, His Truth…His Holy Spirit, the evidence of our betrayal and rebellious behavior, is measured by whether we can see His Face or have Christ living within us, or not. But it is obvious that we can no longer see His Face because we are living away from Him, here on Earth, awaiting our turn to die. And there is no denying it, even if you tried. Most of us have read and/or heard about the ***"War in Heaven,"*** but we never address who we are within this heavenly conflict. We believe that it was Satan and "his angels" that rebelled, or someone else other than ourselves, but the truth is that it was us… You and Me. In fact, all of us who are allowed to be born in the Earth are at fault, which is why we all ***"fall short of the glory of God" (Romans 3:23),*** we sinned and rebelled against Him. As a result, we became Satan's angels when we chose to obey him. Therefore, we were sinners long before Adam and Eve were created on Earth.

However, for the sake of redemption, we purposely do not remember our past Eternal History because we are born into the Earth, in the innocence of infancy. Our state of infancy or our birth as an infant gives our minds a clean slate to only focus on redemption or our eternal choice of eternal life and eternal death: ***"…[with every breath] I have set before you [eternal] life and***

A CLOSER LOOK AT LIFE AND DEATH

[eternal] death, blessing and cursing: therefore, choose life..." *(Deuteronomy 30:19).*

And as we grow older, the choice between *eternal life and eternal death = light and darkness = good and evil = truth and lies = right and wrong,* is ever put before our minds to make choices and decisions that shape our lives. Some will choose to shape their lifestyle based on truth, and others will choose a lifestyle based on the fallacy of lies. But ultimately, the summation of our life's choices and decisions will reveal our eternal choice regarding where we will spend eternity. Therefore, we cannot plan our choice, we must live our choice!

It makes perfect sense that if God created only Spirit Life, first in Heaven, then doesn't that include the Spirits of you and me... our Angelic Spirits, along with Lucifer's Angelic Spirit?

Spirit = Angelic Spirit = Inner Man's Spirit

So, we are **"Fallen Angels"** like Lucifer: ***"The angels which kept not their [our] first estate [did not stay within the limits of authority that God gave us] but left their [our] own habitation [was expelled from Heaven], he [God] hath reserved [us] in everlasting chains [confined us] under [mental] darkness unto the judgment [to determine who will experience the Second the Death]" (Jude 1:6).*** Recall that this mental darkness is real by closing your eyes.

However, as explained earlier, some fallen angels are not allowed to be born into the Earth to participate in the redemption process; some are bound in various locations in and within Hell, which includes Earth. ***The Lost Books of the Bible and the Forgotten Books of Eden: The Book of The Secrets of Enoch 29:2,*** explains how God made some of His Angelic Spirits: ***"And from the rock I cut off a great fire, and from the fire I created the orders of the incorporeal (having no material body; immaterial)*** *troops of angels and their weapons are fiery and their raiment a burning flame, and I commanded that each one should stand in his order."*

God created this troop of Angels and commanded them to their positions because He needed them and their weaponry to expel us from Heaven after Satan sinned, and we followed suit. Remember, there was war in Heaven, so it was this army of Angelic beings who fought against Satan and his angels (us), and thus put us out of Heaven, then guarded its gates. And when Adam and Eve were expelled from the Garden, God assigned these Angels to guard the entrance to the Garden of Eden to protect the Tree of Life, for they had chosen a life that ends in death. The Divine Order of the Lord places angels at various levels of hierarchy and authority. Angels are ranked according to their wisdom and duties, which span throughout the entire universe.

The following angelic hierarchy chart shows angelic rank or status:

Supreme Hierarchy	Middle Hierarchy	Lower Hierarchy
Cherubim	Dominions	Principalities
Seraphim	Virtues	Archangels
Thrones	Powers	Angels

Lucifer was a Cherubim Angel. Which one were you while living in Heaven?

The Duality of Spirit Life Energy

*"...there shall be a resurrection of the dead, both of the **JUST** and **UNJUST**"*
~ Acts 24:15

The former Light Bearer's betrayal of God produced two states of Spirit Life Energy: Divine **(Holy/Just)** and Demonic **(unholy/unjust).** Hence, deriving life's two choices that we ponder within our minds in our situations and circumstances: right or wrong, good or evil, God or Satan, etc. Everything in life can be deduced from the latter two choices. These two choices are posed to our belief system, which establishes what you believe, and your belief system establishes the history of your life, which will determine where you will spend your eternal future… Heaven or Hell.

Furthermore, the division or separation of Eternal Spirit into two separate states of existence manifests on Earth as duality in the form of flowing negative and positive electrical energy. The same oscillating waveform of energy that flows within the Lithium Battery that powers your cell phone and all equipment and devices on Earth also flows through you. And this energy is visibly apparent when you touch someone and shock them with your energy. Therefore, our Spirit Life Energy within our body requires a power source, like our cell phones and other electrical devices. For instance, if your phone is drained of the energy that makes it function, the phone dies. We immediately respond with a quest to find a charger and the nearest receptacle to connect it back to the power source. The same is true for believers and nonbelievers; death drains our bodies of our Eternal Spirit Energy. Life is extracted from us; without this energy, the body can no longer function and is considered dead (James 2:26).

Therefore, we must connect to our eternal power source, the Holy Spirit of the Living God, to live forever.

It is because of duality that Heaven is the foundation of our choice to think and do what is good, true, and righteous, and Hell is the foundation of our choice to think and do wrong or the opposite of good, which is evil. In the Earth, Heaven, and Hell are interwoven into the fabric of our world for the purpose of our two choices according to **Deuteronomy 30:19**. Duality is a form of the scientific word **"Equilibrium."** For it is our world, according to Emanual Swedenborg's book *"Heaven and Hell,"* that is created in equilibrium: *"...it is [the Earth that is] in equilibrium between the good which is from Heaven and the evil which is from hell; and that consequently it is a spiritual equilibrium, which in its essence is freedom [of choice (Deuteronomy 30:19)]; ...it is equilibrium of good and evil, and also the true and the false, [right and wrong] which are spiritual things [within the mind...thought]; ...and of choosing the one in preference to the other, is the freedom of which we now speak and this freedom is given to every man by the Lord, nor is It ever taken away from him."*

Since our sin resulted in the existence of duality, it ushered in monumental changes to God's original plan for Heaven, Earth, and Man. Lucifer's creation of Hell has changed the configuration of our Universe so that it now consists of Heaven, Hell, and Earth. Therefore, God had to plan, create, and redesign His original plan to accommodate the three realms of Heaven, Hell, and Earth for Man's redemption. To establish choice, per *Deuteronomy 30:19*, He declared, *"I call heaven and earth to record this day against you, that I have set before you [eternal] life and [eternal] death..."*

God has to establish and sustain our Eternal Spirit Life Energy states in two separate locations within our Universe. It is from these two locations that the Lord derives our two eternal choices or duality, and He has set each of their consequences... Eternal Life and Eternal Death, per **Deuteronomy 30:19.** These two choices,

A CLOSER LOOK AT LIFE AND DEATH

with each breath, are before us to carry out our choice redemption through Man's bodily composition. Therefore, the coexistence of good and evil in the Earth was required to effectuate our redemption, and God's Physical Presence cannot remain where evil is, so they had to be expelled from the Garden, away from Him.

And through all of this and even until now, Lucifer's Spirit is the same Spirit that committed the first sin and formed the rebellion against God, in Heaven, he will never change. Consequently, he is the same Spirit that exists today, on the Earth, just as you are the same living Spirit now that God first created of you, in Heaven. But since Satan is the opposer of God's Truth, for example, if God created us *"...male and female, and blessed them [us] and called them [us] Mankind in the day they [we] were created" (Genesis 5:2),* then Satan will engage in and promote the opposite behavior, *"Neither shall he [Satan] regard the God of his fathers, nor the desire of women [Gay], nor regard any god: for he shall magnify himself above all" (Daniel 11:37).* Satan will perverse, perpetuate and promote the opposite of what God has established as truth. He contends and teaches humanity that a male should lie with a male and a female with a female and proclaim that "love is love" or that their love is the same love as which God created, instituted, and ordained…No!

The word "Love" is not the same because of the duality of Spirit Energy; therefore, love is regarded as holy unto God and *unholy = self-dependent = Satan,* which relies on the two realms of Heaven and Hell from which holy and unholy love flows. The Spirit Energy of Love is either holy or unholy; thus, we can choose to live a lifestyle based on this. Christ died to make this choice completely up to you. The duality of "love" means that there are two loves, which are far from the same, because one love is between God, one man, and one woman, whereby they consummate their love unto God and populate the Earth as He instructed.

The other **"love,"** same-sex love relationships, do not include the love of God because He did not create, establish, or ordain this kind of love relationship. This love relationship does not and cannot meet the purpose of ***Genesis 9:7, "...be fruitful and multiply..."*** ***God tells us: "If a man lies with a male as with a woman, both of them have committed an abomination" (Leviticus 20:13, EVS).*** Also, consider this direct command from God: ***"A woman shall not wear anything that pertains to a man, nor shall a man put on a woman's garment, for all who do so are an abomination to the LORD your God" (Deuteronomy 22:5).*** No other sin is called an abomination whereby God has destroyed cities due to this behavior.

Therefore, please DO NOT get angry with me or anyone who believes God's truth, or does not agree with your lifestyle, because your lifestyle is designed to be your choice. Your "beef" is not with me because I do not own a Heaven or Hell to put you in, so your "beef" is with your Creator alone. He has given you two choices: either **repent** or accept your choice and your eternal consequence, as you continue to **live what you call "your truth."** We have established that **Truth belongs to God alone**, but these days, many are saying that they are happily living "their truth," which **is Satan's lie.** Truth belongs to God, so when and how did you create your own truth? You can either live your life under God's Truth or live a life under Satan's lies. However, you can change your ways while there is still time, but do so today, because tomorrow may never come.

There is also the duality of the word **"Rapture."** As we have previously discussed being Raptured up to Heaven, there also exists evidence of being Raptured in the opposite direction, as revealed in the Bible. To be Raptured downward, into Hell, is when God sends fire down to consume you and bring you down into the pit of Hell. This was demonstrated by the destruction of Sodom and Gomorrah and four surrounding cities.

There were four out of five cities that received damnation, and the reason that these four cities burned instead of all five was because those four cities had passed a law that gave their sexually perverted citizens the right to put beds in the public square to indulge in homosexual activities for all to see. Nowadays, our public square is television, movies, gaming, etc. Therefore, Fire and Brimstone rained down upon them from Heaven as the fires of Hell consumed them all, and this fire continues to this day, even forever.

This same "Rapture to Hell" phenomenon also occurred in the Book of ***Numbers 26:10,*** *"...when Aaron with the followers of Korah who rebelled against the LORD. "And the earth opened its mouth and swallowed them along with Korah, whose followers died when the fire consumed 250 men. They serve as a warning sign [same as Sodom and Gomorrah]."* ***Numbers 16:32*** *continues, stating: "and the earth opened its mouth and swallowed them and their households—all Korah's men and all their possessions."* **It's Hell being in Hell!**

God, His Holy Spirit, who is His Word made flesh in Jesus, will always remain the same in all realms of our Universe: ***"Jesus Christ [who is God is] the same yesterday, and today, and forever" (Hebrews 13:8).*** However, on Earth, He set aside His Deity (a state of humility) when He came to Earth to die for our sins because He had to follow Earth Rule (1), as every man must follow to participate in the redemption process. He was born and given a name... Jesus, like you, were born and given a name. However, it was in Joseph's dream that God's Angel told him what to name His Son: ***"And she [Mary] shall bring forth a son, and thou shalt call his name JESUS (for he shall save his people from their sins" (Matthew 1:21).*** Subsequently, Jesus died because ***"the wages of sin is death" (Romans 6:23),*** even though He had not sinned. And Jesus went to Hell just like every man before Him: ***"He [Jesus]...descended into the lower parts of the Earth [Hell]?"***

A CLOSER LOOK AT LIFE AND DEATH

(Ephesians 4:9), as you will certainly descend if you choose not to accept Christ as your Savior.

But the kicker for Satan was that Jesus did not remain dead or come under his captivity through death like every human before Him. Jesus Christ's resurrection, according to Genesis 3:15, crushed Satan's head by releasing us from the power of death's grip, thus setting believers free from Hell. When the Holy Spirit within Jesus descended into Hell, He freed the Spirits of all those who had died from the Earth, from Adam to Jesus, who descended into the Paradise section of Hell (see the diagram in the index). **JESUS IS THE ULTIMATE GAME-CHANGER!!!!** Again, none of my relatives or friends has ever returned from the grave. What about yours?

The Lord tells us, ***"But if the Spirit of Him [The Holy Spirit] who raised Jesus from the dead dwells in you, He [The Holy Spirit] who raised Christ from the dead will also give life to your mortal bodies through His Spirit who dwells in you" (Romans 8:11, NKJV).*** If this is not GOOD NEWS, I don't know what is. As prophesied, the Good News of your salvation was and still is being proclaimed and heard around the globe!!! You must understand that God's Holy Spirit, in Heaven, produced His Word in a Seed that became visible in the physical birth of Jesus. His purpose was to defeat that which takes eternal life from God's Creation… death. Death is the only thing that prevents us from living forever. Therefore, it was God's Holy Spirit that raised the body of Jesus to Eternal Life. Please consider inviting God's Holy Spirit (Christ) to live within you today, as His redemption plan will soon end.

The body was created secondary to the Spirit because the body was designed to hold our Spirits, on Earth. Our body is a vessel that allows our fallen spirits born into the Earth to participate in the choice-driven redemption process. This is our undeserved second chance to receive God's Holy Spirit, which will resurrect us to eternal life with the Lord. However, the vessel of the human body is the temple (dwelling place) of God that holds God's Holy Spirit within us if we so choose.

Therefore, our Spirits are involved in all of Eternal History…past, present, and future, as evident in **Revelation 12:7-9:** *"And the great dragon was cast out, that old serpent, called the Devil, and Satan, which deceived the whole world [all spirit life who are born on earth to participate in the redemption process]: he was cast out into the earth [darkness/abyss], and his angels [Satan, his inner circle and all the rest of us who believed his lies] were cast out with him."*

But because of redemption, all believers in Jesus Christ *"… are a chosen generation, a royal priesthood, a holy nation, His [Christ's] own special people, that you may proclaim the praises of Him who called you out of darkness [of the Abyss of Hell] into His marvelous light [on Earth, to participate in God's redemption plan]…" (1 Peter 2:9).* Again, we who are fallen angels…Spirits within a body, whom God has mercifully called forth out of the darkness of Hell (where we were first cast out to), are allowed to be born on the Earth, to experience our death, judgment, and punishment while being offered salvation from The Second Death.

The above revelation reveals the existence and purpose of God's redemption plan by setting an example for us through Christ. The Lord shows us what He will do for us through Christ; He died, and so will you; He was raised from the dead by God's Word (The Holy Spirit of Truth) to eternal life, and so will you. He ascended into Heaven, and so will you if you believe in
Christ. All men will be resurrected to eternal life or eternal death.

I certainly hope that a thorough revelation of God's Divine Redemption Plan has, finally, begun to resonate within your Spirit so that you may know the truth about your life, death, and eternal future. And that you will accept and appreciate God's extension of

A CLOSER LOOK AT LIFE AND DEATH

His love, mercy, grace, and forgiveness of your sin through Jesus Christ so that you may have eternal life with God again. The Lord truly has a plan for your eternal life…keep reading; there are so many more powerful revelations that God reveals throughout this book series. His detailed and simplified explanations are far beyond anything I could have ever learned in church, in books, or from anyone. His truth brings unspeakable joy!

[Side Note]: The fact that we were cast out of Heaven along with Lucifer is, astonishingly, new to me. I am told that this subject matter is not taught in Theology. Also, the part of Hell that is described in Genesis 1:2, and the fact that we face both Natural Death and The Second Death, are grossly overlooked and undertaught. I prayed and asked the Lord why He chose me to reveal this new way of looking at our Eternal History. It is very difficult to change centuries-old, well-established Theology, but then I thought, why not me?

Recalling some prophecies that were given to Daniel **(Book of Daniel 8:26)** and John **(Revelation 10:4),** the Lord ordered that portions of it be sealed up until the end times. So, perhaps He wants this information revealed and explained, in layman's terms, during these end times so that you are fully aware of what is at stake…You! Your Eternal Life!! There are no words to express my overwhelming honor and blessed privilege to be called to write down the revelations of the Holy Spirit for over 28 years (since 1996); to experience God's Holy Divine Presence is beyond mere words! The Lord has completely and utterly blown my mind with His engagement with me and the renewed way of examining our Eternal History. Thank you, Heavenly Father, may your **"Will"** be done. Amen! **[end]**

After our Spirits fell, hence we are called fallen angels from Heaven (Holy Spirit removed), and our Bodies fell on Earth (Holy Spirit removed from the Body), God repurposed the Earth to be the

A CLOSER LOOK AT LIFE AND DEATH

venue whereby we would come to serve out our death sentence (Natural Death) while at the same time, we are being offered the choice to regain our eternal life through Christ. He also repurposed Man to be the vessel to house our fallen Spirit for the purpose of redemption, which is based on our freedom of choice.

However, we think that someone else rebelled along with Satan, but again, it was you and me; our Spirits rebelled. The Spirit that dwells in your body, right now… rebelled. You and I made a conscious decision to turn against our Creator's love, truth, and righteousness to follow a created being (Lucifer). This resulted in a confrontational rebellion which, subsequently, caused us to be separated (death) from His Holy Presence and punished (Hell/Eternal Death). Therefore, our separation from God is the definition of death, and the place where our Spirits are held upon our separation is called Hell. Gehenna leads to eternal death, which is permanent separation from our Heavenly Father.

Again, I remind you that the evidence of your disobedience and revolt against God is your certain death, on Earth, and your cast down shadow to remind you of this event in your Eternal History. And again, due to God's Divine Redemption Plan, Natural Death is really a blessing in disguise because it returns or transitions the Spirits of believers, in Christ, back to dwell with God in Heaven (Thank You, Heavenly Father!!). So, we have the wrong perception of death because we do not understand God's redemption plan. The duality of the Lord's redemption plan gives us the hope of seeing God and our loved ones again: ***"Your dead shall live; their bodies shall rise. You who dwell in the dust, awake, and sing for joy! For your dew is a dew of light, and the earth will give birth to the dead" (Isaiah 26:19, GST).***

God gave us His Word (Jesus) which created **"the way"** for us to **repent** and be forgiven by allowing the Earth to be the place whereby He would create our bodies in His image as a Temple for the indwelling of His Holy Spirit of Truth: ***"Do you not know that your bodies are temples of the Holy Spirit, who is in you, whom you have received from God? You are not your own," (1 Corinthians 6:19, NIV).*** Since we are no longer in Heaven, we do not know God's truth anymore, and because of duality, we must decide what is truth and what is a lie. If we do not study to know God's Truth for ourselves, then we will continue to fall for anything that Satan has to offer. However, if you still cannot fully understand your eternal plight and don't realize that you need Jesus as your Savior, please start back at page one, and re-evaluate and when it sinks in, take a moment to Acknowledge and confess your sins and confess that Jesus is Lord, Believe that God raised Jesus from the dead, **repent** of your sins with your mouth and Call on His name, it is as easy as ABC. He will forgive your every sin, lead you towards His eternal righteousness, and give you the free gift of Eternal Life! But as always, it's your choice.

You! Cast Out Of Heaven
Heaven Became Closed To Us

"The earth [you and me] was without form [of the Image of God], and void [of truth], and [mental] darkness was on the face of the deep [waters (peoples)]"
~ Genesis 1:2

    We have already established that once you and I were cast out of Heaven, Heaven became closed to us. It is similar to if you were at my home and I asked you not to smoke, but you did so anyway, and a disagreement ensued. Subsequently, an altercation occurred that resulted in me telling you to leave, and the door was closed behind you. At this point, I'm sure that you would know that you are not welcome back. However, for you to return to my home, we must communicate using our words of forgiveness and the acceptance of an apology; then I would announce to you that you are welcome back to my home. This is similar to what happened to us when we betrayed (sinned) and rebelled against God, at home, in Heaven, and we had to be thrown out.

    Can you imagine how God felt? However, God forgave us and sent His Word in the flesh (Jesus) to communicate or announce to us by the display of Christ's death and resurrection, that we are welcome back home to Heaven. This is what I call God's ultimate use of the **"Word"** to communicate to Man. Recall that, in Heaven, Jesus was *"the Word, and the Word was with God, and the Word was God" (John 1:1). "And the Word was made flesh [on Earth], and dwelt among us" (John 3:14).*

    Therefore, we transitioned to Genesis 1:2, which describes our chaotic new lifestyle in the darkness of the Abyss of Hell, whereby we now live an alternative lifestyle in darkness as we live separated from the light of God's Holy Spirit. God's Light, which was embedded within us, was from the essence of His Holy Spirit,

A CLOSER LOOK AT LIFE AND DEATH

which is now the darkness within our minds because we are no longer in His Presence; we no longer have His Truth (void). Recall that our separation from God is the very definition of death. Subsequently, we were cast down into the darkness of the Abyss of Hell with absolutely no way of returning home to Heaven.

God, through Archangel Michael, threw Lucifer and his angels (you and me) out of Heaven (Revelation 12:7), thus ridding Heaven of Lucifer's evil and death. God will, in like manner, rid him from our Universe forever at the execution of his eternal Hellfire Punishment which is called The Second Death (Revelation 20:14). This is why Jesus taught us to pray like this: *"Thy kingdom come [to Earth]. Thy will be done on earth [to rid, believers in Christ, of Satan, evil, and death], as it is in heaven" (Matthew 6:10).*

Everything below Heaven is Hell, including Earth, and the darkness of man's mind. Life without the Holy Spirit is the opposite of God's Light... dense darkness. Therefore, we do not have to die and go to Hell; we are already in it! Hell is where death occurs or exists, so if you want to know what Hell looks like, take a look around you and see it...chaos, trials, tribulations, suffering, destruction, graves, and death. However, we are not in the Hellfire portion of Hell, yet; it occurs upon your death unless you profess Romans 10:9-10 and confess your sins.

The only reason that Earth is no longer in the pitch-black darkness of Hell, like when we were first cast out of Heaven (Genesis 1:2), is because God forgave us and said, in the midst of our darkness, *"Let there be light... (Genesis 1:14)."* Then the Lord, *"...called you out of darkness [The Abyss of Hell] into His marvelous light [on Earth]" (1 Peter 2:9 NKJV),* for the purpose of our redemption. He divided day from night *(Genesis 1:18)* to establish the beginning of **"Time"** that would begin our journey towards salvation. We are given the opportunity and time to choose our eternal fate. And because of duality, God's attributes are in the

Earth, in the form of the fruits of His Spirit. ***"Love, Joy, Peace, Forbearance, Kindness, Goodness, Faithfulness, Gentleness, [and] Self-Control" (Galatians 5:22).*** The Lord grants us access to His attributes if we sincerely call on His name.

The Lord displayed His mercy and love to us through Christ because He, desperately, does NOT want us to be separated from Him forever: ***"For God so loved the world, that he gave his only begotten Son, that whosoever believeth in him should not perish, but have everlasting life" (John 3:16)!***

He wishes that not one of us, His creation, should die a Second Death and permanently leave Him. One night, the Lord came to me to reveal how He will feel to lose just one of us… His Children. It was the most tear-jerking experience ever. I never thought about death from God's perspective before (more as the book series progresses). So, please take a moment to feel His insurmountable love for you and His plea to save you. So, again I ask: **How else would we know that Heaven has been opened back up to us (the fallen) unless God communicates it to us with His Word (Jesus)?** His Word manifested in the flesh to tell us and show us that Heaven is now open to the fallen or those of us who believe in Jesus Christ.

A CLOSER LOOK AT LIFE AND DEATH

It's Hell Being In Hell… Our "Tree" Selection

And the LORD God called unto Adam…Hast thou eaten of the tree, whereof I commanded thee that thou shouldest not eat?
*~ **Genesis 3:8-9***

"And they [Adam and Eve] heard the voice of the LORD God walking in the garden in the cool of the day: and Adam and his wife hid themselves from the presence of the LORD God amongst the trees of the garden. And the LORD God called unto Adam, and said unto him, Where art thou?" (Genesis 3:8-9). Hell, on Earth, by virtue of our **"Tree"** selection in the Garden, is an extremely dark part of the Abyss that is a difficult and painful place for humanity to be, both mentally (spiritually) and physically (body), as depicted by God's Words to Adam and Eve just before they were evicted from the Garden of Eden. Notice that God specifically called out to Adam first. This is because, between the two of them, recall that Adam is held directly accountable to God, not the woman.

In *Genesis 3:14-19* NIV, as a result of our two episodes of falling for Satan's lies, in the Spirit and Flesh, God had direct, stern words for the serpent (Satan), Adam, and Eve. God's Words were fueled with condemnation, which brought the advent of Hell into their (our) daily lives, forever, and on top of admonishments, our lives end in death. They changed the landscape and lifestyle of humanity: *"So, the Lord God said to the serpent, 'Because you have done this, Cursed are you above all livestock and all wild animals! You will crawl on your belly and you will eat dust all the days of your life. And I will put enmity [war/opposition] between you and the woman, and between your offspring and hers; he will crush your head, and you will strike his heel."*

To the woman, He said, *"I will make your pains in childbearing very severe; with painful labor you will give birth to children. Your desire will be for your husband, and he will rule over you."* Then to Adam He said, *"Because you listened to your wife and ate fruit from the tree about which I commanded you, 'You must not eat from it,' "Cursed is the ground because of you; through painful toil [work] you will eat food from it all the days of your life. It will produce thorns and thistles for you, and you will eat the plants of the field. By the sweat of your brow [hard work], you will eat your food [from the Earth] until you return to the ground, since from it you were taken; for dust you are and to dust you will return."* All of the above hardships, and on top of this, we die… **It's Hell being in Hell!**

But really, has anything that God said, above, changed to this day? NO! Although we now have nice homes with indoor plumbing, good jobs, money, status, material things, and many technological advances, our mindset of sin and rebellious nature remains the same. Therefore, mentally, we have come no further than the gate at the Garden of Eden that we were put out of.

However, as Eternal Spirit with eternal memory from a past rooted in Heaven with our Creator, here in the body, we still know the goodness of God. This is why we get so frustrated when things don't go our way; we had it all; everything in Heaven was perfect for us. Now that we are living away from home, we get angry and even feel hurt and cry tears of frustration when things go wrong, because our Spirit, within our body, is accustomed to living in the perfection and wholeness of God. So here on Earth, it frustrates us now that we must live life in God's Holy Presence. Notice that as long as things are going well and good with us, we feel good, but the moment that things go wrong, it's a problem, don't you agree?

The deplorable levels of our mental darkness (recall, close your eyes to see the darkness) are broadcast through our news media outlets. They reveal our current state of chaos, in the darkness of the Abyss of Hell, daily. They reveal our mindset…attitudes, and behaviors that drift further away from God, downward into deep deception. Our Spirits sink further downward into the lower depths of our original evil and rebellious nature. Subsequently, our bodies await death and transition into the grave, while our Spirits transition to the Hellfire Punishment sections of Hell. But since Satan has almost banished the reality of Hell from us, due to the suppression of truth, many do not believe it exists and do not want to hear or talk about this certain truth.

However, as Satan's corruption is exposed, you hear more about the elite's New World Order agenda, as well as decades of long-kept hidden secrets like UFOs, which reveal the elite's communication with demons (antimatter) or Aliens (Martians). Pope Francis publicly stated that "he would be willing to baptize aliens if they came to the Vatican, asking, 'who are we to close doors' to anyone, even Martians" (Wow, I can't make this stuff up… Google it). He has also created what he calls the Laudato Si', a 7-year pact or agreement regarding Climate Change and concerns about our natural environment and the inclusion of all religions, as evident by the construction of the Abrahamic Family House in Abu Dhabi, UAE, which consists of three houses, a Catholic Church, a Mosque, and a Synagogue.

Climate Change is the catalyst that will call for all people of all nations and religions to come together in unity. Therefore, in 2021, he met with world political and religious leaders to sign this 7-year agreement. I believe this pact, along with a signed agreement that will divide Israel and the building of the Third Temple, will propel us into the Tribulation and the Great Tribulation. Nowadays, people are publicly praying to Satan (at City Council Meetings, churches, etc.). The Actor, Christian Bale, thanked Satan, while the audience clapped, for his help in playing a role that earned him a Golden

Globe. See the video below:

The elite also use color codes, gestures, certain dates, events, movies, etc., to communicate their agenda. Rituals are publicly displayed in performances (Grammys, concerts, etc.). The Arch of Baal (a god of human sacrifice) is a replica of Baal's original Arch, from where Satan's original throne is located in Turkey. However, it was erected in New York City and toured across the nation as Satan puts himself on display in our faces. But we can't believe it, so we shrug it off and fall into his deception: ***"...Satan, which deceiveth the whole world: he was cast out into the earth, and his angels [you and me] were cast out with him" (Revelation 12:9).***

We are so **"Sleep"** to eternal truth…blinded by the distractions of daily life, lies, secrets, and deceptions. However, again, the truth is that we do live in Hell (on Earth), where Satan was cast and is ruling. If you remember, we were thrown out of Heaven along with him. By now, you should realize the most overt evidential proof is your shadow that follows you around everywhere. Again, your shadow reveals the fact that you have been cast down or have fallen from Heaven and are now living on this fallen Earth… It's Hell being in Hell! Let that sink in for a moment. In fact, go back and re-read this section, and then read the referenced scriptures for yourself.

God, through Christ, has delivered us from the grip of death that the former Light Bearer had over us. He has delivered us from the

A CLOSER LOOK AT LIFE AND DEATH

Hellfire punishment of Hell... Gehenna and the Lake of Fire. And for those who are Raptured, God has delivered them from death altogether, by the power and might of Christ's resurrection! The Rapture supersedes the grave and all of Hell's punishments... Lord, have mercy... Thank You! But for those who do not accept Jesus Christ, by default, they will experience Hell, God's wrath, and the permanent Second Death. Upon your death, they will enter the temporary part of Hell... the Hell fires of Gehenna, then move to the permanent chamber... Eternal Lake of Fire and Brimstone, which burneth forever. However, the sad part is that some of us are so prideful that we can't humble ourselves to admit our wrongs against our Heavenly Father (**repent**) to allow ourselves to be saved... **WOW!**

God has repurposed the Earth and Man for our redemption, so He formed the Garden and Man for redemption instead of His original plan and purpose for both the Earth and humanity. As we progress further through God's Divine Redemption Plan to Genesis 1:3-31, He called forth His Light and separated day from night, He formed the dry land, and planted the Garden of Eden with two specific trees, God's Tree, **"The Tree of Life"** and Satan's Tree, *"The Tree of Knowledge of Good and Evil,"* representing **"Knowledge"** or the act of the pursuit of knowledge, as well as displays our eternal "Choice" that is before their (our) minds with every breath, eternal life or eternal death is before us, more on this later as we explore the design phase of the redemption plan in the book series.

However, God created Adam and Eve (humanity) on the Earth, amid His Holy Presence, which meant that God's Holy Spirit was within them. But when they sinned or fell, in their Spirits and bodies (which housed their fallen from Heaven Spirits), subsequently, they were put out of the Garden and were removed from God's Holy Spirit... His Holy Divine Presence. This fact made them fit to go through the redemption process or the Hellfire section of Hell. Again, living separated from the Lord's Holy Spirit (spiritual death) means that we no longer have His Holy Spirit within our Souls or bodies; we must invite Christ within us. We now know that without God's Holy Spirit, there is no Eternal Life for us, so our body dies and only the penalties of death await us.

Also, not only did we lose the Lord's Holy Spirit, but we lost access to His Divine knowledge. According to ***Jeremiah 10:14, NLT, "The whole human race is foolish [due to mental darkness] and has no knowledge!"*** This scripture reveals that Man is a terrestrial (earthly) being who is blinded by the darkness of the Abyss and that humanity is unlearned. Therefore, humanity must be guided and instructed by celestial (heavenly/Spirit) beings in the spiritual realms of Heaven and Hell.

Freedom of choice is defined in God's Divine Redemption Plan (Deuteronomy 30:19), thus, you are free to either be led, guided, instructed and taught by the Lord, *"I will instruct you and teach you in the way you should go; I will counsel [guide] you with my loving eye on you" (Psalm 32:8)* or we are free to choose to be led, guided, instructed and taught by the father of lies... Satan, according to **"The Tree of The Knowledge of Good and Evil"** that we chose in Garden: *"You [your mindset] are of your father the devil, and the desires of your father you want to [be led to] do...he speaks [teaches and instructs unbelievers accordingly to his desired purposes relating to evil, manmade scientific theories, technology, artificial intelligence, carnal things, paganism, religion, business, politics, etc., using] lies" (John 8:44).*

Subsequently, the knowledge from both trees manifests as fruit in your life towards goodness, wholesomeness, righteousness, and holiness or evilness, unwholesomeness, unrighteousness, and unholiness. The duality of the resulting fruit that manifests in our lives is realized within our actions and others. Satan's knowledge is exchanged for worship, and thus it is distributed through his elite within secret organizations that require you to pledge your soul to societal or Greek organizations, deities, or gods, as well as perform rituals and sacrifices. Members progress through higher levels to gain higher levels of Satan's knowledge and power by performing rituals and certain duties. These organizations operate under the guise of helping the community, building hospitals, schools, feeding the hungry, and other noble efforts.

The purposed fall of Man was inevitable because the Spirit had fallen in Heaven, and thus the body had to fall on Earth. The two must fall together, Spirit and Flesh, which represent the fall of the complete Man. The temptation presented to us by Satan, in Heaven, is the same temptation that was presented by Satan to Adam and Eve, in the Garden, which was to be like God. Can you see the Spirit/Body correlation? Hence, the planting of the two trees in the Garden signifies **"Choice,"** being put before our mind like as was done so in Heaven. Also, based on the nature of our already fallen Spirit, God knew that we would fall, in the body, because of our desire to be like Him exists in the Spirit and in the Body.

So, the evidence of Adam and Eve's **(our)** sinful nature was apparent in the midst of the two trees, whereby Satan approached them to offer them knowledge from his tree, stating that, *"...your eyes will be opened, and you will be like God" (Genesis 3:5).* This symbolizes the same thing that he offered us in Heaven... *"to be like God."* And of course, we fell for it both times. As a result, we were expelled in both realms, so that's two times that we experienced death, once in the Spirit, and subsequently, in the Body, which completes the totality of the composition of Man, which is designed to endure our deaths, judgments, and punishments. It is purposed, in the redemption plan, that the complete fallen Man (Spirit and Body) is destined for Natural Death, Hellfire, and Eternal Death.

Although both our Spirits and Bodies were originally created to dwell with God's Holy Spirit, in Heaven, and on Earth, we lost His Holy Spirit. Therefore, God chose to use the composition of man (Spirit, Body, Bones) to effectuate our redemption and a Shadow that reflects our eternity past, present, and future. He allows our fallen Spirits that were expelled from Heaven, then cast into the darkness of the Abyss, to come to live on Earth by birth, in order to participate in His Divine Redemption Plan. And still, we live in the mental darkness of the Abyss of Hell, we only get 12 hours of daylight and 24 hours to **repent** and receive the Indwelling Holy Spirit each day, through Christ Jesus: ***"…Now is come salvation, strength, and the kingdom of our God, and the power of his Christ" (Revelation 12:10).*** Again, according to God's plan, our eternal future would be based on the two eternal choices of **Deuteronomy 30:19**… Eternal life and eternal death.

"Choice" is an essential part of redemption. There is but one God, and your adversary… Satan fully knows this to be true: ***"You believe that there is one God…Even the demons believe— and tremble!" (James 2:19),*** even though you may not care to believe it. And there is only **"one way"** for us to be saved, and that is through Jesus Christ. God created "the way" for you to return to Him for your salvation to eternal life. You can know that you are being deceived if someone tells you that there are many ways to God, and not just through Jesus Christ. Some high-profile ministers and celebrities have, publicly, said that there is more than **"one way"** to eternal life, however, since Heaven and Hell are in the forever realm, technically, there are two ways to eternal life but one will be, in Heaven, with the Lord and the other is to spend eternal life with Satan in the Lake of Fire and Brimstone, kindled with sulfur, forever, which is eternal death.

Avoid those who worship different gods, tell you about aliens, or other life forms, ask you to pray chants, cast spells, practice human or animal sacrifice, worship idols, revere pastors, pray to Mary (Mother of Jesus) or other Saints, Ancestors, or to Popes, and those who teach false doctrines, things that are contrary to God's Holy Word. Also, beware of necromancy (speaking with the dead), lying signs and wonders that the Antichrist will display in the sky, etc.

Many often ponder whether their ancestors can speak to them or if their deceased loved one knows anything about what is still going on in this life after they have made their transition from Earth, however, the authoritative Word of God answers this question very poignantly in **Ecclesiastes 9:5,** *"For the living know that they will die; but the dead know nothing [about what goes on, on Earth anymore]. And they have no more reward [nothing good is offered to them anymore, i.e., Salvation], For the memory of them is forgotten."* And **Psalms 146:4** says, *"When his [your] spirit departs, he [your body] returns to the ground; [and] on that very day his [your] plans [knowledge of your plans and your memory about all things] perish [are no more]."*

Therefore, *"Do not turn to mediums [who pretend to consult the dead] or to spiritists [who have spirits of fortunetelling, Séance, tarot cards, etc.]; do not seek them out to be defiled by them. I am the LORD your God" (Leviticus 19:31).* Nevertheless, if a supposed **"Medium"** or someone tells you that your deceased loved one is saying this or that to them to relay to you, run! God says that the dead know NOTHING! He knows because He is the Creator of all things; He created it that way.

Don't you think if the dead could speak and do anything, they would still be trying to live as they did to carry out their plans? Therefore, if a Medium is not speaking to God, telling you what He says, then, according to the above scriptures, they are speaking to demons. The Medium's lies may bring you comfort, but now that you have been exposed to the Truth of God, it's up to you to believe

His Word or continue to fall for Satan's lies. I strongly encourage you to see to it that you are not deceived, and DO NOT fear death because Christ defeated Satan's hold over you through death by His resurrection. To die in Christ is to live eternally.

We also wonder: "Are ghosts real? Yes! The answer is yes, in that God is called the Holy Ghost (Spirit), and after Jesus Christ was resurrected from the grave, He came to His disciples, who were in shock, and said, **"Look at my hands and my feet. It is I myself! Touch me and see; a ghost [Spirit] does not have flesh and bones, as you see I have" (Luke 24:49).**

Unbelievers, suppose you did choose to believe that Jesus died for your sins and that He did exactly what the Bible prophesied He would do to defeat death by His resurrection. This would mean that you will only face the death of your body…Natural Death. Then your body would go into the grave, and your Spirit would enter Heaven to dwell with the Lord again forever. You would avoid a second permanent death, and if you are Raptured, you will avoid death altogether!

Although death is devastating for us and seems permanent, it is not, because the plan of redemption calls for all men to be resurrected. Therefore, remember that death is a blessing in disguise because Natural Death returns believers to the Holy Presence of the Lord… **Glory!** This is why God is not concerned about losing you through Natural Death because He knows that you will be returned to Him if you believe in Christ Jesus. His focus is on saving you from The Second Death, which is permanent separation from Him forever; it will be as if you never existed before.

Therefore, I am saying all this to say that according to the authoritative Word of God, our common enemy is death through Satan, the father of lies, evil, death, Hell, and the grave, and more importantly, "The Second Death." So, suppose Satan still has you blinded by his lies. You are still holding on to the belief that life for us began as apes and evolved into humans, or that life began with a Big Bang. In that case, I strongly suggest that you consider the truth from the Word of God and that you, literally, look up the scriptures for yourself, then decide your eternal fate. While there is still time, you do have the option to choose to follow Christ, **repent**, and pray Romans 10:9-10, so that you will continue living your best eternal life with your Heavenly Father.

A CLOSER LOOK AT LIFE AND DEATH

Truth Revealed

Lucifer = Satan = Death = Darkness = Evil = Liar = Unseen = Antimatter = Hidden = Occult = Secret Societies = Fallen Angel = Backwards = Apollyon = Destroyer = Abaddon = Halel = El = Aliens = False = Fake = Artificial Intelligence = Liar = Mental = Hideous = Chaos = Confusion = War = Cunning = Serpent = Devil = Dragon = Monster = Deception = Witchcraft = Magic = Sorcery = Antichrist = Paganism = Unbelievers = Unrepentant = Image of the Beast = Death = Murderer (Takes Away Your Eternal Life) = Hell = New Age = World Power = New World Order = One World Government/ Religion = AI = Beast System = Death = Natural Death = Eternal Death = The Second Death = Burneth Forever = God's Holy Spirit is Absent from Within You!

Lucifer **(Satan)** was the first to turn against God; his disobedience, or sin, and rebellious behavior created a separate place called Hell. Then he persuaded us to turn away from God and disobey Him, and subsequently, join his opposition of rebellion…war, to fight against the Lord for His Sovereignty. This war is the definition of all wars or conflicts, and all circumstances of opposition in our lives.

Therefore, we sinned and transgressed God and became ungrateful sinners and rebels, so don't get it twisted; God does NOT owe us anything!! However, *"because of his great love for us, God, who is rich in mercy, made us alive with Christ even when we were dead in [our] transgressions—it is by grace you have been saved [from the Second Death]" (Ephesians 2:4-5).*

However, Satan does not get to participate in life on Earth, whereby the Lord uses Natural Death, as "the means" to retrieve us back unto Himself. Therefore, he cannot be redeemed because he is the originator and embodiment of sin (evil/lies) and death.

He created the need for us to be separated from God's Holy

Presence, and therefore, he created Hell and Eternal Death, which was first made for him. He became the living definition of evil, death, destruction, hideous appearance, darkness, and the author of lies. Therefore, his death sentence is exponentially worse than Hell (Gehenna), where our Spirits go upon our demise.

Satan knows that he will never receive eternal life back with God because he does not have a body on the Earth to participate in the redemption process. When God created Adam and Eve, He did not create a body for Satan because he cannot be redeemed through God's redemption process. Therefore, he will take every opportunity to attack you...your family, your marriage, and your health, etc., as well as confuse you relative to your sexuality. He will cause you to defile yourself before God through your consent to follow his mindset of hate, violence, murder, lying, stealing, lovers of yourself, pride, fornication, adultery...every sin: ***"But know this, that in the last days perilous times will come: For men will be lovers of themselves, lovers of money, boasters, proud, blasphemers, disobedient to parents, unthankful, unholy, unloving, unforgiving, slanderers, without self-control, brutal, despisers of good, traitors, headstrong, haughty, lovers of pleasure rather than lovers of God, having a form of godliness [attending church service, preaching, teaching, carrying a Bible, etc.] but denying its power. And from such people turn away" (2 Timothy 3:1-5)!***

Satan will kill you (if you don't call on Jesus for protection) by sending weather catastrophes and tribulations your way. He will consume your thoughts with dark thoughts to deceive you so that you will NOT know the truth, and thus you will not regain your eternal life with the Lord. Therefore, Satan is extremely angry at you because you are being offered a second chance that he will never be offered. So, he will stop at nothing until he succeeds at causing you to die without the Lord's forgiveness and His free gift

A CLOSER LOOK AT LIFE AND DEATH

of Eternal Life, which is free for the asking because Jesus Christ paid the price for our sins with His Divine Blood. However, Satan desires you to experience both the Natural Death and The Second Death... the Lake of Fire. You must come to terms with the fact that you face not one death penalty, but two. Again, don't take my word for it; you do the research.

Nowadays, there is more and more bold talk regarding allegiance to Satan. And as well, some are coming forth to reveal their readiness to receive the Antichrist and release his Beast System. His system will exert total population control and includes a cashless society that is linked to your social score (behavior score in China), surveillance, robots, trans-humans, and mind control... Elon Musk's Neuralink is a brain-embeddable machine interface that connects humans to computers or the World Wide Web (Beast System) so that they can use their brain waves to search the web.

The Book of Daniel, Chapter 2:1-49, reveals the dream of King Nebuchadnezzar (604-562 BC), who was considered the greatest king of ancient Babylon. However, one night he had a very disturbing dream that bothered him, so he sought out someone to interpret it. Daniel was the only one who could interpret the dream, which was about a giant statue whereby various sections of the statue represented different world kingdoms from the beginning of God's redemption plan to the end. During the final part of the dream, the statue was destroyed by a rock that represents God's kingdom to come: *"This image's head was of fine gold, its chest and arms of silver, its belly and thighs of bronze, its legs of iron, its feet partly of iron and partly of clay. You watched while a stone was cut out without hands, which struck the image on its feet of iron and clay, and broke them in pieces. Then the iron, the clay, the bronze, the silver, and the gold were crushed together..."* *(Daniel 2:32-35).*

The statue represents major ruling empires that will come to pass during Earth's History. Empires are forged by bloodshed, meaning they are created by killing and capturing. Beginning from the head of the statue to toe, the first empire is Babylon, ruled by King Nebuchadnezzar, down to the last ruling empire, which will be the revived Roman Empire. Britain is part of the Roman Empire, which now includes its offspring, America. The second rule of the Roman Empire is an extension of its first rule, as it will be revived to rule during the last days. The Roman Catholic Church will once again exemplify its dominance. These are the governments that will rise and fall before Christ's return to rule and reign on Earth according to God's Divine Redemption Plan.

However, at the end of King Nebuchadnezzar's dream, a great rock, came down from above, thrown without hands, destroying the statue, representing the crushing destruction of all kingdoms, empires, or governments on Earth when "Thy kingdom come [to earth]. Thy will be done in earth, as it is in heaven" (Matthew 6:10). Then all things will be made new, all believers in Christ and the heavenly hosts will witness New Jerusalem coming down from Heaven to Earth and the Lord will dwell with us, forever... **Glory!**

The statue's head of gold, represents Babylon (modern day Iraq), its arms and chest of silver, represent Persia (modern day Iran), its thighs of brass, represent Greece, two Legs of Iron that split, represent the two reins of the Roman Empire (27 B.C.E. to 476 C.E.), or about 400 years and the resurgence of its reign through its Popes and the Antichrist during the last days], and lastly, Feet made of Iron and Clay with ten toes that many say represents the ten regions that make up the European Union or ten regions that the Antichrist establishes on Earth.

There has been great speculation relative to what the feet on the statue, made of both iron and clay, represent. Per my interpretation, the iron represents man-made machinery and clay represents man's flesh which is made from the dirt or clay of the Earth mixed with the computer driven Artificial Intelligence, robotic artificial limbs, artificial wombs (babies created outside of a women's body, in a lab), robots whereby the darkness of the unseen realm of spirits can inhabit and control. This will result in Satan's creation of genetically modified humans via gene altering and editing techniques like CRISPR and other methods of DNA manipulation to create transhumanism that connects man to Satan's beast system; while others will connect via embedded chips, brain implants, tattoos, or other metallic material embedded into the human body.

And eventually, a Sunday Law will be enacted to force the worship of Satan's image, because remember, he does not have a body, so he will select a human representative called the Antichrist to push his global agenda to the world and to force loyalty and worship to Satan. According to Bible Prophecy, he will, eventually, stand inside the coming third Temple in Jerusalem and profess to be God: ***"He [Satan] will oppose and will exalt himself over everything that is called God or is worshiped, so that he sets himself up in God's temple, proclaiming himself to be God" (2 Thessalonians 2:4).***

Throughout the centuries, Satan, through his elite, has planned agendas to pull us away from God... His Truth and implement ways to counter God's redemption plans as foretold in the Bible. Even before America was created, Satan had planned his agenda for it. Through his elite, he secretly planned America's mission, rise, and fall. However, the plan now is to bring down America by assaulting and obliterating its constitution, democracy, morals (right becomes wrong), and the dominance of its financial system. In Bible Prophecy, there are nations and/or leaders or individuals that fit the criteria to carry out end-time prophecy and bring its truth from the pages of the Bible to life. Therefore, it appears that America may be the Second Beast (nation) that will hand the country over to the Roman Pontiff or False Prophet with its 1.3 million worshipers, the

First Beast (Rome) as prophesied in Revelation 13:14-15. We will delve into why the latter is apparent later in the book series. Still, as I said, Satan's plans and efforts are designed to counter God's every move... Pay attention!

Satan, through his elite, will bring down the current world financial system to create chaos... "order out of chaos" through war, food shortages, famine, and economic collapse to culminate with a one-world religion whereby all world political and religious leaders will unite together to worship the image of the former Light Bearer. Then they will bring about the man with the plan... the Antichrist, to solve the world's problems (including the division of Israel) and will bring about a false sense of peace and order. Again, the elite will use Aliens (lineage of the fallen angels of Noah's day...Nephilim) to explain away those missing from the Earth due to the Rapture...read the entire book series for more in-depth details. And please do your own research and choose accordingly, don't go to Hell, and experience The Second Death by default.

Although we may not all agree on Creation, the existence of God, Angels, Satan, Hell, Jesus Christ, Religion, or various man-made theories: The Theory of Evolution or the Big Bang Theory, we can all agree that we do all fall and succumb to death. Therefore, religion and artificial theories seek to divide and confuse us; they only distract us from our true, common enemy... Death, and, more importantly, The Second Death or eternal death, which is to come. There is no denying God's Truth as evident in Genesis 2:17... again, surprise! We do surely die.

Motive

"I [Satan] will ascend to heaven; I will raise my throne above the stars [all Creation] of God; I will sit on the mount of assembly [amongst Heavenly Dignitaries] In the remote parts of the north exalted above [where God is located]"
~ Isaiah 14:13

We were all created as members of God's family, living under His Divine Government, in Heaven. However, suppose one of us, a created being, believed that we could be God with all power and be worshiped by all, without being the Divine Creator of all Eternal Spirit Life. One who cannot create or sustain eternal life but desires to exalt himself above and rule over all Creation for his own selfish gain and self-worship. This mindset puts him in complete opposition to the righteousness of God. The jealous, prideful, and rebellious one is Cherubim Angel Lucifer with a devious evil plan to defeat God and take over His Sovereignty: ***For thou hast said in thine heart, I will ascend into heaven, I will exalt my throne above the stars [all Creation] of God: I will also sit upon the mount of the congregation [amongst Heavenly Dignitaries], in the sides of the "north" (Isaiah 14:13).***

Although Lucifer was initially cast down from Heaven along with us, still he was allowed access to the Presence of God: *"…when the sons of God [Angels] came to present themselves before the LORD, and Satan came also among them to present himself before the LORD". (Job 2:2). However, at some point, Satan's access to God was denied altogether. I believe Luke 10:18 (NIV) refers to the juncture when Satan was cast out of Heaven by himself: "I saw Satan fall like lightning from heaven." Unlike other verses that mention Satan and "his angels"* being cast out, this one refers to Satan alone.

So, ever since the former Light Bearer's fall from the very

heights of Heaven, he clearly intends to get back there. He persuaded men by saying, *"Let us build us a city and a tower, whose top may reach to heaven" (Genesis 11:4).* Therefore, he continuously uses humanity to achieve this end. For instance, the former Light Bearer used man to build the Tower of Babel, trying to reach back into Heaven. He still uses man today, for this same purpose. God would not allow the Tower of Babel to be completed; he caused all who were building the tower to suddenly speak different languages so that they could not communicate and understand each other in order to complete the structure: *"Now the whole earth had one language and one speech…Therefore is the name of it called Babel; because the LORD did there confound the language of all the earth [caused us to speak different languages]: and from thence did the LORD scatter them abroad upon the face of all the earth" (Genesis 11:1, 9).*

"When the Most High assigned lands to the nations, when he divided up the human race, he established the boundaries of the peoples according to the number in his heavenly court [or 12 sons of Israel (Jacob)]" (Deuteronomy 32:8, NLT). For this reason, we speak different languages; we are of different races, and we are scattered throughout the Earth, over all seven continents. You didn't realize that this was God's doing? Hmm, do your research!

The former Light Bearer continues to use man through the knowledge of technology that he provides, for instance, space flight programs… **NASA,** the European Space Agency, and others worldwide. The elite launch telescopes, satellites, etc., and **CERN,** whose Scientists are seeking to create and open portals, is trying to find a way for the former Light Bearer to get back into the heights of Heaven, to collect antimatter, release demons into our realm and from the bottomless pit (Revelation 9:11). He desires to raise himself above God and be worshipped by all. He also uses the above technology to look for signs in the Heavens that the Lord specifies in His written word: *"I will show wonders in heaven above, and signs in the earth beneath; blood, and fire, and vapor of smoke: The sun shall be turned into darkness, and the moon into blood, before that great and notable day of the Lord come" (Acts 2:18-19).* He watches for all anomalies in the sky.

And to further expand my point, since God confounded or changed the language of men so that they could no longer communicate and understand each other, over the centuries, Satan has steadfastly continued his defiant mode of operation. He created the World Wide Web to unite the languages of the world. Today, using computer technology, and now through more advanced Quantum Computing, Databases, Artificial Intelligence, etc. He has guided man to create software and Apps for the co-mingling of people of all different languages and tongues worldwide using readily available AI language translation in real time. He has also navigated the creation of software and Apps that teach us to speak other languages, one of which is called Babel, named after the Tower of Babel of Biblical days. Again, **"Satan Drives Technology to Meet His Desires."** Later in the book series, you will discover how man communicates and ascertains knowledge from Satan, as evidenced by our **"Tree"** selection in the Garden.

The Bible says, as in the days of Noah, so shall it be in the end times, there were giants in those days and we also have our giants, today in the sectors of technology, corporations, and governments and we recognize them as such, we call them **"Big Tech," "Big Pharma," "Big Brother,"** etc. However, the Nephilim giants will also return to usher in the tribulation, False Prophet, and Antichrist rule. They will do signs and wonders, as well as offer humanity healing and eternal life, but of course, this will be a lie.

In search of mind control, Scientists have allowed computer technology to invade our brains. I saw the headgear apparatus for this new technological advancement demonstrated on the news, where a man sitting in front of a computer screen proceeded to think of a website, and then that particular website that he thought of, suddenly, appeared on his computer screen. I guess we will be able to **"think search."** Scientists, through their **"correspondence"** with the dark side, have developed the ability to detect electrical brain activity through the scalp and control it. Wow, they want to know what we are thinking... Really. They want Mind Control!

Also in 2016, Elon Musk developed Neuralink, where chips are designed to be implanted into our brains and may be implemented in 2022. However, he says that it is for medical applications like neurological disorders, but of course, the reason is always hidden. Their appetite for knowledge and technology is disturbingly endless, to the point that it decimates our freedom by imprisoning us through surveillance, which destroys our lives and leads to death.

Ever since Genesis 11:1, when the Lord caused us to speak different languages, the former Light Bearer has been on a quest to break the language barrier and unify the world under his global rule. And eventually, he will assert himself as God; he wants to be worshipped for all the knowledge that he has provided to humanity. However, if he has the power to be God, as he leads many to believe, then why isn't he still in Heaven doing what he said he desires to do… exalt himself above God? Because he is a created and defeated being, he is not God; therefore, he CANNOT and will never be able to achieve the desires of his heart!

Since we have experienced death (separation from God) and live in exile from Heaven and the Garden, we have been marked as fallen (fallen to Satan's lies), evil, and labeled a Sinner (a prisoner to death). We are destined to serve out our death penalty, which is eternal Hellfire, unless something happens to change our course, which it did in Jesus Christ. So, seek Him now, if you choose, while there is still time. Also, since Lucifer is cast down from where God resides and there is no going back there for him, you can believe that he knows God's plans as written in His Word…the Bible (the Book of Redemption), so that he will know God's every move in order to plan his defense and countermoves. He uses his witchcraft to counterfeit, impersonate, manipulate, and intimidate you to deceive you out of your eternal life. Again, Satan knows the Bible better than you, and he knows your moves too, through constant surveillance using your electronic devices. **Wake up** and pay closer attention!

Satan attacks your thought life to adversely control your behavior, leading you into the darkness of his evil mindset. He uses you against yourself so that your behavior before God and your fellow man will defile you and cause you to be unfit for eternal life! [**Exercise**]: I employ you to take the blinders off and allow yourself some time to put away or separate yourself from the attachments of your phone, social media, friends, family, and all the things (the secret things that you do) and all of the voices through radio, TV, etc. that you allow to flow through your ears. Then commit to studying by completing the exercises at the end of this book; meditate on some of the scriptures, and do your own analysis. And lastly, **wake the Hell up because Hell awaits you!** [end]

Sinner, in one word, is disobedience. It has led you to spiritual death or the removal of God's Holy Spirit… His Presence. We followed Lucifer's mindset to oppose God, which caused us to become prisoners to him through sin and death. We are imprisoned away from God's domain where He sits on His Throne, so that we can no longer see His face. Being a sinner results from believing and living a lie instead of the truth that comes from God alone.

A lie comes from a created being, i.e., a fallen angel or human. Let us evaluate this truth as it unfolds at the Tree of the Knowledge of Good and Evil amid the Garden of Eden. Satan knew that God had commanded both Adam and Eve, who represent all of humanity, not to eat from this tree: *"Now the serpent was more crafty [sneaky] than any of the wild animals the Lord God had made. He said to the woman, "Did God really say, 'You must not eat from any tree in the garden'?" The woman said to the serpent, "We may eat fruit from the trees in the garden, but God did say, 'You must not eat fruit from the tree that is in the middle of the garden, and you must not touch it, or you will die. You will not certainly die," the serpent said to the woman" (Genesis 3:14, NIV).*

So, the cunning serpent (a created being) came to Eve with his forked tongue, signifying his ability to twist the truth of God's Words with his lies, saying **"...unto the woman, You shall not surely die: For God doth know that in the day you eat thereof, then your eyes shall be opened, and you shall be as gods, knowing good and evil" (Genesis 3:4 NKJV).** Now, which statement became the living truth: Do we die or not? Yes, so it is best that you believe the words of your Creator over the words of any created being, don't you think?

The Big Lie

"Satan has guided humanity to believe that there is no God, no Devil or Satan, no Jesus Christ (God in Flesh), and no Hell. He would fool us into believing that there is NO Death if we do not get to witness it happening with our own eyes"
~Tracy Jones

The former Light Bearer has humanity believing that he is a red devil caricature with horns and a pitchfork, so that you will believe that he is simply a figure of your imagination. He has guided humanity to believe in idols and other gods to prevent us from believing in our Creator, whose Holy Word manifested as Jesus Christ to save us from his impending death sentence and penalty.

Although in the Bible, Satan is called the devil, an old dragon, and a serpent…a cunning snake, he is also the author of hideous appearance, evil thoughts, and acts. His new appearance is associated with his transition from the name Lucifer, the beautiful Cherubim Angel of Light, to being named Satan, a liar and adversary of God. He formed Hell with his thoughts, attitude, and actions. Recall that Hell is where darkness (our night sky), evil, destruction, and death exist.

Satan is now damned to exist in every hideous form portrayed in movies, video games, television, and in real life. He also makes real-time appearances as he manifests in our thoughts, propelling our hellish thinking and actions. Satan will appear as **"you"** when you think and do evil, i.e., lie, cheat, steal, act pridefully and selfishly, garner negativity, fear, commit crimes and corruption, spew hate, practice witchcraft, or anything contrary to holiness, goodness, and righteousness! After you have done wrong, look in the mirror at who thought the thoughts or committed the act, yes, it's you.

Since photo cameras were created using mirror technology, jail mugshots represent **"the person"** in the mirror who got caught, so the photo represents who? Ironically, it's no coincidence that Hell rhymes with jail... Hmm. By design, your thoughts and actions create your life's history, and eternal memory, and the color of your Spirit (darkness or the light of Christ) that is released from your body will determine your final destination into one of the eternal realms upon your death. Therefore, it is imperative to keep **"your man in the mirror"** in check to reflect the attributes of God... goodness, truth, and righteousness when you look in the mirror.

Satan has successfully waged war against our belief system in his effort to suppress truth and our belief in our Creator. He has guided humanity to believe that there is no God, no Devil or Satan, no Jesus Christ (God in Flesh), and no Hell. He is so cunning that he would fool us into believing that there is NO death if we do not get to witness it happening with our own eyes.

We have already established that there are only two (2) Life Forms or Beings that God Has Ever Professed to create...Angelic Spirit and Human Beings. Humans were created with an exterior of flesh to carry out the thoughts and actions from our mind, which reside within our inner Spirit that manifests in the brain. The inward part of man is the indwelling or manifestation of the angelic Spirit that God created of you when He created you in Heaven. Therefore, today, your fallen Angelic Spirit or your Spirit, which resides in your human body, is one and the same.

Because of duality and the spiritual equilibrium of good and evil, Eternal Spirit Life Energy now exists in two separate states... Divine (Holy) and Demonic (Unholy). Therefore, the two entities must live and thrive in two separate environments, or places in the realm of eternity, based on whether Spirit Life.

Energy is holy or unholy unto God. Divine Spirit Life Energy lives in the Holy Presence of God, and Demonic or negative, dark Eternal Spirit Life Energy must live in a separate place away from the Holiness of God. This established and created Satan's domain called Hell. The same division applied in the Garden of Eden when Adam and Eve were expelled from the Holiness of God; they had to go live and dwell somewhere else, away from God and the Tree of Life.

The difference in these two Spirit energies is why the Lord tells us, *"For we wrestle not against flesh and blood, but against [Spiritual] principalities, against [Spiritual] powers, against the [Spiritual] rulers of the darkness of this world, against spiritual wickedness in high places" (Ephesians 6:12)*, he also warns us, *"... do not believe every spirit, but test the spirits, whether they are of God..." (1 John 4:1).* Therefore, you must test the Spirits that reside in the bodies of those whom you know, as well as those whom you choose to hear the Word of God from or those you associate with.

Since God has only created two Life forms, Angels and Humans, each composed of our original nature, all other beings, i.e., aliens or other life forms that man finds himself foolishly searching for, are not of the Divine. They are Demonic Eternal Spirit Energy or antimatter, and again, your eternal life is under assault.

Seek to grow in the knowledge of God, seek His face and wisdom to make better, informed decisions in life and your eternal future. You must pay close attention to the nouns **(people, places, and things)** that you allow in your life and limit what you allow others to impart into your Spirit. Walk away from the negative, practice self-control... control your actions and reactions with others, and be slow to anger **(Psalm 86:15)**. Your choice between Life and Death, light and darkness, good and evil, or right and wrong, truth and lies matters. These two choices take on different forms relative to your daily situations and circumstances; your life's choices will ultimately reflect your eternal destiny. But they all boil down to the same connotation, which ties into our eternal choice regarding our spiritual future... Heaven and Hell, God or

Satan.

However, the former Light Bearer busies us with the distractions of daily life, so that we won't pay attention to the truth regarding himself and his determined agenda to destroy you and me, therefore, *"Be alert and of sober mind. Your enemy the devil prowls around like a roaring lion looking for someone to devour" (1 Peter 5:8)*. Satan knows that his time is short for his impending eternal death penalty; but you now, have a chance to avoid it **(shhh, you don't suppose to know this)**. However, the eternal choice in **Deuteronomy 30:19** is yours alone, but first, you must know and understand your two choices and each of their consequences so that you can make an informed decision about your eternal future. Hopefully, you know this by now.

Therefore, you must either invite the Indwelling Holy Spirit of the Lord to reside within you or accept the known consequences of living without Him, which is eternal death… simple. This choice will not always be available; time is running out, so I suggest you decide now. Don't risk eternal separation from God.

As you continue to read, you will realize that God is NOT to blame for all the ills in the world, for his objective was to establish a choice…between eternal life and eternal death (the second death), which equates to our choices of right and wrong, or good and evil, and so on. So, when someone commits murder or shoots up a school or commits any evil act, it is their choice to do so. God is not to blame. Again, by design, God allows both good and evil to co-exist in the Earth to be the two foundations that give us freedom of choice. However, this choice is only put before sinners who are certain to die; it is not put before those who remain in Heaven, where the purity of truth resides.

Unlike in Heaven, on Earth, we must determine what is truth or a lie, and we die, whereby our lives will speak for themselves… righteous or unrighteous, but guess what? It doesn't matter whether you believe in God or Jesus or not, because your impending death also speaks for itself as the Word of God's Truth. Death is the brick wall that we all run into, no matter what. You can't go over it, you can't go through it, nor can you go around it, but you can go 6 feet under it without belief in Jesus Christ, whereby your grave will lead you to Hell and Eternal Death… You decide!

Sinner Symptoms

"But rebels and sinners will both be broken [crushed], and those who forsake [desert] the LORD will perish [die]"
~ Isaiah 1:28 NIV

Jesus, as He spoke to His disciples, called us evil: ***"If you then, being evil..." (Luke 11:13 NKJV);*** now, let that sink in. We are both rebels and sinners, two distinct violations that have transferred to Earth, whereby we must face the consequences of our sinful and rebellious nature and actions.

Our undeserved second chance, whereby we are allowed to come to live on Earth to choose to receive Christ or not, is a great gift. While Christ, God's Indwelling Holy Spirit, leads us back to eternal life, it is the greatest gift ever given. However, Satan has glorified the acceptance of sin among men, so now we think that we can live any way that we want with no repercussions. Laws are passed to make sin publicly accepted, whereby the use of enforcement to obey is lawful. It doesn't matter what is acceptable to God anymore; it only matters how we "feel" and how those around us accept our feelings. If your government, friends, and family accept you and your sin, then all is well; however, all is not well between you and your Creator-God.

Therefore, humanity has created a culture where sin is perfectly acceptable based on the passage of laws and the suppression of truth. They don't want to hear about the consequences of Hell, which is sure to come; it's all about **"how we feel,"** and what **"I"** want to do. Don't bring up wrongdoings, Hell, eternal death, or God's coming wrath that will be poured out upon all unbelievers. The latter is not taught in churches or in our homes anymore.

We used to stone people for adultery, burn witches at the stake, rebuke same-sex activity, etc., but now we have been conditioned to accept these sins using laws that force us to bow down to acceptance or be punished. Sin is displayed on television, in video games, and in movies for us to see, and on the radio, for us to hear. And the more we see and hear it, the more we give in and accept it as the norm. Even priests, bishops, pastors, and pontiffs indulge in the cover-up of sin, keeping secrets until they stink their way into courtrooms. Then they are judicially forced to pay damages to hurt victims and/or receive jail time.

These days, governments are in bed with the church (through 501c3, tax breaks) so that governments can control what is allowed to be preached to congregations in their effort to stamp out teachings of the truth of God regarding Hell and unrighteousness. Ungodly behaviors are promoted because the former Light Bearer doesn't want you to know that you have already experienced two death sentences: **1.** Separation from God in Heaven, **2.** Separation from God, on Earth in the Garden. This is why you are awaiting your two (2) respective Hellfire Punishments. One of which is Satan's permanent, eternal punishment, The Second Death.

I suppose the only sins left that offend us are murder, bestiality, human trafficking, and pedophilia. However, society will probably soon seek to make those acceptable. You know the pattern: someone or a group will become an advocate for the change, and then they make commercials, video games, movies, and television programs about it so that you will begin to accept this behavior. And if the ungodly behavior causes illness or death, Big Pharma will create medication to allow you to continue to indulge in the ungodly, hideous behavior. Then, laws will be passed to force it upon society as the norm, thus sinking us to another new spiritual low.

But remember, it is by design that it is your choice to indulge in unrighteous behavior or not, no matter what the law says. There appear to be no consequences for sinful, ungodly behavior in society nowadays, so when you bring up Hell or talk about its punishments, no one wants to hear it. However, when the reality of

God's Word brings your punishments to pass, it will be too late; you will immediately return before the Lord, whereby your lifestyle will tell Him where your Spirit belongs…with those who love to do evil, like you. So, you will immediately go to Hell to await eternal death with no time to change your mind, your ways, or **repent**.

Your two eternal choices, Heaven or Hell, and their equivalent dualities… good/evil, etc., along with the resulting two Hellfire consequences, are firmly in place for believers and unbelievers; you can change your belief between either, at any time. However, remember, you must still experience Natural Death, the death of your body, no matter what. Therefore, your death or funeral must take place because of your sins committed in Heaven, or when unbelievers get to Hell, they will curse God and blame Him (for the choices they made) as they continually burn. You know how it feels to burn yourself; you have burned your hand or some part of your body before to know exactly how fire feels… yes, I'm talking about that same feeling, but exponentially and incomprehensibly worse. However, along with the intensity of your body burning, your sins will continually burn through the thoughts of your mind.

Do you remember that time you killed someone, or the time that you stole a car, were revengeful and disrespectful, spread gossip, cursed someone out, or even the time when you refused to forgive someone or to *"…love your neighbor as thy self (Leviticus 19:18)?"* Your consequential punishments were written in the Bible **(long ago)** to advertise exactly what would happen to you based on your two choices. Everything on Earth, starting from the Garden of Eden to now, has been made known to you, but you don't seek the truth, pay attention to, or take your eternal life seriously. Mentally, you prefer to remain the same as Satan, desiring to be like God by controlling your own life.

However, the good news is that **you still have time to repent** and change your ways toward righteousness. Christ's resurrection means that Divine Blood was shed for you to give you a second chance to regain your eternal life with the Lord. Take this chance now to choose before your Natural Death occurs… choose ye now this day.

The fact remains that those of us who live life away from God's Holy Spirit or have His Presence within their physical body because they have not asked Christ to live within them, or more specifically, if you are not located where God's Throne resides, in Heaven, whereby you can see His Holy Face, then you are a sinner because *"…all [who are born on Earth] have sinned [in Heaven and on Earth] and [have] come short of the glory of God. (Romans 3:23).*

I am a sinner (**repentant sinner**), and you can tell that you are a sinner too by analyzing the sinner symptoms below. You are welcome to circle those that apply to you, but be honest with yourself. Many do not think they are a sinner because they are puffed up with pride, caught up in deception, or the distractions of daily life that have you disillusioned. All sinners have shadows, and they die; some go to Heaven, and some go to Hell: *"For man goes to his eternal home [Heaven or Hell], and the mourners go about the streets" (Ecclesiastes 12:5).*

Some sinners are good people, but they also hate, fear, doubt, exhibit guilt, anger, jealousy, lie, are deceitful, etc. Sinners do charitable/good deeds, and some do bad deeds. Some are proud of their jobs, power, homes, cars, technological advancements, knowledge, money, etc. Some gamble, do drugs, smoke, drink alcohol, have sex, etc., to levels of addiction. Some worship God, and others worship other gods and idols. Some believe in God's truth, and others accept false doctrine. Sinners require rest/sleep, and they dream. Some commit murder, rape, robbery, and other atrocious crimes and go to jail or prison, and some don't. Sinners age and become ill. All sinners expel waste from their bodies and constantly accumulate trash that fills landfills with their filth.

A CLOSER LOOK AT LIFE AND DEATH

Some sinners believe in God but don't believe in Jesus or the devil, even though they are clearly revealed in the Bible, and the duality of characters is portrayed as good and evil in movies, games, the news, etc. Sinners are programmed by the societies in which they live… school, religion, government, politics, the media, i.e., radio, television (tell-a-vision, meaning authoritative leaders tell us the vision that they want us to see and believe). Some sinners, like the wealthy elite bankers, politicians, and government officials, as well as corporate officials, have Satan's mindset to control the world, while others are jobless and can hardly make ends meet.

Sinners are members of churches, secret societies, and the secret religions of the former Light Bearer, they desire to control the population and financial systems, exhibit supremacy over other races/people; and exert control over others through religious brainwashing of others using a photo of a white, blue-eyed Jesus, instead of the bronze-colored man with wool-like hair, as depicted in Revelation 1:14; they purposefully twist and suppress the truth of God's Word… The Bible.

Sinners create and use laws with insidious agendas to segregate and discriminate, take land and valuable resources (especially and intentionally in Africa per Satan's elites' agenda to keep Africans poor and most other countries rich, especially the West), and enforce slavery of mind and body, unapologetically. For decades, they have planned agendas to ensure perversion by enticing the population to defile themselves before God using television, movies, video games, music, etc. They promote vile behavior like abortion, sexual immorality, unholy matrimony, etc. Sinners have babies and don't care for them, speak with a foul mouth… every other word is a curse word.

Some sinners love everyone and make time for God, and some make no time for Him. Some love pets more than they love their fellow man. Although thought is spiritual, they try to separate

A CLOSER LOOK AT LIFE AND DEATH

church and state to push God away and sink society further down into more sin (Sodom and Gomorrah). They substitute God with money, business, and politics. Some sinners are drug users/dealers, drink alcohol, are con artists, bribers, manipulators, partakers of pornography, and all sexual perversion. Some know that they are living a life contrary to the ways of God, but think that they will have time to change before their death to turn their lives around. Some never **repent** or change their ways.

Sinners who are atheists lack the belief that God exists, and some are agnostics who believe that there is nothing known or can be known about God's existence or nature. Some sinners think they do nothing wrong; they give to the churches, good causes, help the poor; they build hospitals, schools, etc. (to get tax write-offs, not true giving). Some sinners live decently and in order; some do not; some break laws, cheat, steal, hate, fight, argue, are warmongers, rape, kill, think wrongfully, enslave and oppress others, talk evil and negatively; some keep their word, and some do not and are habitual liars. Some sinners participate in spiritual manipulation of witchcraft, and some do not; they produce and live in chaos and confusion; they hide and deny the truth; they make right wrong and do all things opposite to God's righteous ways and truth…And the list goes on and on.

Still, the adamant says, **"I AM NOT A SINNER!"** So, are you saying that you are not a prisoner to death, or that you will not die and leave Earth, or that you do not have a Shadow that follows you everywhere to remind you of your eternal past, present, and future? Unfortunately, the latter is undeniable and is coupled with many of the sinner symptoms above, requires the following diagnosis: If you do not live life in the Divine Presence of God, whereby you can see His Face or His Throne, in Heaven, then **YOU ARE A SINNER (in my Maury Povich voice)!**

You are either a **repentant sinner**, like me, or an **unrepentant**

sinner, but you are still a sinner, and many of the things listed above are a reality in your life. Sadly, you will allow yourself to be tricked out of your eternal life with God. However, the good news is that you can change your mind to live for Christ today by reading and following the instructions in Romans 10:9-10. Otherwise, your body is certain to die and experience the consequences of two death penalties, but no one can make the decision but you.

The goal is not to dissuade or persuade you to believe in Jesus Christ but to highlight your choices in regard to what you have been taught in school/science and the **"Choice"** that God has set before you, eternal life and eternal death **(Deuteronomy 30:19)**;
as well as the respective consequences of your choices. Again, Christ died to make this choice completely up to you.

However, the first step to recovery, for unbelieving, **unrepentant sinners**, is to admit the answer to the last question above with a **"Yes,"** my death is certain because of my sins, and I need a Savior. Then confess your sins and that Jesus is Lord; believe that God raised Jesus from the dead to forgive you of your sins **(pray Romans 10:9-10)**! Ask and accept God's forgiveness and the Indwelling Holy Spirit or Christ into your heart. But if you still choose not to accept that you are a sinner or deny Christ, it's ok because it is designed to be your choice, alone; just simply accept your known consequences for an eternity in Hellfire.

But in the meantime, be truthful with yourself relative to what you truly believe, and either accept the Lord's known consequences for your sins… Hellfire or God's way back to Eternal Life through Christ. Please compare what you have been taught, most of your life, versus what God has told you in His Word…the Bible and shown you by His visible Word (Jesus Christ) so that you can determine if what you believe is *"fake or fiction"* regarding your life, death, and eternal future. Remember that **"Time"** is of the essence because your time on Earth will run out. As prophesied, we are living in the end times and last days of the Tribulation, the fast-approaching end of God's redemption plan; therefore, ***"Seek ye the LORD while he may be found, call ye upon him while he is near" (Isaiah 55:6).***

By design, your conscience is your God-given sin barometer. When you first do something wrong, it bothers you; you may feel something in the pit of your stomach or feel uneasy, that's your conscience. However, suppose you continue to do wrong, overlooking your gut feelings or conscience; in that case, you subvert what your conscience is telling you. When you are thinking or doing wrong and do wrong anyway, and repeatedly, it becomes normal behavior for you. Then you start to do even more wrong and fall further away from the Lord; you change and become no longer sensitive and respectful of others: ***"Because of the increase of wickedness, the love of most will grow cold" (Matthew 24:12, NIV).***

So, now you are surprised when the lawless one **(Satan)** shows himself to you in the news, in this Hell where you live? He shows up in the form of increasing shootings (even killing very young school children), violence, disrespect, anger, etc. He acts through people to steal, kill, and destroy you by defiling yourself before God through abortion, same-sex marriage, drugs, sex trafficking, pedophilia, murder, slavery, etc., and pornography. It has been reported that America produces over 65% of the world's pornography. However, you don't seem to understand or care that you need God's TRUTH in your life because He says that His people are destroyed due to a lack of His knowledge (Hosea 4:6). Yet, we continue to deny His Truth, thus we continue the same news cycles that announce more of the same lawlessness.

For the sake of redemption, duality exists whereby you can include God in your life through prayer and faith, and God will show forth the fruits of His Spirit, or you may choose to follow

Satan's mindset. Remember, Heaven is wherever God is, so when you no longer include God in your life, you get the opposite of where He is…Hell. What else do you expect? Satan and his elite don't care about your life now or your eternal future…**wake up!!** Remember that everything below Heaven is Hell… The Abyss… the bottomless, which includes Earth and the darkness of our human mind. Therefore, in the section within Hell that is called Earth, your only hope is Jesus Christ. However, if you choose NOT to **repent** and continue living a life rooted in sin and rebellion, Satan has sealed your destiny in Hellfire…Gehenna and the **Eternal Lake of Fire and Brimstone (Revelation 20:10-14).** You are simply living your best life now while bidding your time to go there if you do not accept Jesus Christ.

Many of you don't believe that there is life after death, but again, I reiterate that our Spirits live forever. Therefore, your Spirit never stops living, even though your body returns to dust from which it came. So, when people say Rest in Peace (RIP), they seem to think we are simply resting or asleep in the grave, but the Bible reveals the contrary. Some of you rely on a Pastor to tell you what God says, instead of studying for yourself. The Pastor cannot stand before God for you, but oh yeah, you are too busy…right?

You never take time to explore what life, death, and your eternal future are all about, so you would rather go to Hell by default…smh. But you can start taking your life as seriously as your death, right now, by studying the diagram and completing the exercises at the end of the book: *"Study to shew [show] thyself approved unto God, a workman that needeth not to be ashamed, rightly dividing the word of truth" (2 Timothy 2:15).*

Take the Lord seriously and study His Holy Word that He provides for your instruction, correction, to give you His love, truth, His promises, and especially to express to you that He wants you back in His Eternal Life!

Works & Deeds Cannot Save You

"He saved us, not because of righteous things we had done, but because of his mercy. He saved us through the washing of rebirth and renewal by the Holy Spirit [that raised Jesus Christ]"
~ Titus 3:5 NIV

Although you may do good things for others, your **"good deeds and works"** cannot save you. It is only because of redemption that we can pray to the Lord and have faith in Christ, which leads to the righteousness of **"doing good,"** according to God's righteousness. Outside of that, "doing good" on your own means nothing because you are not depending on God through Christ. Therefore, you can "do good" and go straight to Hell. *I [God = Jesus] am He who searches the minds and hearts [of Spirits/Man]. And I will give to each one of you [Heaven or Hell] according to your works"* **(Revelation 2:23).**

Your faith means that it is not by sight or the fact that we, literally, saw Jesus Christ on the cross, but that we believe the evidence as told to us by those who were present. Therefore, we can live our lives with the passion of believing and knowing in our hearts that Jesus Christ completely fulfilled God's Holy Word.

Nonetheless, know that only your confessed belief or faith that Jesus Christ is Lord who paid your sin debt, not your works, will save you: *"For by grace you have been saved [delivered from judgment and eternal death] through faith [in Jesus], and that not of yourselves [your works/deeds]; it is the [undeserved] gift of God, not of works, lest anyone should boast [I put forth more effort than you so, I can have eternal life but you can't!]. For we are His workmanship [designed to do good works], created in Christ Jesus for good works [to perform Christ's good work, not our own]"* **(Ephesians 2:8-10, NKJV).**

Some sinners regard Christmas as a time of "goodwill" or doing

A CLOSER LOOK AT LIFE AND DEATH

"good deeds" to others, which cannot save you. This annual holiday season is known for giving and helping others. However, most do not understand the duality of this popular celebration, where some regard it as the celebration of the precious birth of our Lord and Savior Jesus Christ, while the duality, or the other side of the same coin, is that this holiday is cloaked in darkness. It is reported that the Catholic Church named this holiday by mixing Satan's pagan traditions **(lies)** with the truth of God (like he did to Eve in the Garden), which is evident in the word **"CHRISTMAS,"** which co-mingles the word **"Christ"** with the Catholic Church's **pagan** worship service called **"Mass." Wake up!**

Although some of us will never believe that we fall for Satan's lies or admit that we are a sinner, it doesn't change the truth of God, especially regarding your death to come, whereby Eve (you and me) was beguiled to believe the lie that if she believed Satan by disobeying God, she would not die…WRONG! The fact that we do fall for Satan's lies is evident by your death. However, the plot thickens with the belief in Santa Claus and the Easter Bunny. We celebrate and push the lie that there is a *Santa = Satan* (letter scramble trick), who flies in the air guided by horned reindeer carrying toys that are made by little green elves (representing supernatural creatures with magical powers) that fill this festive season with Christmas Joy… yeah, right.

Then there is the duality of Easter, the celebration of Jesus Christ's death and resurrection for the payment of our sins, and our deliverance from **"The Second Death."** But, on the other side of the same coin, many only celebrate the Easter Bunny with decorations of bunnies and colorful Easter eggs, disregarding the Lord altogether. Some take their children to sit on the lap of a stranger, dressed in a bunny suit for a photo op…smh…why? And these lies are intensified by the billions made through merchandising for gift giving, decorations, and movies and television programming celebrating old Saint Nick, the Easter Bunny, witches and monsters, not Jesus.

And of course, we cannot exclude the tradition of celebrating Halloween, with costumes and decorations that include skeletons, graves, cemeteries, tombstones, skulls, etc., that signify and glorify Satan. Remember that you and your children are captive to Satan by death, which is certain to come. One day, you and your children will descend into Satan's domain...a grave, as your Spirit descends into his abode of Hellfire. The only time a human skeleton is exposed is when the body decomposes after death; therefore, *skeleton = death*. Even churches celebrate with the intention of providing a safe environment for children, yet the children still come dressed as witches, skeletons, and other gory costumes, as well as a gory mindset set by the very nature of the father of death... Satan.

The Word of God tells us that death is considered unclean: ***"Whoever touches any dead body will be unclean for seven days...Anything the unclean person touches will become unclean, and anyone who touches it will be unclean until evening" (Numbers 19:11, 22).*** This holiday is known for the ceremonies of the dark works and deeds of witches and warlocks who cast spells and summon demons. It is common knowledge that children are abducted to participate in sexual rituals or sacrificed during Halloween. So, ask yourself, why do I, and my children, celebrate death, child sacrifice, and the things that are an abomination to God, in any shape or form? What is godly about this so-called holiday? Absolutely Nothing! Everything about it is ungodly; the duality of celebrating this holiday is to participate in it at all because it is not of God.

However, it never ceases to amaze me that believers, unbelievers, the uneducated, as well as the educated, and the advanced intelligent, doctors, attorneys, engineers, scientists, etc., and those with Master's and PHD degrees, and even Ministers practice these traditions. Nonetheless, God said that *"...[you] are holding on to human traditions [that are ungodly]" (Mark 7:8).* Are you willing to risk your eternal life by following the above worldly traditions? And the kicker is that these traditions are a subliminal lie that you, as an adult, pass the dark side of these traditions down to your children.

At Christmas, parents eagerly hand their babies over to sit on the lap of a complete stranger in a red suit (reportedly representing blood), as most children scream and cry. This practice is semi-representative of the age-old pagan ritual of child sacrifice where children were handed over to idol gods, screaming and crying as they are offered up for sacrifice by putting them on the alter flaming with fire: *"And they built the high places of Baal...to cause their sons and their daughters to pass through the fire unto Molech; which I commanded them not..." (Jeremiah 32:35).* Wow, the outlandish things that we do because of the lack of the knowledge of God's Truth. Children would be just as happy if parents told them the truth about Jesus, explaining that His birth is the reason for the decorations and gift-giving.

So, ask yourself: Why do I continue to fall for or believe Satan's lies, then knowingly pass this lie of a tradition down to my children? And finally, when your lies catch up with you, your children are crushed as the truth is exposed that there isn't a real Santa Claus who comes down their chimney bearing gifts. I saw a lady on the television show, Botched, who consulted the doctors on the show because, after several nose surgeries, her nose still looked horrible. She explained that her nose became disfigured because she told her eight-year-old son that Santa Claus is not real, so he hit her on the bridge of her nose with his fist and broke her nose.

This lie can have serious consequences; you don't want your children lying to you, so why lie to them? The real purpose of this lie is to distract us from the truth of God. Satan's holiday agendas are programmed into the minds of our children throughout their formative school years via cartoons, movies, television programming, games, store merchandising, etc. Can you see the great extent to which Satan goes to ensure that his programmed agenda steers you and your children away from God? Paradoxically, when you pass on these lies, you become a liar, along with Satan… the father of lies!

What does the belief in Santa Claus, the Easter Bunny, skeletons, witches, and warlocks do to enhance your life? Do they save you from eternal death by offering you the free gift of eternal life? I suggest that you seriously reevaluate the traditions that you and your family celebrate relative to what you believe is the truth of God or Satan's lie, straight out of Hell. Also, evaluate the fact that you are actually lying to your children, which will have a detrimental impact on them… think about it.

Personally, I do remember how crushed I was when I found out that there was no such thing as Santa Claus. This lie really did have an impact on my feelings, my understanding, and my future experiences of Christmas were never the same. However, I do celebrate the birth and resurrection of Jesus Christ. I never did tell my two children about Santa Claus, the Easter Bunny, or witches and monsters; they learned about them from others, at school, and the media. I had always explained to them about Jesus and that He is the reason for celebrating the season, as I took them over to our nativity scene to teach them about each of the attendees at Jesus' birth. I would tell them that the Three Wisemen brought gifts to baby Jesus, who came to save the world, and that this is why we give and receive gifts. While my children opened their gifts, they expressed the same exhilaration as if I had told them Santa had brought them.

However, some say that Jesus was not born on December 25th,

but evidently, the actual date was not important because if it were, God would have specified it. They say that December 25th coincides with the pagan winter solstice celebration. Nonetheless, if you don't believe this is the correct date, then do some research and pick another date to celebrate His birth. Some of us spend so much time and effort spewing opposition that we never allow the great joy of the following scripture to become a reality of celebration in our lives: ***Matthew 2:9–11, "When they [the Wisemen] had heard the king, they departed; and, lo, the star, which they saw in the east, went before them, till it came and stood over where the young child was. When they saw the star, they rejoiced with exceeding great joy.***

And when they were come into the house, they saw the young child with Mary his mother, and fell down, and worshipped him: and when they had opened their treasures, they presented unto him gifts; gold, and frankincense, and myrrh." Therefore, if you do not celebrate King Jesus' Birthday on December 25th, when do you celebrate the most extraordinary birth in Earth's History?

If you cannot understand why Jesus came as a baby to rest in a manger, then you do not understand your plight. You do not understand that your problem is death and that the solution to your death problem is Jesus Christ. His birth is the greatest reason to celebrate. You celebrate your own birthday, don't you? However, I always found it perplexing that Jehovah's Witnesses celebrate the resurrection of Jesus Christ at Easter but do not celebrate the miracle of His birth, as both were prophesied in the Word of God. So, the question becomes: How do you celebrate Jesus' resurrection but deny the celebration of His blessed birth, which had to occur first?

The realities in this next section will further bear witness to our status of being "Sinners."

Sinners Are Subject To...

DIRT/A BODY:

"The body that is sown [created] is perishable, it is raised imperishable [never die]; it is sown in dishonor [sin], it is raised in glory; it is sown in weakness, it is raised in power; it is sown a natural body [Jesus], it is raised a spiritual body [Christ]..." (1 Corinthians 15:42-44). Sinners are subject to a body to be able to participate in God's redemption plan so that they are able to function in the Earth, to live their lifestyle choice towards righteousness or unrighteousness. As established earlier, sinners must enter the Earth through birth because they must have a body, made in God's Image, created from the dirt or clay of the Earth: *"The LORD God formed man from the dust of the ground" (Genesis 2:7).*

And to make this even more of a reality for you, go outside to a grassy area, kneel, and dig down into the dirt or underneath the grass (remember that we associate Heaven with upwards, while the grave and Hell are downward). Now, please pick up a handful of dirt, notice its dark color, and feel the texture of it... Yes, this is what you are made of, the darkness of the dust as detailed in the latter scripture. Better yet, you can even take this exercise further, gather a pile of dirt and add water to make a paste, then mold it into the figure of a person and allow it to dry... That's you, minus God's Breath of Life, which is our life.

Upon our demise, most of us are lowered back down into the ground from which we came, into what God calls a grave. Dirt is tossed on top of us, which confirms the Truth of God's Word: *"Then shall the dust return to the earth as it was" (Ecclesiastes 12:7).*

Grave = Mausoleum = Cremation = Buried at Sea = Anywhere a Person is Dead

A CLOSER LOOK AT LIFE AND DEATH

Therefore, there is no sense in you trying to deny the Holy Word of God because you have witnessed burials firsthand, and you know that this is exactly what happens. But you may not have known that the reason that burials occur is because it is predicated in the Word of God regarding something that you did against Him. So, what good is all the money, power, and fame in the world that you sold your soul for, now? You can't take any of it with you, and you surely cannot buy your way out of death because eternal life with God is not for sale; it is free for the asking…enough said.

Does any of this ring true to you, or do you still believe what you were taught in school: **The Theory of Evolution** which claims that we evolved into humans from apes **(although there are no human/ape fossils that prove this transformation… NONE!)**, OR do you believe in **The Big Bang Theory**, whereby a big explosion occurred in outer space to, supposedly, create **"Life"** on Earth OR do you believe that you were created by God, with purpose, as a holy, intelligent, loving Spirit… in His likeness; designed to live forever? Nonetheless, you disobeyed and rebelled, but you have been forgiven through Christ… You decide!

However, if you really think about it, **a big bang is an explosion, and we know that explosions cause destruction, chaos, and death.** Bangs do not create governed, functional societies with intelligent beings, ecosystems, weather, animal and vegetable kingdoms, marriage, family, or eternal life. **And if we evolved from apes, shouldn't we have evolved into something else by now, or have we stopped evolving into other species?** None of man's theories are authoritative because they are from the mindset of a fallen, created being…Satan; they are simply lies of unproven, made-up words and assumptions to teach us in school under the guise of "Science" to distract us from God and His Truth.

Recall that my definition of the word **"Science"** is: *"Science is* *the study of what God has already created and established."* However, the former Light Bearer provides man his scientific and technological knowledge that we pass along to our children to frame their minds throughout their formative school years to ensure that they believe what his ruling world authorities (Secret Societies, Politicians, Scientists, Engineers, Corporate Officials, Doctors, World Organizations, etc.) put before them to believe, instead of having them believe the Holy Word of God.

None of man's scientific myths, assumptions, or secular inferences describe how Man was created with our Eternal Spirit Life Energy within or how it is sustained; nor do they explain the source of truth and lies, or even where our Spirits come from, and why Spirit resides within us and is gone the moment that we die. And they dare to explain how death fits into the mystery of eternal life. However, it is your choice to believe as you wish. Still, whether you believe it or not, we are filthy, dirty, mentally tainted sinners who need a Savior.

In Genesis 1:1, the moment that we sinned, God's Holy Spirit was removed from us (the definition of death), and we were expelled. Therefore, His Holy Spirit became no longer available to us, and Heaven was closed to us forever. Again, the Lord says that we have become like Satan, who is now your father: ***"You are of your father the devil, and the desires of your father you want to do. He was a murderer [taketh away eternal life; taketh away from God's Presence] from the beginning and does not stand in the Truth because there is no truth in him. When he speaks a lie, he speaks from his resources, for he is a liar and the father of it"*** *(John 8:44, NKJV).*

Remember that Jesus' life, death, and resurrection availed God's Holy Spirit back to us so that our souls can be regenerated towards truth, based on our choice. It is up to you to invite Christ's Indwelling Holy Spirit to come live within you. However, we still, automatically, have God's Eternal Breath of Life within us, which belongs to Him alone, and it will return to Him upon our demise. However, we no longer automatically have His Holy Spirit within us, as we once did in Heaven; here on Earth, we must ask for it.

I hope by now, I have drilled into your mind: **"Who God is," "Who you are,"** and **"What you are facing."** But again, I will reiterate that we are fallen from Heaven, sinners in the Spirit, and now fallen humans who were expelled from God's Divine Holy Presence, in the Garden, on Earth. And for the purpose of our redemption, we reside in a fallen body that holds our same fallen Spirits that were first created in Heaven. Nevertheless, we are sinners living on Earth to be given an eternal "choice" while awaiting our turn to die.

We are made of dirt, and as a result of this fact, we constantly deal with dirt: We must clean our bodies, wash our clothes, and our belongings, we must clean our homes, and all places where humans dwell. **Sinners leave a ring around the bathtub** as the Truth of God's word is ever-present. However, some sinners love to think and act like they are superior to the dirt they were made from, and even more superior than you. But we are no better than others, as one pile of dirt is no better than another.

We build buildings, homes, and structures from the Earth's dirt, on top of the dirt of those who have passed on before us. Dirt is always circulating through the air, so we are constantly cleaning because this is the Word of God confirms to you that you were created from the dust or dirt of the Earth **(Romans 10:9-10)**. Therefore, clean up your mind or thought life, and choose to operate in the righteous ways of God. But again, I will continue to remind you that it's your choice regarding how you prefer to live. It is your choice to search for God's Truth about your life, death, and eternal future because you can certainly believe that the Truth of His Holy Word **(Genesis 2:17)** will find you when it is your turn to be lowered back down into the dirt from whence you came.

EARTH: THE "SHOW AND TELL" PLACE
(*EARTH = THE WORLD*) / JUDGMENT

Sinners are subject to the duality of truth and lies that are revealed before our eyes, for all to see, while we live our temporary life on Earth. Everyone has a story and a history; therefore, every life has a book in God's heavenly library with their name on it. Now, let's go back over this again. This world is where Satan's evil mindset, motives, and intentions are exposed as he and his inner circle rule Hell and Earth. He is the overseer over all of us who sinned and rebelled against God while our Spirits lived in Heaven. For this reason, we were cast down to the prison of Earth where the grave, the pits of Hellfire **(Ephesians 4:9)**, the darkness of the Abyss **(Genesis 1:2)**, or the bottomless pit exists.

This World is where everything has a beginning and an end, including the humanity portion of your eternal life, while your body enters the grave; your Spirit returns to God who gave it **(Ecclesiastes 12:7)**. So, when we come to Earth to serve out our death sentence, then we pay for our sins and rebelliousness against God in Heaven with our Natural Death because God said: *"For the wages of sin is death" (Romans 6:23).* There is no way around this truth, and you know it, as well as I. We established that there is only one way to enter the Earth, birth, and only one way to leave is death, with one exception, if you are Raptured or taken away to Heaven by the Lord, like Enoch and Elijah.

The World is also the "show-and-tell" place where truth is revealed before our eyes. As well, the evidence of Satan's lies, in words, deeds, and his actions, is exposed against God's truth. Earth is where God set the atmosphere for redemption with the birth, death, and resurrection of Jesus Christ. He overcame the world of death, where every human life ends in the death of the body. It is the place where God has literally set life and death before us with each breath that we take (**Deuteronomy 30:19**). Miss your next breath (or few) of "His Air" and see what happens, you transcend from the finite realm of Earth into the infinite realms of before life on Earth and after life on Earth... Heaven and Hell, with your lifestyle determining your final eternal destination (see diagram in the index). This scripture defines our reason for being here in our present fallen state. Therefore, at the beginning of creation, the Lord set the foundations of Heaven and Hell, which sustain good and evil that must co-exist to create our present state of duality that endows us with freedom of choice, in the Earth.

Recall that Satan was cast down to Earth to be given his wish to become like God and to establish his evil government with the foolish plan of returning to Heaven to exalt himself above God. While in the Earth, his aim is to create a world without the God of Heaven so that he is God with total control. He desires to create his own beings and destroy humanity. And when Christ returns to Earth (The Second Coming) to avenge His physical death, in the flesh, Satan's army of unbelievers desires to defeat Jesus Christ in the coming final War of Armageddon. Even still, Satan will portray the depth of his satanic nature within God's redemption plan to save us from the permanent, Eternal Second Death, so that there will be no excuse and no doubt that the former Light Bearer deserves the fate of his impending punishment in the Lake of Fire.

Earth is also a prison where we are held until our Natural Death occurs and as well a prison for the worst of Satan's fallen high-ranking generals who fought against Archangel Michael and lost (**Revelation 9:14**). It is the abode of those who chose to join Satan's quest to disobey and attack God's Sovereignty which subjects us to tribulation, death, Hell, and the grave. I remind you once again that Satan is the father of all lies: *"Ye [you] are of your father the devil, and the lusts of your father ye [you] will do. He was a murderer*

A CLOSER LOOK AT LIFE AND DEATH

from the beginning, and abode not in the truth [hated truth], because there is no truth in him. When he speaketh a lie, he speaketh of his own: for he is a liar, and the father of it" (John 8:44).

Whereas, we were only subject to God's Truth, in Heaven, and in the Garden of Eden, we fell from grace and became subject to two streams of thought voices, the truthful words of our Creator, and the dishonest, evil words and thoughts of a created being...Satan. Therefore, here on Earth, we must listen to both and then decide which one we will believe, follow, and the thoughts that we act upon, which will define who we ultimately worship.

Earth is the place where all humans will be resurrected to conjoin their same Spirit back with their same earthly body, for judgment: *"And I saw the dead, small and great, stand before God; and the books were opened: and another book was opened, which is the book of life: and the dead were judged out of those things which were written in the books, according to their works" (Revelation 20:12).* Again, your life, all your thoughts, decisions, and deeds are written down in heavenly books, including all that you have hidden will be found and revealed during your face-to-face meeting with your Heavenly Father. Therefore, it doesn't matter whether you believe these revelations or not; just know that they are as certain as your Natural Death is to come.

Just as God has His Throne in Heaven, so it is that Satan has his throne on Earth. It is located in Pergamos, Turkey, as recorded in *Revelation 2:12-13, "And to the angel of the church in Pergamos...I know thy works, and where thou dwellest, even where Satan's seat [throne] is..."* In Pergamos, the devil exercised great power and influence; he is *"the god of this world" (2 Corinthians 4:4).* Most of its citizens lived and died in unbelief as Satan was their king, ruling from his invisible throne; however, he makes himself well known to his elite agents and followers.

A CLOSER LOOK AT LIFE AND DEATH

We often wonder where the Antichrist will come from; however, it is plausible that he could come from where his original throne resides, in Turkey, since the Lord will come from where His Throne resides, in Heaven. The point of departure is the point of return. The return of the offspring of the Fallen Angeles, the Nephilim, will again inhabit the Earth, as well as inhabit or possess transhuman bodies, clones, babies created in artificial wombs, robots, etc., and will assist the Antichrist with the display of lying signs and wonders in the sky.

BLOOD SACRIFICE (Graphic Content Advisory):

Just as Satan's government, on Earth, uses money as payment for debt, God's spiritual currency system uses payment by blood, hence the blood shed by Jesus Christ on the cross. Animal sacrifice was prevalent from Adam and Eve, after they were expelled from the Garden of Eden, until Jesus was sacrificed, which ended the custom. However, Satanists continued to use blood sacrifices, cannibalism, and pedophilia in their ritual worship dedicated to the former Light Bearer. Thus, he copies God's system for his followers, but in an inverted form, which includes grotesque ways of eating human flesh and drinking human blood.

Aborted fetuses, infants, and children are a delicacy for Satan's elite at the higher levels of his pyramid organization structure. However, Jesus paid the ultimate price once. Still, Satan continues to use blood sacrifice **(including abortion)** because it employs his followers to profess their allegiance to him visibly. He will bring this custom to the forefront during the last days. They worship him with human blood, which is life, because again: *"For the life of the flesh is in the blood" (Leviticus 17:11).*

In 2017, famed Hollywood actor and movie producer, Mel Gibson, in a shocking exposé, spoke out about those who control Hollywood and their prevailing practice of child sacrifice and pedophilia. Below is an excerpt from his statements during the following interview **(Graphic Content Advisory)**: *"Hollywood studios are "drenched in the blood of innocent children"* according to Mel Gibson who claims the consumption of "baby blood is so popular in Hollywood that it basically operates as a currency of its own… every studio in Hollywood is bought and paid for with the blood of innocent children… this isn't anything new. If you do some research, you will see it's a metaphysical, alchemical phenomenon, and you can find it behind the scenes in all the dark eras in history.

Blood sacrifice is a dark, multidimensional *occult = hidden* art and practice, used by secret societies in the last few hundred years for social programming and mind control, and raised to a zenith by Hollywood in America in our era…The secret society referred to is the Illuminati, the globalist cabal that controls our media of communication. Their objective from the beginning is to instigate a revolt against the institutionalized Church and to submerge the nations under a communist one-world government and religion. Part of the ritual of this satanic one-world religion is pedophilia, which is promoted by homosexuals, which ties in with the cannibalism that it leads to. According to Gibson, **"Hollywood is an institutionalized pedophile ring,"** but for some children, it is but a stepping stone to be drawn fully into Satanic covens where they are sacrificed. This is where many of the missing children have disappeared to." --Article reported (1/15/18) on TLDM by David Martin.

Occultists believe that blood is very powerful, which concurs with the Word of God… The Holy Bible, however, their sinister mindset regarding blood is the focus of the following article featured on www.occult-world.com, called **"Blood"** by Lux Ferre on September 8, 2019: Aleister Crowley, according to the article below, reportedly "had a formidable encounter with a Demon named Choronzon. The Demon was evoked in a ritual that involved slitting the throats of three pigeons and pouring their blood upon the sand.

Many mystics who dabble in the Demonic Supernatural mind of the former Light Bearer believe that **"Blood"** is a source of power unleashed in ritual sacrifices to appease gods and conjure Demons and other Spirits...**Animal Blood** is used in folk Charms and spells.... Some sources of blood are considered to be more powerful than others. **Human Blood** is identified with the soul and carries the greatest power. Ingesting human blood is believed to confer the powers and strengths of the victim upon the conqueror.

The blood of executed criminals is said to be a powerful protector against disease and bad luck, because of the energy of resentment and fury, which is released upon execution...Human blood was believed to strengthen the foundations of buildings, and sometimes sacrificial victims were walled up in temples, forts, and other structures...**Menstrual Blood** has a long history of being feared by men, and prescriptions have been given against associating with, touching, or having sex with menstruating women, for their blood has the power to harm...In Christianity, menstrual blood was believed to spawn Demons and to defile altars." However, since *Leviticus 17:11* states that the *"life of man is in the blood,"* you can see from the above that blood, and specifically, human blood is an integral part of Satan and his followers' diet and worship. Also, sexual perversion is key to their rituals. It's Hell Being in Hell!

Unfortunately, the Abyss of Hell or the Bottomless Pit is even more sinister than we could ever comprehend, but this next topic is a new low for me. Prominent news outlets report that the use of human aborted baby fetus cells and tissues, which are ingredients in our food to provide flavor... REALLY! They said that an ingredient called Senomyx creates flavour enhancements for companies like Pepsi, Kraft, Nestle, and Campbell's. It goes on to say that Senomyx grafts kidney cells from human aborted fetuses, replicates these cells, and puts them in products including Gatorade, Lay's chips, Pepsi, Tropicana (all made by PepsiCo), Dasani water, and Minute Maid (both made by the Coca-Cola Company).

Of course, all of the above food manufacturers deny this claim, but if this claim has been tested and proven true, then why would the state of Oklahoma and Texas introduce and pass bills that ban the use of aborted human fetuses in food? According to ABC News: **"Bill Would Ban Aborted Fetuses"** in Food By Katie Moisse January 26, 2012: An Oklahoma bill that would ban the sale of food containing aborted human fetuses has some people wondering: What food currently contains aborted human fetuses? The bill, introduced on January 18, 2012, by State Sen. Ralph Shortey, prohibits the manufacture or sale of "food or any other product intended for human consumption which contains aborted human fetuses in the ingredients, or which uses aborted human fetuses in the research or development of any of the ingredients."

ALSO: TEXAS LEGISLATURE Online (.gov)
https://capitol.texas.gov › html 88(R) SB 314 - Introduced version - By: Hall S.B. No. 314 A BILL TO BE ENTITLED AN ACT relating to required labeling of certain products that contain or are derived from aborted human fetal tissue.

BE IT ENACTED BY THE LEGISLATURE OF THE STATE OF TEXAS:
SECTION 1. Subchapter D, Chapter 431, Health and Safety Code, is amended by adding Section 431.085 to read as follows: Sec. 431.085. LABELING REQUIRED FOR FETAL TISSUE FOOD PRODUCT:
(1) "Fetal tissue food product" means a food or food additive that:
    (A) contains human fetal tissue;
    (B) is manufactured using human fetal tissue; or
    (C) is otherwise derived from research using human fetal tissue.

A CLOSER LOOK AT LIFE AND DEATH

(2) **"Human fetal tissue"** means tissue, cells, or organs obtained from an aborted unborn child.

OMG, can you believe this? The vileness and cunning ways of the serpent, whose goal is to trick us into unknowingly eating humans... aborted babies!!!!! This exponentially unbelievable atrociousness is available for our consumption at our local grocery store... WOW!!! Satan's mindset and agenda are from the pit of Hell and are in action against you, me, and our children, with the approval of your government. Can't you see his devices at work to deceive you and bring harm and death to you? Recall that his only goal is to steal, kill, and destroy. It is beyond words... **WAKE UP AND PAY ATTENTION!** And we, the public, not knowing this, spend our hard-earned money buying and consuming these products, making these company executives billions. Then they lie and deny it to our face, as tests prove otherwise. It makes my stomach turn...just sickening. It's the most astonishing, horrific horror ever imagined...eating babies!!! However, once you know these things, you can't unknow them. Just think about the abortion doctors, medical workers, researchers, and major company execs who work together and have meetings behind the scenes to bring these products to market... surely Hell awaits!

At high-level meetings, behind closed doors, they work to commission and implement their plans to push them forward to harvest and logistically distribute these products that contain the ingredients of aborted fetuses for our consumption. This is beyond insane madness; it is extremely sickening and truly infuriating. Thank God that Hell exists for those who think they are getting away with such atrocities... surely Hellfire awaits them. The Abyss of Hell is astronomically dark and deep...**It's Hell being in Hell!** Then they do television commercials to promote these products straight out of Hell. Again, there are no words to adequately express this Hell that we live in.

And the killing part is that many of us idolize celebrities, especially our children. As adults, we continue to fall for Satan's lies and do not seek God's Truth, so how are we to teach our children the truth if we don't know it for ourselves? Please stop falling for Satan's Government and Hollywood's lies, and stop your children from falling. Do your own research, don't just simply believe your government, pastors, and celebrities, believe the Word of the living God alone. Don't follow the crowd, follow God's Word, turn inward within your Temple and talk to Him as you would anyone else, ask Him about things in your life instead of your family, friends, or any created beings... think, research the scriptures, pray, **repent**, and invite Christ to live within you and for protection during these last days. Look forward to the blessed hope of the Rapture, that is the cure for death!!!! But I can tell you this: If you are not looking for the Rapture, the Rapture certainly is not looking for you, according to ***Hebrews 9:28, "...so Christ was offered once to bear the sins of many [on the cross]. To those who eagerly wait for Him. [to come in the clouds] He will appear a second time, apart from sin, for salvation."***

Again, life is about choices, and you must be ready to make a choice because the ultimate eternal death test... **"The Mark of the Beast"** using biometrics in your right hand and on your forehead is coming, as certain as your death will come. Therefore, do NOT allow Satan to intimidate you by threatening to kill you if you do not accept the mark because Christ has defeated death so that when you give your life as Christ gave His for you, you will receive the gift of eternal life... **Glory!** We do NOT bow down, we stand for Christ, forever.

The elite will soon collapse the current economy and the established world cultures, all our conveniences will shut down, and we will come back up with the Beast System in place. At this juncture, you must make the ultimate choice to stand for Christ or submit to Satan through his Antichrist so that you can **"buy and sell"** and get back to living with a sense of normalcy, but it will require you to reject Christ and sell your soul to Satan. Are you ready?

Hell, witchcraft, blood consumption, and the worship of Satan are real, and so are his followers who carry out his plans, magic, and rituals. They are plentiful and stand ready, willing, and able to do Satan's bidding. Eventually, many will willingly choose to receive the mark on their hand or forehead and will publicly worship the beast and his image, which is waiting in the wings for rollout using Artificial Intelligence (AI), 3D, and Holographic Technology. (Revelation 14:9) However, all will be forced to do so if you want to participate in society and buy and sell. So, what will you do? Is your Soul for sale? I hope that you prepare yourself and resolve those questions for yourself because we have been forced to do things right now (masks, quarantine mandates, vaccines, etc.), and God has revealed where we are headed, so it is on you to decide. One thing about it, you cannot blame God for the consequences that you will receive as a result of your own decisions to turn away from His truth!

IDOLATRY:

Sinners are subjected to **"Idolatry."** This is the worship of a cult image or **"idol"** as though it were a deity like God. In Abrahamic religions, idolatry connotes the worship of something or someone other than the Abrahamic God as if it were God" (Wikipedia). Idolatry became a very public and profound custom that the fallen angels and their offspring, the Nephilim, taught man. They were Satan's dark arts (idolatry, magic, makeup, science, technology, etc.) or the teachings of unrighteous ways of living and conducting themselves in ways that led his followers to worship him.

The most popular story regarding idolatry occurred when the Hebrews were captive slaves to Pharaoh. But when Moses was elevated to serve in Pharaoh's government, God raised Him from the dead to save His people. After Moses freed the slaves, he was subsequently told by God to come up to the top of Mount Sinai, where he spoke with God and received His Ten Commandments. However, when he came down from the mountain, he found that the people had created a golden calf to worship. They wanted to worship something that they could see, instead of the living God who had delivered them after 400 years of slavery in Egypt. *"The whole human race is foolish and has no knowledge! The craftsmen are disgraced by the idols they make, for their carefully shaped works are a fraud. These idols have no breath or power"* **(Jeremiah 10:14, NLT).**

The end times and last days will take us full circle or back to the times in Noah's day, whereby Satan will bring back idolatry and sacrificial worship from its current secret status into mainstream society so that this behavior will be, once again, on public display. Recently, in America, a 90-foot statue of the Hindu monkey god called Lord Hanuman was erected in Sugarland, Texas (same height as King Nebuchadnezzar in the book of Daniel). This monkey god also aligns with the narrative that we are taught in school, the Theory of Evolution, which states that we evolved from Apes, while at the same time, ironically, there is a recent plague called "Monkeypox." This is not a coincidence; it's an agenda.

Furthermore, the former United States Vice President, Kamala Harris, of Hindu origin, interestingly, during the 2024 Democratic and Republican Conventions, both parties allowed Hindu prayers. They were embracing religious pluralism or the worship of other gods. Also, America's southern borders are flooded with many immigrants who are bringing their idols with them: *"**They provoked Him [God] to jealousy with foreign gods; With** *abominations they provoked Him to anger. They sacrificed to demons, not to God, to gods they did not know…And He said: 'I will hide My face from them, I will see what their end will be, for they are a perverse generation, Children in whom is no faith…' For a fire is kindled in My anger, and shall burn to the lowest hell; It shall consume the earth with her increase, and set on fire the foundations of the mountains" (Deuteronomy 32:16-17, 20, 22).* Now, that is what I call the epitome of ANGER… WOW!

As prophesied, the world is returning to the days of Noah, which includes the return of the Nephilim, blood sacrifice, idol worship, and the public worship of Satan. Again, none of the above is a coincidence; it's an agenda. Therefore, I urge you to determine if what you believe is fact or fiction before your certain date with death.

If you do not get anything else out of reading this book series or the Bible, please understand that your works and deeds cannot save you. You are saved by God's Divine Grace or the temporary **"Grace Period of Time"** that He has extended to you, while you live on Earth, and participate in His Divine Redemption Plan whereby salvation is offered through faith in Jesus Christ. Christ paved the way back to eternal life with our Heavenly Father; no other way exists: *"Jesus said 'I am the way, the truth, and the life. No one comes to the Father except through Me…" (John 14:6).* I hope that you will gain wisdom and understanding regarding the seriousness of your eternal life and eternal death situation, recall that *"Wisdom is the principal thing; therefore, get wisdom: and with all thy getting get understanding" (Proverbs 4:7).*

The end times and last days will take us full circle or back to the times in Noah's day, whereby Satan will bring back idolatry and sacrificial worship from its current secret status into mainstream society so that this behavior will be, once again, on public display. Recently, in America, a 90-foot statue of the Hindu monkey god called Lord Hanuman was erected in Sugarland, Texas (same height as King Nebuchadnezzar in the Book of Daniel). This monkey god also aligns with the narrative that we are taught in school, the Theory of Evolution, which states that we evolved from Apes, while at the same time, ironically, there exists a plague called "Monkeypox." This is not a coincidence; it's an agenda.

Furthermore, the former had a Vice President, who also ran for President of the United States, and is of Indian descent. It is known that the Hindu culture has many idols of gods. Interestingly, during the 2024 Democratic and Republican Conventions, both parties allowed Hindu prayers, thus embracing religious pluralism or the worship of other gods. Also, America's southern borders are flooded with many immigrants who are bringing their idols. As prophesied, the world is returning to the days of Noah, which includes the return of the Nephilim, blood sacrifice, idol worship, and the public worship of Satan. Again, it's not a coincidence; it's an agenda. Therefore, I urge you to determine if what you believe is fact or fiction before your certain date with death.

If you do not get anything else out of reading this book series or the Bible, please understand that your works and deeds cannot save you. You are saved by God's Divine Grace or the temporary "Grace Period of Time" that He has extended to you, while you live on Earth, and participate in His Divine Redemption Plan whereby salvation is offered through faith in Jesus Christ. Christ paved the way back to eternal life with our Heavenly Father; no other way exists: *"Jesus said, 'I am the way, the truth, and the life. No one comes to the Father except through Me..." (John 14:6).* I hope that you will gain wisdom and understanding regarding the seriousness of your eternal life and eternal death, recall: *"Wisdom is the principal thing; therefore, get wisdom: and with all thy getting get understanding"(Proverbs 4:7).*

OUR LIFE IS IN THE BLOOD/BLOODLINES:

Sinners are subject to blood that runs through our veins: *"For the life of every creature is its blood: its blood is its life. Therefore, I have said to the people of Israel, you shall not eat the blood of any creature, for the life of every creature is its blood. Whoever eats it shall be cut off" (Leviticus 17:14).* During the course of Earth's History, family bloodlines were of the utmost importance to Heaven because the bloodline of the lineage of Jesus must remain pure. The bloodline of His family, throughout generations, could not be tainted with the bloodlines of the Canaanites, fallen angels, or the Nephilim Giants. For 4000 years, God had to navigate bloodlines to ensure that the right people were mating to keep His bloodline genuinely pure and fit for the King of Kings to be born. The same is true relative to keeping the integrity of God's Word... The Holy Bible. For thousands of years, through His many prophets, God had to navigate the sacredness of His Holy Word so that it would remain undefiled with lies.

Although many may criticize the 66 books of the Bible that were selected to be included in the King James Bible version, by the Nicene Council under the Roman Emperor Constantine, in the year of our Lord 325, the core point of God's Holy Word is will never change as revealed in the Old Testament, Genesis 3:15, where God said that He would send us a Messiah to save us from The Eternal Second Death, then the first chapter of The New Testament, Matthew 1:1 begins by revealing the family lineage leading up to the birth of the Messiah, which God said He would send. Then the chapter continues with the birth of the Messiah. Thus, God has kept His Word from the very beginning of the Bible by introducing the visible body of Jesus with the Light of God's Holy Spirit within Him as the Messiah to effectuate Christ's resurrection of Christ; therefore, no one can call God a liar.

Therefore, we are all subject to the consequences of sin, which are death, the grave, judgment, and Hellfire; thus, we need a Savior from the Eternal Second Death or permanent separation from our Creator, the giver and sustainer of eternal life. By now, you should know that He forgave us and promised to send us a Savior, Jesus Christ, whereby through Him we are provided a second chance and a pathway back to eternal life with our Heavenly Father. God wishes that **"not one"** of us should perish but have everlasting life (John 3:16). He wants none whom He created… His Children, to experience the Eternal Second Death that was first created for the first one to sin…Satan, but was eventually availed to all unbelievers. The Lord tells us to choose eternal life through Jesus Christ. Consequently, you are subject to what the Lord has said, as written in His Holy Word, no matter if you believe in God, Jesus, or Satan, or not, because His Word defines your death that is certain. We already know that it is certain, as recorded in ***Romans 14:11,*** *"every knee shall bow"* unto King Jesus, and *"every knee"* includes you.

GOD'S WRATH:

Unrepentant Sinners are subject to God's wrath. According to His redemption plan, He will **"pour out"** His wrath upon the Earth during the Tribulation and Great Tribulation. However, God's unbridled, fierce wrath was shown when Man became so evil and corrupt that He decided to destroy the inhabitants on Earth with a flood that decimated all things, people, and the giants, except for Noah, his family, and the animals specified by the Lord. God's global wrath will occur again, directed at all unbelievers and rebels when the Day of the Lord soon cometh. Logically, a just God would have a just system to handle the righteous and unrighteous, as we do in our justice system. Justice is served when the judge has the scales that balance freedom and punishment. Based on evidence, the judge can issue a sentence to an individual that sets them free

(Heaven) or sends them to jail **(Hell)**, which is the definition of **"Justice."** Therefore, in Heaven's Universal, Most High Supreme Court, Hell is what makes God just!

The opposite of God's goodness appears as anger, so when we do not accept God's goodness through Christ, guess what? We get His opposite, which is the anger of His wrath. When we don't listen to Him, just like when our children don't listen, they receive your chastisement or punishment. God's wrath or punishment is always designed to produce **repentance** and restoration and encompasses the eternity of each of our Souls, specifically, our future eternal consequences: Heaven or Hell. For unbelievers or the **unrepentant,** your consequences ain't pretty:

Romans 2:5 (NIV): "...But because of your stubbornness and your unrepentant heart, you are storing up wrath against yourself for the day of God's wrath, when his righteous judgment will be revealed."

Nahum 1:2 (NIV): "...The LORD is a jealous and avenging God; the LORD takes vengeance and is filled with wrath. The LORD takes vengeance on his foes and vents his wrath against his enemies."

Rom 1:18 (NIV): "...The wrath of God is being revealed from heaven against all the godlessness and wickedness of people, who suppress the truth by their wickedness, since what may be known about God is plain to them, because God has made it plain to them. For since the creation of the world God's invisible qualities—his eternal power and divine nature—have been clearly seen, being understood from what has been made, so that people are without excuse. For although they knew God, they neither glorified him as God nor gave thanks to him, but their thinking became futile and their foolish hearts were darkened. Although they claimed to be wise, they became fools and exchanged the glory of the immortal God for images made to look like a mortal human being and birds and animals, and reptiles. Therefore, God gave unbelievers over in the sinful desires of their hearts to sexual impurity for the degrading of their bodies with one another. They exchanged the truth about God for a lie, and worshiped and served created things rather than the Creator— who is forever praised" (Romans 1:18-25, NIV).

So, if you don't know the above, now you know! **Unbelievers, BEWARE** as God's global wrath comes down to punish you. Believers will be lifted up to Heaven while God's wrath comes down because they are NOT appointed to go through the tribulation. God has allowed us time to **repent**, pray for the healing of our world and our land, have revivals, etc., to get our lives right with Him for almost 6,000 years. Now, we are living in the end-times… in the last days, whereby, as it states in the latter scripture, we are at the stage where time is up! It's time out for revivals or prayers that seek to turn things around. God is tired; our filth has reached His nostrils in Heaven, so He has removed his mercy from unbelievers and has given them over to the sinful desires in their hearts.

The Lord has given unbelievers over to their sins, especially idolatry and sexual impurity, for the degrading of their bodies with one another, for he knows that you have exchanged good for evil and the truth about God for Satan's lies. You worship and love created things… idols [devices…cell phones, social media, your job, money, friends, family, your lover, sports, material things, celebrities, animals, Satan, etc.] rather than your Creator. Please be advised that whatever is most important to you in life, over spending time and having an intimate relationship with Jesus Christ (who is God), is your idol.

And for those who didn't get caught, thinking that they have gotten away with murder, theft, mistreating others, sexual perversion, habitually lying to others about their gender, because they have had a sex change, or thinking of themselves as better than others, due to the corruption of their wicked wealth… Think again! And for those with bunkers underground as a means to escape… think again… there is no escaping God: ***"Nothing in all creation is hidden from God's sight. Everything is uncovered and laid bare before the eyes of him to whom we must give account" (Hebrews 4:13, NIV).*** Your time is up! It is now time for God's wrath to come against you, unimaginably and inconceivably strong and fierce with anger!

The Lord says that at His return in the clouds, just before **"The Day of The Lord,"** it will be like in the days of Noah and Lot. First, the water deluge that covered the entire Earth, then fire will come down from Heaven, like it did in Sodom and Gomorrah. We have made a 360° return to the same place in our Eternal History, but this time, the progression is described in Matthew Chapter 24, as "Birth Pains." However, when a woman goes into labor, the contractions are nonstop, but first her water breaks. So, at what point can we officially say that her water has "broken" when compared to end-time events?

I believe that her global water broke with the severe worldwide flooding and earthquakes that defied Man's scientific and technological analogy. Every continent on Earth reported multiple earthquakes, flooding, and they also report that there has been a 5-degree pole shift, along with the reversal of our ocean/river system flow over the span of 9-12 days at the beginning of July 2025. On July 16, 2025, the Source reported: *"A major ocean current in the Southern Hemisphere has reversed direction for the first time in recorded history, in what climatologists are calling a "catastrophic" tipping point in the global climate system."* However, since her water has broken, the birth pains will only intensify until they culminate with God's wrath raining down on all unbelievers during the Tribulation and Great Tribulation.

When the filth of our sins reaches God's nostrils to the point that our filth becomes so overwhelming that He can no longer suppress His anger, I believe that ***Psalms 18:7-15, NIV***, depicts the progression towards the approach of **The Day of the Lord's Wrath:** *"The earth trembled and quaked [from birth pains (Matthew 24), and the foundations of the mountains shook; they trembled because he [God] was angry. [so very angry that] Smoke rose from his nostrils; consuming fire came from his mouth, burning coals blazed out of it. He parted the heavens and came down; dark clouds were under his feet. He mounted the cherubim and flew; he soared on the wings of the wind. He made darkness his covering, his canopy around him—the dark rain clouds of the sky.*

Out of the brightness of his presence, clouds advanced, with hailstones and bolts of lightning. The Lord thundered from heaven; the voice of the Most High resounded. He shot his arrows and scattered the enemy, with great bolts of lightning, he routed them. The valleys of the sea were exposed and the foundations of the earth laid bare at your rebuke, Lord, at the blast of breath from your nostrils." Who can withstand the anger of the Lord?

SATAN/SIN/DETERIORATION:

Sinners are subject to the former Light Bearer, now known as Satan, who is an immensely powerful, created spirit being and was given high-ranking status by God. And within the redemption plan, he was purposefully given much authority on the Earth by God, as you will see later in the book series. However, we have established that the former Light Bearer's rebellious mindset flows as dark or negative energy through our thoughts, speech, and actions. The duality of Spirit Life Energy, on Earth, is graphically and mathematically shown as a Sine Wave or Sin wave with an **"e."**

A CLOSER LOOK AT LIFE AND DEATH

This waveform reflects the duality of good and evil, or the co-existence of good and evil, in our world. It manifests as light waves, tidal waves, sound waves, electrical power (positive and negative), or current. It reveals that good and evil are allowed to co-exist on the Earth, which is also evident by the tree that we chose in the Garden, *"The Tree of the Knowledge of Good and Evil."*

Therefore, a Sine wave graphically shows the flow of light wave energy moving upwards (towards Heaven), called the positive direction. And since we can no longer reach Heaven, it reverses and flows back downward and below zero, in the negative direction (towards Hell). Many may remember this wave from math class, or by working with power systems instruments that diagnose electrical power issues within electronic devices, which reveal this waveform before your eyes. However, you will never learn this truth about the Sine wave in textbooks like you will in the Word of God.

Since Genesis 3:1 identifies Satan as a serpent, ironically, a sine wave resembles a serpent in shape or form. In mathematics, sine wave equations can model many real-life scenarios. Visually, an ideal sine wave is an S-shaped, smooth wave that oscillates (moves up, down, or side-to-side) above and below zero. This wave is the source that carries sound, radio, and television waves, tides/tidal waves, and musical tones through the air. It produces electrical currents that supply energy to energize all of our electrical systems and electronic devices.

God's light waves are emitted in units of frequency to meet our eyes and ears, as we listen to the radio, television, and all media. But be careful what you listen to and watch on TV, and monitor what you allow to penetrate your spirit and your children's, because you have an enemy that never sleeps. The former Light Bearer is called the Prince of Power of the Airways: *"...according to the prince of the power of the air, the spirit that now worketh in the children of disobedience" (Ephesians 2:2).* His elite reportedly

A CLOSER LOOK AT LIFE AND DEATH

determines and controls what you see and hear and who gets to the top in the entertainment industry, as well as who will receive one of his stars on Hollywood Boulevard based on those who are willing to pay and/or compromise their Soul.

[**Side Note**]: Recall that God associates us... His children, as **"Stars,"** Lucifer was called the **"Morning Star,"** and in ***Revelation 22:16,*** Jesus is referred to as *"**The Bright Morning Star.**"* Also, there was a specific star that was associated with the birth of Jesus, which is called the **"Star of Bethlehem."** Again, Satan copies everything that God does; therefore, he has his own stars. God calls Satan **"the great dragon" (Revelation 12:9);** thus, you see the Red Dragon displayed on the front of the Grumman Chinese Theatre in Hollywood, CA, with his stars beneath him along the sidewalk. There is always a price to pay in Hollywood to reach the upper echelon of fame. [**end**]

In school, I was taught about the sine wave and worked with it during my career as an Electrical Engineer; however, I never thought about it in this manner until I received the Holy Spirit's wisdom and revelation associated with writing this book. I am truly amazed and thankful for what God is sharing with you through me.

To harness God's Light Wave Energy, so that it becomes visible to our eyes, Sine wave energy is captured utilizing an oscilloscope that displays the continuous wave form on a monitor that uses backlit LED technology so that we can see the wave in the darkness of the Abyss. In school, I was taught about the sine wave... how to graphically draw and analyze them based on certain parameters over time and to do trigonometry calculations to find heights, distances, and angle measurements. Sine waves are also used to analyze sound and tune instruments, model economic and financial data that exhibit cyclic or periodic behavior. Sine waves are the foundation of quantum mechanics and are used to solve the Schrödinger equation, which describes how quantum systems evolve over time.

During my career as an Electrical Engineer, I used sine waves to calibrate electrical equipment, to write and solve mathematical equations within computer programming languages, etc. However, I never thought about the sine wave as using God's Light to solve, analyze, and discover answers that solve real-world matters for the betterment and advancement of mankind. Ironically, they don't teach you about that part in school… Hmm. I received the Holy Spirit's wisdom and revelations in correlation to writing this book. I am truly amazed and thankful for what God is sharing with me in order that I may share His knowledge, as applicable to my real-life experiences, with you… **Glory!**

The former Light Bearer's spiritual method of operation is built into the sine wave or light wave energy as it is used to broadcast radio, television, and broadband (internet) straight to our eyes and ears. Satan's frequencies are below zero. The airways allow him to plant his cunning words of deception and his doctrines of lies (serpent, secular, pagan energy) to persuade and convince individual belief systems against God's righteousness. So, who owns the media companies? The answer will reveal the allegiance of those whom the former Light Bearer has placed in high-ranking positions within his secret societies and religious organizations.

Sin causes deterioration of the body, mind, and Spirit. The body ages and experiences illnesses, aches, and pain. Sin causes suffering for believers and unbelievers because we are all sinners due to our disobedience that had already transpired in Heaven. Our fallen Spirits, which encompass our mental state or mentality, manifest within our thought life and derivative actions to cause adverse outcomes in our lives, plus adverse medical conditions. The effects of death weigh on us like the heavy cross that Jesus carried up to Calvary to die for our sins.

Inherently, a sinner's Spirit Energy deteriorates through various life circumstances, including depression and other conditions that lower our vibration. Everything that sinners create, or build deteriorates… structures, technology, infrastructure, equipment… everything! Nothing we do or create on this fallen Earth lasts forever or is sustained to eternity, but our words do last for all eternity. Recall that our word is the only thing that we are born with, and it is the only thing that we leave here with, so that our words can and will be judged against God's truth. Therefore, I reiterate that our Spirit, which encompasses our word, is the only thing that is eternal.

During the end times, the Lord says, ***"The coming of the lawless one [Antichrist] is according to the working of Satan, with all power, signs, and lying wonders, and with all unrighteous deception among those who perish, because they did not receive the love of the truth, that they might be saved. And for this reason, God will send them strong delusion, that they should believe the lie"*** (2 Thessalonians 2:9-11). Furthermore, ***"Just as they have chosen their own ways, and their soul delights in their abominations, so will I choose their delusions, and bring their fears on them; Because, when I [your Creator] called [you], no one answered, When I spoke, they [you] did not hear; But they [you] did evil before My eyes…"*** (Isaiah 66:3).

This is a stark warning from your Creator to all unbelievers! In these **"Last Days,"** strong delusion is the result of God completely removing Himself…His Holy Spirit, from the Earth, which is within all believers whom He Raptured, dead and alive. It is at this juncture that God turns you over to yourself…your will, and the lifestyle that you chose, hence you must suffer the consequences of His Divine wrath. Our descent into deception sinks us deeper into the Abyss of Hell. We cannot decipher what's true and what is a lie because what is right is now wrong, and vice versa.

We live in a state of chaos and confusion, ***"For God is not the*** *author of confusion but of peace...," Corinthians 14:33.* We are utterly deceived, however, the Bible explicitly tells us to see to it that we are not deceived, *"Let no one deceive you with empty words, for because of these things the wrath of God comes upon the sons of disobedience" (Ephesians 5:6).*

Unlike God, who is all-powerful, all-knowing, and omnipresent, Satan is not. He cannot be everywhere or omnipresent, or omniscient, all-knowing. So, his goal is to create this ability for himself, utilizing computer technology within his autocratic Beast System. He has guided man to create massive computer systems and databases to collect and store information about all of Earth's inhabitants to establish total population control. Satan's all-knowing era will be a surveillance-driven technological totalitarian system centered around Artificial Intelligence and imagery that fulfills Revelation 13. Since he does not have a human body, creating his image is necessary so he can be worshiped.

Satan will select a human, the Antichrist (soon to be revealed), whom he will give power to rule and control his worldwide Beast System. The Light Bearer's goal is to totally control you and the entire world so that he, via his image, will be like God, and he will be all-knowing about all things and all people. So that, ultimately, he is worshiped by all. Halfway through the Tribulation, he will assert himself in the Third Temple (reportedly is prepared to be built in Jerusalem now) and proclaim himself to be God: *"He will exalt himself and defy everything that people call God and every object of worship. He will even sit in the temple of God, claiming that he is God" (2 Thessalonians 2:4, NLT).*

As you continue to read, you will see that God, for the purpose of redemption, has granted the former Light Bearer his wish to establish his own kingdom and to assert himself as God on Earth. Again, he has established his dark, sinful government over fallen humanity through deception, perversion, hate, fear, tribulation, death, Hell, and the grave. Life, as we know it, on Earth, will culminate with a one-world government and religious system, a final battle (The Battle of Armageddon), then all men being resurrected with the Book of Life being opened. Again, Satan and all unbelievers in Christ will receive their eternal punishment to end the 7,000-year redemption process: ***"And the devil that deceived them was cast into the lake of fire and brimstone, where the beast and the false prophet are, and shall be tormented day and night forever and ever" (Revelation 20:10).***

SATAN'S NUMBER (666):

The number 6 is attributed to man or sinners because man was created on the 6th day. The number 7 represents perfection, and since man is less than perfect, we fall just below perfection at the number 6. I also heard a pastor explain that man consists of body, spirit, and soul, and without the indwelling of the Holy Spirit within, man is only two-thirds of a man, 2 divided by 3 = .666; when God blew His breath into Adam, he became a living Soul as if his entire inner body is the Soul. The Soul is where your fallen Spirit resides with the selfishness of Satan's mindset, or *your Spirit = your selfishness*; hence, we are living in the "Selfie" generation. However, you can invite God's Indwelling Holy Spirit to dwell within your Soul. So, does our entire ***"Inner Body" = Soul?*** I believe so, but read Genesis 2:7 and see what you think.

Revelation 13:18 (NKJV) says, "Here is wisdom. Let him who has understanding calculate the number of the beast, for it is the number of a man: His number is 666." The mark will not be given in secret or unbeknownst to you; it will be received by your cognitive and verbal consent. This "buy and sell" mark system is similar to that of Emperor Julius Caesar of Rome, who required loyalty from his citizens by having them verbally recite a pledge.

I saw a video that explained the pledge: "In order to buy or sell

A CLOSER LOOK AT LIFE AND DEATH

in the Roman market, one needed to pledge allegiance to Caesar, and upon making this declaration, they would receive a mark on their right hand and forehead... There are a few paintings that depict this mark." Since God states that *"...there is no new thing under the sun," Ecclesiastes 1:9,* invariably, we will return to this same system on a global scale during the end times and last days.

The elite, dignitaries, entertainers, and all those aligned with the former Light Bearer show their allegiance through handshakes, logos, and gestures like those in the photos below:

Acronym wordplay: NASA = SATAN, the red tongue makes a "T" = Satan
https://ifunny.co/picture/never-told-oldyou-the-truth-nasa-hebrew-5377-nw-nasa-zolwcnrjb
The Above Photos Are from the Public Domain

The latter confirms that the alignment with the serpent and his number associated with the number 6 or "666" is real, according to

A CLOSER LOOK AT LIFE AND DEATH

the truth of the Bible. As you can see above, these logos are everyday fixtures in our society, but again, we don't pay attention even though they stare us in the face as truth. The elite use the number **666** to solidify their worship of Lucifer, but we pay it no mind, instead of realizing that what you are seeing is Satan ruling his fallen world and that he is real.

You have been deceived by the fairytale lifestyle of celebrities that many look up to, yet they cannot save you. You know nothing of the truth of God, nor do you care about God and His Holiness; you are shrouded in disbelief or simply don't care. However, it is time for you to **wake up** and take responsibility for your life, death, and eternal future because God (who is Jesus), Satan, Heaven, and Hell are real. Hell is as real as the logos and hand gestures that correlate to the number 666 as described in the Bible, as the number of "A Man," and this spiritual man is Satan. These facts are as certain as your death is to come.

Although there have always been Antichrists, there has been much speculation surrounding who might be the global, end-times, and last days Antichrist. Some believe that the Antichrist may come from the Middle East or the revived Roman Empire, however, the Author of the book *"The Antichrist and a Cup of Tea Charles, Prince of Whales Foretold,"* by Tim Cohen, points his finger at Prince Charles whose crowning ceremony, in 1969, was surrounded by pictorials of the Dragon and is also depicted on his Coat of Arms. King Charles III is now the new royal on the throne, and Cohen details many reasons to support his theory, including the English and Hebrew Gematria calculation of the name: Prince Charles, Prince of Wales, which he says equals 666. Also, he is King over the elite secret society members who hold the highest-ranked and most powerful positions worldwide within lower-order secret societies, corporations, the military, world health organizations, the arts, entertainment, banking institutions, and governments.

During the King's coronation ceremony on May 6, 2024, an enormous, red-hued, pale-faced portrait of the King of England was unveiled. And upon gazing at it, it begged the question: "Is he portraying himself as the devil?" Uncannily, King Charles III spoke and oversaw the 2022 Commonwealth Games in Birmingham, England, whereby a 10-meter bronze bull commanded center attention as the act of worship was displayed during the theatrical performance.

However, in the 2024 Paris Olympic Games, the opening and closing ceremonies were equally demonic. At the opening ceremony, the Olympic Committee portrayed Jesus and His disciples during the biblical depiction of **"The Last Supper"** with drag queens seated at the supper table, as well as other blasphemous scenes throughout the night. It was so blatantly offensive that, due to the outrage and complaints, they were forced to take down the video of the ceremony from their official website. Equally as demonic was the closing ceremony, which depicted the Antichrist being revealed to the world…WOW! Ironically, it was reported that later that night, Paris experienced a blackout across the city. God spoke… Hmm. Why is it that, instead of uplifting the true purpose of celebrating the enormous talents of athletes from around the world, Luciferins use large, televised events to display their allegiance to Satan? **It's Hell being in Hell!**

Throughout the ages, the elite have banished books that reveal the fact that we do live in Hell. They have purposely focused our attention on material things, sports, social likes, and prosperity, without mentioning Satan and Hell. However, unfortunately, we do live in Hell, where we see lies disguised as truth, destruction, tribulation, death, and satanic ceremonies, as well as companies, celebrities, politicians, and others showing their allegiance to Satan. Is it just a coincidence that Jared Kushner and his family reportedly own(ed) the 41-story building at 666 Park Avenue, New York, New York?

In regard to "buying and selling," the number 666 is already embedded within barcodes and QR codes associated with buying and selling goods. Earth is where you encounter Satan and the fallen part of yourself...your dark, sinful Spirit... your Shadow and your fallen body. Earth is where you experience tribulation, devastation, and death happening all around you at the hands of Satan. The latter doesn't happen in Heaven, as evidenced by you, me, and Satan being cast down to Earth. However, in this part of Hell, God has made His goodness available to us through Christ; He is our only hope or way out of The Second Death... you decide!

Recall that ***Matthew 24:37*** says, ***"as in the days of Noah, so shall the end times be, the Lord saw that the earth was filled with violence and that men were corrupt, and so the same is true now. So, like in the day of Noah, Man is corrupt, filled with violence [and doing unnatural things...killing each other, pornography, abortion, homosexuality, sex trafficking, unholy matrimony, etc.], and committing every evil...And the LORD said, I will destroy man whom I have created from the face of the earth; both man, and beast, and the creeping thing, and the fowls of the air; for it repenteth me that I have made them."*** However, it was Noah who pleaded with God not to destroy humanity from the face of the Earth.

When our vile behavior is coupled with receiving the mark of the beast and the altering of our DNA (for example, the mRNA Vaccine), whereby man will no longer be of the same human quality or state that God created, this means that man will not be able to be redeemed to eternal life with God, like the giants in Noah's day. As prophesied, the end times or when Christ returns will be as in the days of Noah: ***"But as the days of Noah were, so also will the coming of the Son of Man be"*** *(Matthew 24:37).*

WORSHIP TO THE IMAGE OF THE BEAST:

Sinner will be forced to worship Satan's image. Since God the Father is a Spirit and is not physically located in Earth's realm anymore, He has an Image which is you, in both Spirit and Bodily form. Satan is a Spirit but has no body; therefore, he must exist as an image in the Earth to propel worship unto him. He achieves this through computer technology, whereby he has always guided man's intellect in ways that allow communication with those who are in the darkness of the Abyss.

To live on Earth, you need a body to function; however, on the sixth day, when God made man, male and female, He gave them each a body, but did not fashion one for Satan. Satan could not create a human-like God; the closest he could only manifest through animals, like the serpent in the Garden. The closest he could come to creating humans is half-human, half-animal creatures. For instance, the god Dagon, half man and half fish, or a mermaid body (Yes, mermaids are real). However, since God said: ***"Let us [those in Heaven during the planning stage of God's redemption process] make man in our image, after our likeness," Genesis 1:26,*** meaning to make man in an image that can lead him towards truth and righteousness, complete with a Soul or Temple whereby the Holy Spirit can come to dwell within man.

Our Heavenly Father decided to create man in the image of Divine Order instead of leaving man in the image of Hell or to exist in a state prepared for eternal death with no need for a Soul, Temple within a Body, because there would be reason to invite Christ in, and no place for the Holy Spirit to dwell, thus no chance of man's redemption. It is in this state of existence that would allow our Spirits to burn forever in the Lake of Fire and Brimstone with no option to return to eternal life with God, ever again. Those are the only two options, according to **Deuteronomy 30:19**, that were available at the time that God was conversing with those in Heaven in Genesis 1:26. There are only two choices in our present Universe ...*God/Satan = light/darkness = good/evil = truth/lies = right/wrong*, and so on. Therefore, God created our bodies in His Holy Image, and He will never allow Satan to take on a body that is modeled in His Divine Image, EVER!

To save us, the Lord, used the human reproductive system for His Son to be born (the only way to enter Earth) as baby in a manger, not to be God but for the purpose of defeating death which presents eternal life for humans like you and me: ***"Since the children have flesh and blood, he [Holy Spirit] too shared in their humanity so that by his [Jesus] death he might break the power of him [Satan] who holds the power of death—that is, the devil—and free those who all their lives were held in slavery by their fear of death. For surely it is not angels he helps, but Abraham's descendants. For this reason, he [Jesus] had to be made like them [us], fully human in every way, in order that he might become a merciful and faithful high priest in service to God, and that he might make atonement for the sins of the people. Because he himself suffered when he was tempted, he is able to help those who are being tempted" (Hebrews 2:14-18, NIV).***

This is Divine Love to the nth degree, so that you don't have to experience a permanent second eternal death. During the grace period of redemption, natural death is a temporary state because the dead shall rise to either reward or judgment, but it is designed to be used as our pathway back to Heaven. So, it is eternal death that you must avoid, but it is contingent on your belief in Jesus Christ, which was designed to be your choice alone; no one can make this choice for you. Only you can examine God's truth against what is truly in your heart, in order to make your eternal decision. However, the Body or Temple, in which God would come to dwell within each of us, has to be Holy and Pure; the same is true regarding Jesus' bloodline or lineage. Again, Mary had to be pure as a virgin because nothing of God can be defiled. Thus, our body, which was created in God's Holy Image, could never be the habitation of unholy Satan, who would only defile it.

Also, the Holiness of the Father's Holy Word, as transcribed by many prophets, will remain intact forever, no matter how many may declare that the Bible has been changed, or certain scriptures have been removed or modified. No one can change Genesis 2:17 or Hebrews 9:27, which defines your death to come; therefore, until someone can disprove that they are NOT going to die, there is nothing to discuss regarding the truth of God's Word. If you believe that death is real, that would mean that His Word is true, then all of God's Word is true. Do you think that God cannot keep His Word of Truth Pure and Holy forever and ever? Think again…everything about God and everything that surrounds Him must be pure and Holy or be separated from Him.

Since God fashioned our bodies in His Image, Satan does not have a body, and consequently, is shut out of participating in living life within God's Divine Redemption Plan, on Earth, and why he is ineligible for eternal life with God, like you and I: ***"…none of them [His children] is lost, but the son of perdition [Antichrist]; that the scripture might be fulfilled" (John 17:12).*** Nevertheless, everyone in the Earth who is allowed to be born into a body, has the opportunity to receive eternal life back with God, except all unbelievers and the Antichrist whom Satan will yield his power to during the end times: ***"…and the dragon [Satan] gave him [the Antichrist, his image and his beast system] his power, and his seat, and great authority" (Revelation 13:2).***

The Body is key to the redemption process because the human body which houses our fallen Spirit, fell in the Garden, recall that it was at this juncture that God promised that He would send us a Messiah to save us as He spoke directly to the serpent in the Garden: ***"And I [God] will put enmity [strife] between thee***

[Satan/his church] and the woman [Christ/his Church], and between thy seed [Satan's children] and her seed [Christ's Children]; it [Satan's defeat] shall bruise thy head [on Calvary or Golgotha, a skull- shaped hill where Jesus' Cross was driven down into the ground thus crushing Satan's head/skull or mental state] and thou shalt bruise his heel [by nailing Jesus' feet to the Cross]" (Genesis 3:15), to save us from The Eternal Second Death.

In summary, the Bible is a book with various stories about sinners who are in need of a Savior, and it reveals our interactions with both Satan and God (who is Jesus) for the purpose of our redemption. This is why the Old Testament is ultimately used to prophesy and proclaim that God would send us a Messiah to set the stage for our two eternal choices (**Deuteronomy 30:19**). Subsequently, the New Testament follows with Matthew 1:1, the introduction of our Messiah… The Lord Jesus Christ. The New Testament goes on to reveal the birth and life of Jesus, and His death, which defeated death by His resurrection… The Good News that Reverberated Around the World!

The New Testament culminates with the fulfillment of the law and all the promises that God gave to our ancestors in the Old Testament through the coming of Jesus Christ. Therefore, the promised Messiah is introduced first so that God's Word, Genesis 3:15, would come from the written truth of the Bible, to life for our salvation. The final book, is the Book of Revelation, and is: *"The Revelation of Jesus Christ, which God gave Him [John] to show His servants—things which must shortly take place" (Revelation 1:1).* This book reveals our Universal History stating: *"I [Jesus = God's Word = God] am Alpha and Omega, the beginning and the end, the first and the last" (Revelation 22:13), "Behold, the days come, saith the LORD, that I will make a new covenant with the house of Israel, and with the house of Judah: Not according to the covenant that I made with their fathers in the day that I took them by the hand to bring them out of the land of Egypt; which my covenant they break...this shall be the covenant that I will make with the house of Israel;*

After those days, saith the LORD, I will put my law in their inward parts, and write it in their hearts; and will be their God, and they shall be my people...they shall all know me, from the least of them unto the greatest of them, saith the LORD: for I will forgive their iniquity, and I will remember their sin no more" **(Jeremiah 32:31-34).** As well, the Book of Revelation reveals our eternal future in Christ Jesus. It concludes with the coming of a New Jerusalem, as well a New Heaven along with a New Earth: *"And I saw a new heaven and a new earth: for the first heaven and the first earth were passed away; and there was no more sea" (Revelation 21:1-2), more later as the book series progresses.*

[Side Note]: Per the above, we are discussing the end of God's redemption plan on Earth, or the OMEGA. Recall the discussion in Chapter Two, where I questioned why Google and NASA shut down their high-level advanced project that integrated Quantum Computing with Artificial Intelligence? Interestingly, their project was computing with the intelligence of AI, and as a result, data was processed faster than any known device, providing answers to their quest for higher-level knowledge until their data started disappearing, causing system reboots with every effort. Thus, they could not retrieve higher-level, advanced information to realize their goal.

As a result, God revealed to them the OMEGA Code, the **OMEGA** pattern or symbol, or in other words, He is saying: "I am not allowing you to go any further because this is THE END of the finite knowledge that you so desperately seek from Satan." Therefore, every effort with every attempt yielded the OMEGA Code, **THE END... GOD SPOKE!** The authoritative work of the Lord caused the deletion of their data and a hard reset of their devices. **God** alone is *"the beginning and the end <u>AND THERE IS NO OTHER</u>" (Isaiah 45:13, Revelation 22:13).* Enough said!

Again, we are fast approaching the end of God's Divine Redemption Plan, with the ultimate, sole purpose of providing you and me a second chance to get right with God by choosing Christ for eternal life or default to eternal death, which is Hell and the eternal fires of the Lake of Fire and Brimstone. **OMEGA... "The end,"** is showing up everywhere, in our increasingly unsustainable atmospheric temperatures, catastrophic weather events, volcano eruptions, earth quakes, devastating fires, mudslides, plagues, diseases, hearts growing cold, corruption, wars and rumors of wars, violence, globalization of a one-world currency, one-world government/religious system, the opening portals, Christ-like persecution, etc. (Genesis 6, Matthew 24).

Furthermore, OMEGA is even showing up to Scientists and Engineers within their quest for secular knowledge to produce more advanced technology. The OMEGA pattern and symbol have been revealed, and when it shows up, it wipes out data and resets all systems so that data cannot be retrieved or questions answered from the darkness of the unseen realm, causing a complete shutdown. Again, God's Word is forever true; no matter what man seeks to do, God is in complete control. Study these things for yourself! What more do you need to see God's Truth? It is staring you in the face. Therefore, it's decision time: Where do you choose to spend eternity? **[end]**

For the purpose of our redemption, Christ had to be born as a human to visibly show us His death and His return from the grave to retrieve His same Body, whereby at the command of the Living God in Heaven, Jesus was raised from the dead. Jesus, with His Human Body and Spirit intact, ascended into Heaven to be "Glorified," or His Human Body was made prepared to receive and dwell in the Glorious Divine Light of our Heavenly Father. After which, our Father sent down to us His Indwelling Holy Spirit (Christ), so that the fulfillment of *Colossians 1:27 NLT: "For God wanted them [us] to know that the riches and glory of Christ are for you...And this is the secret: Christ lives in you. This gives you assurance of sharing his glory."*

The fulfillment of the latter scripture gives each of you the ability to invite Christ to live within you, so when it is your time to be resurrected, at the command of God, the Indwelling Holy Spirit (Christ) will activate your resurrection from the grave. And upon your Rapture from the Earth or your Resurrection from your grave, your human body will be changed to an immortal, incorruptible body befitting of living life in the midst of God's Holy Divine Light, in Heaven, and in the restored Earth forever. Our spirits and bodies will follow the pattern of Jesus Christ, as one day, our bodies will be changed: "in a moment, in the twinkling of an eye, at the last trumpet. For the trumpet will sound, and the dead will be raised incorruptible, and we shall be *changed" (1 Corinthians 15:52)*. Jesus is our example!

Nevertheless, the only way that Satan can enter into a human body is by possession, whereby a person, knowingly or unknowingly, allows him into their life based on their thoughts, decisions, and actions; either way, it means that they do not have the Indwelling Holy Spirit (Christ) living within them. However, because of redemption, the only way for God's Holy Spirit to live within you is by invitation only; you must choose to ask or invite Christ to indwell within your **repentant heart**.

I hope that you can understand why Satan does not have a body. And since he does not have a body in this world, he will use Computer Technology to create for himself an image that has the power to be both audible and visible. The former Light Bearer's power manifests throughout the Earth through his technology. The Antichrist and Satan's image, the Son of Perdition, will be worshiped: ***"And they worshipped the dragon [Satan] which gave power unto the beast [system and Antichrist] He [Satan] was granted power to give breath to the image of the beast, that the image of the beast should both speak and cause as many as would not worship the image of the beast to be killed" (Revelation 13:15).*** The video below reveals a 10-story-tall giant sculpture (by The Giant Company) that reveals the chilling technology that seems to bring Revelation 13:15 into reality... WOW!

SLEEP:

Sinners are subject to sleep. However, there are various states of sleep, for instance, there is "Deep Sleep" that occurred to Adam when God took one of his ribs to create woman: ***"And the LORD God caused a deep sleep to fall upon Adam, and he slept: and he took one of his ribs and closed up the flesh instead thereof" (Genesis 2:22).***

Then there is **"Natural Sleep,"** which is designed to give us daily rest to rejuvenate us. However, when we sleep, we really don't know what goes on, spiritually, but we know that physically our bodies retire to rest. Doctors have studied human sleep to derive and establish various levels of sleep and/or patterns (REM sleep, deep sleep, Theta Sleep, etc.), and we know that humans experience dreams; however, we know nothing about what happens with our Spirit Life Energy while we are asleep. Since we are always attuned to or are connected to the two universal realms, here's a thought: Suppose that when you are asleep, your Eternal Spirit Energy, which is always in constant motion, continues to interact within either Heaven or Hell based on what you love to do during waking hours, righteousness or unrighteousness.

If you love the righteousness of God, then your heart's desire resonates and attunes with the frequencies of the goodness and the delights of Heaven, so your Spirit continues to live and do righteousness in the Holy Realm of Heaven. Consequently, if your heart desires to live a lifestyle that perpetuates evil, then as you sleep, your Eternal Spirit Energy resonates and attunes with the frequencies of Hell, whereby you live, dream, and act there; then you awake to consciousness ready to raise hell again in Earth's realm. What do you think?

Subsequently, there is **"Dream Sleep,"** a spiritual state that draws from the two eternal realms of Heaven and Hell, just like when we are awake in our limited body, because again, thought is spiritual. We are continuously sustained by these two realms for the sake of our redemption. Dreams pacify the carnal mind while the Spirit continues its never-ending existence... movement, consciousness, and functionality in the Spiritual realm that aligns with your character, lifestyle, or whatever you love to do, here on Earth. If you love to do evil, then your eternal Spirit continues to function in the darkness of Hell, and if you love to do righteousness through Christ Jesus, then your eternal Spirit continues to function within the realm of Heaven.

If you have gory, ghostly, or monstrous nightmares meant to torment you, which realm do you believe these dreams flow from? And consequently, when you sleep well and have peaceful, heavenly dreams, these flow from the blessings and protection of God, hence the phrase **"Sweet Dreams!"**

I remember one night, during my teenage years, I dreamed that I was running through a dense forest, and Satan was running after me, throwing fire at me and in my pathway trying to kill me, but I escaped his every attempt. Then I turned and looked back at him and said, "You are a defeated foe!" I then woke up. Dreams can be so obscure that you don't see the presence or face of someone, but you know exactly who you are interacting with. I say that to say that I could not tell what Satan looked like in my dream, but I knew that it was him. I attributed this dream to victory over Satan by Christ's resurrection, thus making Satan a **"defeated foe"** so that we do not have to fear death ever again.

Lastly, there is seemingly permanent sleep or **"Death Sleep"** as a result of Natural Death; I call it the **"Great Sleep."** This is the sleep state of the dead, like in a morgue, or anywhere a person is deceased. It is this sleep that is the shadow or representation of our permanent sleep called The Second Death (Revelation 20:10). It is the Sleep where you appear in your last posture or your state of being when you are found to have taken your last breath of God's air. In many cases, this is when you lie in your last pose, on Earth, as mourners come to view you to pay their last respects.

It is this "Great Sleep" that the disciples tell us ***"…we do not want you to be uninformed about those who sleep in death, so that you will not grieve like the rest, who are without hope. For since we believe that Jesus died and rose again, we also believe that God will bring with Jesus those who have fallen asleep in Him" (1 Thessalonians 4:13-14, BSB).*** Upon falling into this "Great Sleep," your sinful lifestyle or your **repentance** and professed belief in Christ will determine where your Eternal Spirit will transition to… Heaven or Hell.

War... We Are At War!

"...we do not wrestle [war] against flesh and blood, but against principalities, against powers...against spiritual hosts of wickedness in the heavenly places..."
~ Ephesians 6:12

Sinners are subject to war. The "Spiritual War" that began in Heaven established the definition of the word **"War,"** and every war is merely a shadow of the heavenly war. This war has also transcended to the mind of man, whereby our opposing thoughts (duality) are a result of spiritual warfare between God's Divine Light and Satan's demented darkness that he exerts over the human mind. Remember, close your eyes, what do you see? The darkness that you still are! Hence "...we do not wrestle [war] against flesh and blood, but against principalities, against powers...against spiritual hosts of wickedness in the heavenly places..." (Ephesians 6:12). Let that sink in again!

Since our fallen Spirit is now held within a fallen body, this spiritual war has transcended into Earth's physical realm. Man is made of both Spirit and Flesh, so that our same fallen Spirit carries our same sinful and rebellious nature that was demonstrated in Heaven but is now seen in the Abyss. Our fallen Spirit resides in a body and has the mental capacity to spiritually process thoughts from both realms, and our bodies include bones that are designed to endure everlasting Hellfire.

Therefore, the War in Heaven is, concurrently, being waged both in the spiritual realm of the mind of man and in the physical (Flesh) realm on Earth, where we carry out actions based on our thoughts. This war that began in Heaven will continue until it ends, in the Flesh, during the final battle between Jesus Christ and the former Light Bearer called **"The War of Armageddon" (Revelation 16:16).**

As a result, this war transcended into Earth's realm, whereas man is made of both Spirit and Flesh, so that our same fallen Spirit will carry our same sinful and rebellious nature that was demonstrated in Heaven and in the Abyss. Our fallen Spirit resides in a body and has the mental capacity to spiritually process thoughts from both realms, and our bodies include bones that are designed to endure everlasting Hellfire.

In preparation for this monumental war to take place, certain things must happen in the Spirit, for instance Jesus and His Raptured Saints will return from Heaven, as well as in the physical realm…the prominent River Euphrates will dry up to create the pathway, by land, for the King(s) from the East are able to travel by land to the battlefield called the Valley of Megiddo.

The **"War"** that we participated in Heaven set the definition for all wars wherever opposition is present. Recall that since thought is spiritual, the human mind reflects the duality that manifests as thoughts that equate to *light/darkness = eternal life/eternal death = good/evil = truth/lies = right/wrong = 1/0 (math and computer technology)*. The thoughts that we ponder originate from these two eternal realms of our Universe, which establishes opposition between Heaven and Hell. The war in heaven formulates our thought structure to produce thought life, or how our minds are designed to process thought. The conflict between our Spirit and the Flesh is reflected in our actions that first began as a thought. We act and react from thought, then we see the visible results in our physical world.

Our minds carry out this war through opposing thoughts that our minds ponder, which fuel our will and actions. Due to the Duality of our minds, we war within ourselves, we war against each other in relationships, and nations rise against nations. We are at War! Suit up with the full armor of God: **"…*take up the full armor of God, so that when the day of evil comes, you will be able to stand*** *your ground, and having done everything, to stand. Stand firm then, with the belt of truth buckled around your waist, with the breastplate of righteousness arrayed, and with your feet fitted with the readiness of the gospel of peace…take up the shield of faith, with which you can extinguish all the flaming arrows of the evil one. And take the helmet of salvation and the sword of the Spirit, which is the word of God. Pray in the Spirit at all times, with every kind of prayer and petition. To this end, stay alert with all perseverance in your prayers for all the saints" (Ephesians 6:13-18).* War/opposition is what fuels the chaos that we live in daily within the darkness of the Abyss of Hell. **It's Hell Being in Hell!**

We are living near the close of God's redemption plan… the End Times and last days of God's Grace Period of Salvation. The Bible tells us in Matthew 24 about wars and rumors of wars that will grip the entire world, with World War III being the catalyst that sets the stage to lead up to the final War of Armageddon at the Second Coming of Christ. If you have been paying attention to world news and noticed that Russia has come forth on the world stage to begin a series of wars at the behest of the Catholic Pope, that brings Ezekiel 38-39, or the Gog Magog War, which is written truth to life. Gog represents a person or leader, with Magog representing a land or nation. The **"Man"** is clearly Putin in the land or nation of Russia. Although "Man" represented by Russia, the Pope, the United Nations, the EU, or any nation or world leader may think that they are in charge of planning end-time events (or any events for that matter), it is quite the contrary.

God is in charge of Biblical Prophecy and all that happens on the Earth is in His complete control, as evident in *Ezekiel 38:3-4, "…the Lord GOD says: Behold, I am against you, O Gog…I will turn you around, put hooks in your jaws, and bring you out with all your army— your horses [planes, tanks, etc.], your horsemen [armored vehicles] in full armor, and a great company armed with shields and bucklers, all brandishing their swords [guns, drones, bombs, nukes or military equipment].* God makes it crystal clear who is in charge, and it is certainly not Satan, man, or any created being. He alone sets the events on His Divine Calendar and their timing whereby each event in biblical prophecy is used to reveal who is for the God of Heaven, represented by Israel, and who is against Him.

Modern-Day Persecution Of "The Christ-Like:" The Seven Noahide Laws

"If they have persecuted me, they will also persecute you"
~ John 15:20

Unbeknownst to us, the Seven Noahide laws are already in place worldwide in support of the persecution of believers in Jesus Christ. America will become an accessory of the coming Beast System or global New World Order with the Antichrist and his False Prophet at the helm, along with the public worship of the Image of the Beast. Therefore, it's One World Government will become shrewd and persecute the **Christ-like:** *"Remember the word that I [Jesus] said unto you, the servant [you] is not greater than his lord [God]. If they have persecuted me, they will also persecute you" (John 15:20).* In preparation for the persecution of the Christ-like, they will bring back the Guillotine, but more technically advanced, a now computer-based version called the **"Smart Guillotine"** that can precisely cut heads off with the click of a button… Next!

The laws to support the persecution of Christians are called the seven (7) Noahide Laws, which were quietly signed into law by George W. Bush Senior. These laws are based on the post-diluvian covenant God made with Noah and his descendants (Genesis 9:8-17) and are incumbent on all human beings; and their violators are subject to the death penalty. The Babylonian Talmud (Avodah Zarah 64b) interpreted the stranger to be all gentiles who accept the seven Noahide commandments, constituting the basic laws of morality that are punishable by death:

1. To worship God, not idols
2. Not to curse God
3. Not to commit murder
4. Not to commit adultery or sexual immorality
5. Not to steal

6. Not to eat flesh torn from a living animal
7. To establish courts of justice

The falsehood is, just like **"In God We Trust"** on the back of the American dollar bill, the word **"God"** refers to the former Light Bearer, and intolerance of worshipping any idol or god other than Satan will be punishable by death. The New Orleans legislature has passed a law to allow the Ten Commandments into public schools, and the Texas School System has passed a law to allow Chaplains into their schools. While this sounds like they are planning to bring the God of Heaven back into our school system…WRONG! The word **"God"** will be none other than the former Light Bearer, the man of lawlessness… the Son of Perdition, his image, his Beast System, his Antichrist, and the False Prophet.

In preparation for the persecution of the Christ-like, the development and the implementation of the computerized Smart Guillotine is already on display in the elite circles: "It was decided that all seven Noahide laws are capital crimes. Under Noahide law, one may be executed based on the testimony of one witness or a confession, and without a prior warning. According to one opinion, a criminal might be executed under Noahide law based on circumstantial evidence. According to Maimonides, non-Jews are required to establish a judicial system using the imposition of capital punishment.

It would appear, then, that American courts might be required under Noahide law to impose capital punishment for the violation of any one of the seven Noahide laws based upon one-witness testimony, circumstantial evidence, or a defendant's confession" (http://www.wikinoah.org/). They don't talk about this because the goal, as usual, is to suppress the truth. Do your research and pay attention to what is really going on; your eternal future depends on it.

A CLOSER LOOK AT LIFE AND DEATH

America: The Second Beast Turns Cruel

THE FIRST BEAST: *"And I saw a beast rising out of the sea, having seven heads and ten horns, and on his horns ten crowns, and on his heads a blasphemous name"*
~ ***Revelation 13:1 NIV***

THE SECOND BEAST: *"Then I saw a second beast coming out of the earth. It had two horns like a lamb, but it spoke like a dragon"*
~ ***Revelation 13:11 NIV***

  The First Beast rising out of the sea signifies the rise of a government… Satan's Government, rising out of the sea of the Abyss of Hell. And the Beast has seven heads, representing the entire world that consists of seven continents (Asia, Africa, Europe, North America, South America, Australia/Oceania, Antarctica), so when some say that America is not in the Bible, according to Revelation 13:1, America is one of the seven continents on Earth. The 10 horns and crowns represent the dominant world leaders during the end times and last days. Satan's government absolutely and completely hates God and is the global ruler of the Earth with a blasphemous name, like Satan. Upon the seven land masses, major empires will rise and rule on Earth. The First Beast has also been equated to the Roman Empire, which was the dominant governmental empire that is credited with the crucifixion of Jesus Christ.

  It is this empire that would have two separate rulerships during two separate times in Earth's History, according to King Nebuchadnezzar's dream (Daniel 4:18). The only person who could interpret the dream for the King was Daniel. He explained that the statute in the dream foretells each ruling empire or superpower that would come to exist and rule in the Earth, as well as the coming Kingdom of God that will descend from Heaven to destroy all earthly kingdoms. However, the portion of the statue that represented Rome was the statue's two legs, indicating two separate rulerships during Earth's History or two Beasts. The first Roman Empire that ruled during Christ's life on Earth would later become less dominant at the defeat of the French, who captured Rome and exiled the Roman Catholic Pope, which represents a "deadly wound." The territory and governance of the Papacy were eventually reduced to a small plot of land in Italy called Vatican City.

The resurgence of the Roman Empire would return during the end times and would be associated with the rise and fall of the United States of America and Mystery Babylon, the Second Beast: *"I [John] saw a second beast, coming out of the earth [or coming forth out of the land]. And I saw one of his heads as if it had been mortally wounded [the fall of Rome/Papacy], and his deadly wound was healed [Second rule of Rome/Papacy]. And all the world marveled and followed the beast. So, they worshiped the dragon who gave authority to the beast; and they worshiped the beast, saying, "Who is like the beast? Who is able to make war with him?" And he was given a mouth speaking great things and blasphemies..." (Revelation 13:3-5).*

America is the last continent to rise to superpower status in the Western part of the Earth, and therefore, is purportedly called the Second Beast: *"...I saw another beast coming up out of the earth, and he had two horns like a lamb [seemingly Christ-Like] and spoke like a dragon [became shrewd or cruel like Trump separating mothers from their babies at the southern boarders]. And he exercises all the authority of the first beast [Roman Papacy] in his presence and causes the earth and those who dwell in it to worship the first beast [Roman/Papacy], whose deadly wound was healed. He performs great signs [Project Blue Beam], so that he even makes fire come down from heaven on the earth in the sight of men. And he deceives those who dwell on the earth..." (Revelation 13:11-14).*

As the AI Beast System ramps up, more unprecedented adverse behavior will ensue, like deporting non-citizens and citizens, do away with free speech, cut programs to help the poor, take their income, put citizens in detention centers, militarize the police, utilize robots for law enforcement, persecute believers in Christ, etc., and eventually the enforcement of the worship of the image of the Beast. America's behavior under President Donald Trump aligns with Bible Prophecy in that the Second Beast (America) will turn power over its citizens to the First Beast (Rome). The 1.4 billion global Roman Catholic Church parishioners will be led by the False Prophet and the Antichrist to worship the image of the beast.

As I write presently, we see the framework of this happening now because we have two empires clashing, the Western World's New World Order or the deep state that President Donald Trump is currently dismantling, and the Revived Roman Empire (Vatican/Putin); President Trump is with Rome. Ironically, the passing of Pope Francis brought about the election of the first American Pope, Robert Prevost, from Chicago, Illinois, on May 8, 2025. The emergence of Pope Leo XIV, on the balcony, is certainly befitting of Revelation 13:15... Hmm.

America's **"Cruelty"** is becoming more prominent as President Trump's quest for dictatorship through militarization of the police force will lead to the coming worship of the image of the beast, the Antichrist, his Beast System, and the False Prophet. Perhaps the new American Pope Leo XIV, who for the first time brings the United States and Vatican City into extremely close ties, for a reason. President Donald Trump is shrewd enough to do what the elite wants him to do, along with the complicity of both congressional parties.

A CLOSER LOOK AT LIFE AND DEATH

Also, gun violence is prevalent under the guise of the Constitution's Second Amendment, which gives citizens the right to bear arms. So, when this amendment is coupled with the purposeful influx and influence of alcohol and drugs, it creates the foundation of the elite's agenda to become the bedrock of gun violence through lobbyists like the NRA, who have Congress in their back pocket. And no matter how parents and citizens protest, calling for gun control, the lawless lawmakers continue to expand Satan's **"killer"** agenda by making military-grade assault weapons readily available to the public. Some states allow open gun carry with no gun permits required, like in the Wild, Wild West. Then they hunt down the perpetrators that they enable, and then put them in jail. They create the chaos, and subsequently, enforce a solution for what should have never happened in the first place… sinister!

At this juncture, what we have is two empires clashing, the Western World's **"New World Order"** (Trump calls them the deep state or shadow government) and the "Revived Roman Empire" (The Vatican/Putin), and President Trump is with Rome. Therefore, he is dismantling the United States Government and is performing a controlled demolition of the American economy. Now, per their agenda, mass shootings, terrorism, people of color killing each other, racial profiling, police officers getting away with killing minorities, the mass killing of school children, police brutality, gang violence, etc., are the norm. Ironically, gangs started as a means to protect their neighborhoods, but they were later infiltrated to purposely create rivalry and opposition between gangs in various neighborhoods. The *"man of lawlessness," 2 Thessalonians 2:8-9*, is clearly amongst us, and things will only get worse as he brings idolatry, blood sacrifices, the persecution of the Christ-like, and worship of himself into mainstream. **It's Hell Being in Hell!**

Subsequently, the Second Beast will turn power over to the first beast, the revived Roman Empire…the Papacy, the Antichrist, the

False Prophet, and the Beast System: *"The second beast [America] was given power to give breath [life] to the image of the first beast [Rome], so that the image could speak and cause all who refused to worship the image to be killed" (Revelation 13:15).* Ironically, the United States...the Second Beast will fall due to its overt unholiness before God. The New World Order will assert the image of the beast so that citizens are forced to worship Satan, or they will be killed. *All who dwell on the earth will worship him, whose names have not been written in the Book of Life of the Lamb slain from the foundation of the world" (Revelation 13:8).*

All of Earth's global citizens must accept the "Mark of the Beast" or be killed and be mandated to take vaccines, be surveilled, and honor the coming Sunday Law for worship of the image of the beast. I can envision the Giant Company's 10-story statue being introduced in America as a new state-of-the-art form to enjoy and later morph into a dictatorship image of the beast, along with the revelation of the Antichrist. Then the Second Beast will yield United States worshippers over to the Pontiff's control.

"Mystery Babylon," alluded to *Revelation 17:5,* some believe this equates to America or the Nation with a female statue called the Statue of Liberty, a gift from the country of France, which defeated Rome. The mystery is the co-mingling of nations on a global scale who drink from her cup of iniquities throughout the world's economics and politics: *"The woman [the country symbolized by the Statue of Liberty (Woman = God's Church; Satan = The Corrupt Church = America and Global Mystery Babylon)] was arrayed in purple and scarlet, and adorned with gold and precious stones and pearls, having in her hand a golden cup full of abominations [detestable] and the filthiness of her fornication [intimate corrupt financial dealings with unholy world governments, like we see happening today as President Trump is pimping out the Whitehouse by giving meetings and* *business deals to the highest bidder]. And on her forehead a name was written: MYSTERY, BABYLON THE GREAT, THE MOTHER OF HARLOTS [PROSTITUTES] AND OF THE ABOMINATIONS OF THE EARTH. I [John] saw the woman, drunk with the blood of the saints and with the blood of the martyrs of Jesus" (Revelation 17:4-6).* The Babylon of old (modern-day Iraq) will return to reclaim its title on a global scale: *"They spend their days in wealth, And in a moment go down to the grave" (Job 21:13).* **[Side Note]:** The word "Women" represents God's Holy Church through Jesus Christ and the duality is Satan's corrupt church, whereby he is worshipped. However, once Christ comes to remove His Church from the Earth at the First Resurrection and Rapture, then "Woman" refers to Israel (Revelation 12:6): *Women = Israel.* **[end]**

China will soon replicate its authoritarian Beast System with face and right-hand recognition, a citizen surveillance-based behavior score system, and a one-world digital currency that will replace all fiat. I understand that there will be a system in place that will replace America's current credit score system, which will be called a Social Score (currently called Behavior Score in China). It is a system that will quickly evolve into a more robust global totalitarian system. It will combine an individual's behavior score (online) with their criminal, credit history, vaccine status, surveillance, global ID, and monetary use tracking…. a global cashless society.

During the end times, America, along with the revived Roman Empire, the Antichrist, and the False Prophet, will institute the Beast System and will begin the persecution of the Christ-like.

THE SERPENT:

Because God denied Satan (and many of his angels) a human body to participate in His redemption plan, Satan could only manifest in the Garden, on Earth, as an animal.

The Vaccine (Snake Bite)

"The serpent was more cunning than any beast of the field"
~ ***Genesis 3:1***

The former Light Bearer manifested in the Garden of Eden as a serpent. The serpent is described as the most cunning of all, meaning sly, tricky... a liar. After lying to Eve, which resulted in the fall of man, the serpent was cursed to crawl on the ground, so again, God's Holy Word holds true, as evident every time we see a snake crawl. Ironically, since the 16th Century, a serpent appears in official government emblems, a staff with two snakes and some with one snake coiled around it, called a caduceus. However, we never pay enough attention to question its origin and significance. Many Public Health Services, as well as other nations and world organizations, use this symbol. You may notice the caduceus displayed on the emblems, signs, flags, etc.

The caduceus, or the stick down the center, represents the magic wand carried by the god Hermes (known by the Romans as Mercury), the messenger of the gods. Therefore, we can see the covert allegiance to the Light Bearer. **[Side Note]:** It is said that the magic wand is made from the wood of a Holly Tree, hence the word, **"Hollywood,"** which adorns a mountain top in Hollywood, California… Hmm. [**end**]

Of course, snakes with venom are poisonous and deadly, which personifies Satan's character, so let's take a closer look at the ingredients that make up venom or Satan's other attributes. Snake venoms are a complex mixture of enzymes, proteins, amines, lipids, nucleosides, and carbohydrates. Snakes inject venom. Let's take a closer look, venom contains various metal ions that are presumed to act as cofactors, and include sodium and calcium, potassium, magnesium, and zinc. Satan's cunning ways are the same today as they were in the Garden of Eden, as he sought to get something (food from Satan's tree) into the body of man, or in this case, Eve's body, to change the state of her molecular **DNA**, which caused man to fall. In the Garden, he wanted to "inject" the forbidden fruit or get Eve to ingest the fruit because Satan knew that God told both Adam and Eve not to touch or eat, and he succeeded. We fell to sin yet again in our flesh and were then removed from the presence of the Lord, for the purpose of redemption.

This same scenario is once again taking place as the execution of Satan's death penalty is fast approaching. Now, during the end times, due to the push for worldwide total population control through the Beast System, Satan desires to get his metallic characteristics into our bodies through chemtrails, water systems, implants, or other advanced technology. He has guided man to create "The Internet of Things," so that everything and Everybody can be connected, activated, or deactivated at the control of the Antichrist and his AI computer matrix. To accomplish this, **CERN,**

Big Tech, spearheaded by Bill Gates' ID2020 with their agendas, are in place to serve their roles with the implementation of 5G technology hardware infrastructure (Satellites, Cellular Towers, Alexa, Ring Doorbells, Embedded Chips or Metals within Humans, etc.) that will lead to 6G technology with worldwide advanced AI software running **"The Internet of Things."** Google it.

I am not saying that the current vaccine is the Mark of the Beast, but it is definitely a precursor that lays the groundwork for it. ID2020 vaccine technology is designed to place a special metal called a Quantum Dot Metallic Digital Dye Tattoo, Graphite, etc., into us, underneath the skin, through an administered vaccine. The Quantum Dot is one way to make us connectable to the WWW, like your cell phone and other devices. ID2020 is a Certification Mark that, according to pymnts.com, utilizes "immunization to serve as a platform for digital identity" using a Quantum Dot Digital Tattoo implanted within us through vaccine technology. Gates says the mark is for vaccination tracking, but it will ultimately make us an Internet-connected device. Also, notice that Luciferins, who use color codes, signs, symbols, and gestures, associate the colors yellow and blue with the vaccine advertisement, and ironically, these same colors are associated with the country of Ukraine, their flag... Hmm.

The Quantum Dot Tattoo, delivered with vaccine technology, is a type of Luciferase enzyme or Luciferase Bioluminescence Technology, named after the former Light Bearer, which emits light, similar to a firefly. Satan's light comes from that which he creates through man, like the invention of the back-lit screen, which is evident in televisions, computer monitors, cell phones, etc. The vaccine delivery system consists of micro-needles and a digital identification mark, in the form of a dye underneath the skin, creating a tattoo that can be detected with special light and/or scanners. These quantum dots emit near-infrared light that can be

A CLOSER LOOK AT LIFE AND DEATH

detected by a smartphone equipped with an app.

Those who do not take this mark, in their hand or forehead, will not be able to buy and sell goods (Revelation 13:17). Another possibility of metal suitable for injection or conductive ink tattoos on or under the skin is graphite to create the "Mark." These types of technologies or something similar will be used to create the **"Mark of the Beast,"** and we will be forced to make a conscious and verbal decision to take this mark under the coming Beast System.

CERN, in conjunction with universities around the globe, has identified what they call the **"God Particle,"** called the Higgs Boson, and they have also identified the **"God Gene,"** called Vesicular Monoamine Transporter 2 (VMAT2). This gene is in the frontal portion of our brain and may be associated, in some way, with the Pineal Gland. The Pineal Gland is a pinecone-shaped gland located in the center of our forehead, which cannot be duplicated. It is commonly called **"the third eye,"** which connects us to the spirituality of God. Consequently, the VMAT2 gene is also known as **"the God gene."** The VMAT2 gene affects the frontal lobe area of the brain that deals with your emotions and your spiritual connections to the Creator. Therefore, the VMAT2 gene is what COVID-19 vaccines are designed and engineered to attack. These vaccines are called mRNA or messenger Ribonucleic Acid in nature.

This is the technology that is used to weaken this gene or our spiritual connection with God, within us. This is an abomination before the Holy God of Heaven that is effectuated through the mRNA vaccines and continuous booster shots designed to weaken and eventually destroy this gene, over time, and will break our spiritual connection with God. Due to the significant change to the natural state of Human DNA by mRNA vaccines, the United States Supreme Court ruled that people who receive mRNA vaccines are no longer human or **"transhuman,"** WOW!

There was a 2013 court ruling in the case Pathology vs. Myriad Genetics, INC. (use your phone to scan the QR Code for more information). The court stated that if the human genome is modified by mRNA vaccines, it has been removed from the internet in order to hide the truth. mRNA vaccines are widely in use now, so the changed genome can be patented, meaning that you are now a **"thing"** and no longer a person.

Of course, some medical professionals have objected to the court ruling. However, we know that humans are not patentable; only inventions, designs, or items for sale are patentable. So, as a transhuman, all you need is your **"Mark"** on your hand or forehead as foretold in Revelation 13:7; therefore, you are ready for the beast system. Accepting the mark will render you humanless or no longer human according to God's design and specifications; hence, you are unfit to be saved by the Lord's redemption process. It is Satan's goal to steal, kill, and destroy YOU! However, his prime target is our children... keep reading to explore more on this subject. Like in the Garden of Eden and in the days of Noah, Satan now seeks to alter human DNA by ensuring that the population's genomes are manipulated through various techniques and vaccines, the pineal gland is destroyed, metal implants, etc.

He wants your DNA to be altered, along with receiving his coming **"Mark,"** so we will be rendered fit for his system and unfit to gain your eternal life back with God! If he can get the adults to fall for his agenda, it's much easier for him to get to your children.

There is a method to Satan's mad scientist mindset that seeks to counter God's plan for your good and deliverance and destroy you. Satan, through his elite, has always sought to destroy our Pineal Gland within our brain, which is our connection to God. Furthermore, the Dragon has a history of trying to attack our Pineal Gland; he has guided man to utilize our drinking water, toothpaste, mouthwash, dental cleanings, etc., by using the ingredient called fluoride, which causes calcification. Calcification occurs when calcium salt deposits build up within soft body tissues and cells that contain DNA, to harden and/or destroy them. This agenda, like the mRNA vaccine agenda, seeks to target and destroy that which God created as a direct connection link between you and your Heavenly Father.

By affecting or destroying the Pineal Gland with calcium build up, it allows the former Light Bearer's agenda to disrupt you both spiritually, as well as physically, by affecting your health…your sleep cycles, melatonin production, neurologically, fertility, etc. Think, it's a game if you want, but you are under spiritual and physical attack by God's enemy, which makes Satan your enemy, who, for the sake of creating choice within the Lord's redemption plan, has been allowed to establish his government on Earth. Therefore, again I suggest that you do your own research to determine if what you believe is fact or fiction before your certain date with death.

The Bible reveals that there will be signs in Heaven or the sky, and of course, the copycat… Satan will use Satellites and Drone Technology within Project Blue Beam to create lying wonders in the sky. However, God defines His signs that include the sun, stars, moon, and constellations that foretell certain events, warning indications, and display future things to come, in our night's sky, for instance: **Revelation 12:1, "And there appeared a great wonder in heaven [Sky]; a woman clothed with the sun, and the moon under her feet, and upon her head a crown of twelve stars:"** This sign was reportedly seen in the sky on September 23, 2017. ***Revelation 12:3, "And there appeared another wonder in heaven [Sky]; and behold a great red dragon, having seven heads and ten horns, and seven crowns upon his heads."***

This sign foretells Satan's plan whereby he will guide the world leaders to a one world system, seven heads…seven continents, ten horns = 10 nations (The European Union, United Nations, BRICS, or others; crowns upon their heads…kingdom rulership over specific areas or nations leaders. These signs are taking shape now, during these end times. Some constellations in the Sky have a constant, cyclic pattern. There are approximately 48 constellations, 12 of which are zodiac constellations that are meant to reveal the 12 roles of Jesus Christ:

CONSTELLATION	NAME	ROLE OF CHRIST
1. Maiden	Virgo	Messiah
2. Scales	Libra	Redeemer
3. Scorpion	Scorpius	Judge
4. Archer	Sagittarius	Savior
5. Sea-Goat	Capricornus	Great Sacrifice
6. Water Bearer	Aquarius	Lawgiver, Master
7. Fishes	Pisces	High Priest, Holy One
8. Ram	Aries	Resurrection
9. Bull	Taurus	Lord of Hosts
10. Twins	Gemini	Son of God
11. Crab	Cancer	Deliverer
12. Lion	Leo	King of Kings

A CLOSER LOOK AT LIFE AND DEATH

Ironically, my zodiac sign is Libra. I find it very interesting that Libra is associated with **"Redeemer,"** whereby the Lord has called me to write this book about Him as the Redeemer and to detail His plan of redemption…Wow! The number 12 is associated with the "complete" 12 tribes (all of God's people), Jesus' 12 disciples, 12 months in a year, which completes time for each year. However, the appearance and some will appear at certain points in Earth's History, like the Revelation 12:1 sign. Also, there are Blood Moons that appear in stages of four (4) consecutive Blood Moons, called a Tetrad. Each of the four Blood Moons coincides with Jewish Feast days and is said to be a sign for Israel and the Jews; Lunar Moon Eclipses are said to be a sign for Gentiles. However, the Sky declares Jesus as King of Kings and Lord of Lords.

The constellation below caught my attention as it directly relates to the coronavirus and the serpent narrative above.

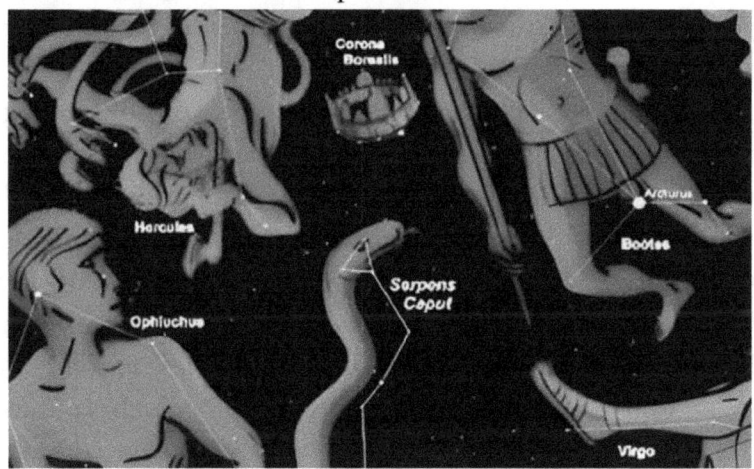

www.bestdoubles.wordpress.com

Notice the Serpent Bearer or the constellation of the man intertwined with a snake. Above the snake's head is a crown called "Corona Borealis," meaning Northern Crown. The name of the crown is called Corona, so with it being over the head of the snake, it intrigues me to wonder if they pulled the name **"Coronavirus"** from out of the Sky. Could the name of the virus be associated with the Constellation Corona Borealis, relative to a snake being connected to the disease that now plagues us? That could not be just a coincidence. Coronavirus is also molecularly similar to the common cold, which has been without a cure or vaccination since we have been alive on this planet. Is the Sky revealing something to us in these end times?

Perhaps they have taken our lifelong enemy… the Common Cold, and weaponized it, knowing that there is no cure. The Coronavirus has been with us forever, as it is a component in the molecules of the common cold; however, we have never been able to create a vaccine against it. Some Scientists have revealed that it takes years of research and testing on animals and the population. However, due to **Satan = Sorcery = Phramakeia (Greek) = Pharmacy = Drugs = Vaccine = "Operation Warp Speed,"** we are supposed to have created, tested, and implemented a vaccine for the coronavirus in 12 months or so…Really?

The Greek word **Pharmakeia** is the root word of the English word **"Pharmacy."** Pharmakeia is **"Sorcery"** which appears in Galatians 5:19-21, *"Now the works of the flesh are evident, which are: adultery, fornication, uncleanness, lewdness, idolatry, sorcery, hatred, contentions, jealousies, outbursts of wrath, selfish ambitions, dissensions [disputes], heresies [contrary to religion], envy, murders, drunkenness, revelries, and the like;"* and as well Sorcery is also **"Witchcraft"** which appears in *Revelation 18:23, "Babylon [and Mystery Babylon (Revelation 17:5)…the end time, last days global Babylon] is described as deceiving all the nations by her witchcraft."* **Pharmakeia** is a term that refers to the administration of drugs, Poisoning, Potions, Spells, and Witchcraft. Of course, not all drugs are used for this purpose; the duality of drug use is their use for the good of mankind, but consequently, those with Satan's mindset are using them to harm or kill you.

In the Bible, pharmakeia is related to occult and pagan worship practices. It suggests various forms of drug abuse, such as using drugs in pagan worship, addiction, the use of poison to kill, manipulation to control others, and using substances to alter a person's perceptions, which are acts of unrighteousness within the Kingdom of God. Therefore, you must think, pray, test the Spirit, and research… stop continuing to fall for Satan's lies! When did you or your children become guinea pigs for vaccines?

During the course of a vaccine's development, there are years of testing, including both animal and human specimens that yield volumes of data to be submitted to the **FDA** for rigorous analysis before approval. However, now we only have an Emergency Use Authorization (EUA) without any proven data. In fact, the data that Pfizer must provide had to be forced into the public domain through a FOIA (Freedom of Information Act) request, filed by Public Health and Medical Professionals for Transparency in the fall of 2021. However, it is reported that the data presented by Pfizer, per the request, had no numerical data to analyze and provided incomplete information. Also, it reported that the leaflets for the vaccine, which accompany the medication that is provided to the public to explain the ingredients, precautions, etc., are completely blank for the vaccine. What are they hiding? The Truth!

We were told that we would need one or two doses for adequate protection, but now we must take boosters whenever the W.H.O. requires it. They are now developing an international vaccine to force it on all humanity, and they desire to give health organizations, such as the W.H.O., etc., control over the population to usher in a global vaccine-based society. Therefore, please evaluate what you believe. Are you taking the vaccine because you are afraid of dying, or do you believe that through Christ, death has no hold on you, so you do not have to be afraid to die? I prefer to die through natural causes, whether it be COVID, a car accident, etc., not by bowing down to lies and fear. You can believe the government and these health organizations and do what they say, but still die anyway. However, you can't go back and change the fact that you believed their lies instead of the Word of God, right? Fear is Satan's same MO.

However, the most hair-raising information I have seen regarding the Coronavirus Vaccine is testimony by medical professionals who testified before the **Texas State Senate**, stating that they had to stop the testing of animal specimens because all of them had died. Therefore, the people who take the vaccine are now the guinea pigs.

In the end, everyone must make a choice to worship Jesus or Satan, the image of the Beast. If you choose to bow down to Satan, then you must do what the Beast tells you to do and say only what the Beast allows you to say. So, it is better to understand your choices now and make an informed decision while there is still time. The Lord warns us in *Matthew 24:4, "Watch out that no one deceives you!"*

The Ultimate Death Test

*"If anyone worships the beast and its image and receives its **mark** on their forehead or on their hand, they, too, will drink [receive] the wine of God's fury..."*
*~ **Revelation 14:9***

Death tests are nothing new; the first death test occurred in the spiritual realm of Heaven and caused us (Eternal Spirits) to receive an eternal death sentence and penalty, and we, subsequently, received the exact same death test which occurred in the flesh. In the Garden of Eden, God warned Adam and Eve not to eat of **"The Tree of the Knowledge of Good and Evil,"** or they would surely die. And of course, we failed or fell for Satan's lies instead of God's Truth.

Since then, death tests have continued to be brought into the forefront, which test us regarding situations that require the choice between life and death. For instance, during times we are in a position to choose to have an abortion or not, or in the case of Christians persecution, do we choose to give our life or bow down to authority, even plaques that require vaccines or anything that put your faith or your life in imminent danger, do you choose to stand firm on Christ or do you save your life by following the elite's protocols that force you to deny your belief in your Creator.

Death tests are designed to test your accountability to God based on your belief system when you are at the moment of facing death. You must decide if you will do what you want, which equates to doing what Satan or his elite, within his government, want you to do, like our ancestors, Adam and Eve did amongst the two trees in the Garden. The bottom line is that Life on Earth is about the choice between eternal life and eternal death, and more specifically, it is about your Eternal Second Death. **Do you fear death** even though Christ has taken the fear of death away from us by His resurrection?

Recall that the second chance that we have been given is solely for you to choose between eternal life and eternal death. Death tests are designed to test your belief in God and his provisions through Jesus Christ versus *Satan = self-centered man = you = your fallen from Heaven Spirit*, whereby your lifestyle choices lead to eternal life or eternal death. Nevertheless, life is about whether you believe God's Words or Satan's words, which are spoken by unbelieving men.

During the Pandemic or **"Planned-demic,"** death took the spotlight as death totals around the globe were broadcast to the masses as a result of the first planned, biomedical designed worldwide pandemic of Coronavirus aimed at beta testing total population control. The mounting death toll was plastered on the news as a constant reminder that life, here, is not eternal. However, many seem not to refer to what God said in ***Revelation 6:8, "And I looked, and behold a pale horse: and his name that sat on him was Death, and Hell followed with him. And power was given unto them [From Satan to the Antichrist and Beast System] over the fourth part of the earth, to kill with sword, and with hunger, and with death, and with the beasts of the earth."*** This prophecy has been around for eons, but we don't read and study so that, when these things come into our reality, we are not caught off guard, confused, or living in chaos and fear.

However, this is what the government and news media call **"Conspiracy Theory,"** and also the fact that they will blame the deaths associated with the rollout of 5G technology, with its high radiation, on the coronavirus. Reported on May 27, 2019 —"Wuhan, capital of Hubei, is one of the first pilot cities of the 5G network in China," (news.can). "The largest 5G network - CNN: Nov 1, 2019 — The country's [China] three state-run telecom operators launched services for the next generation of wireless technology on Friday." Then it is said that cases of the Coronavirus were reported soon after, but we are not supposed to be able to add

1+1 and get 2 because when the truth is hidden, it's a conspiracy theory, right? But we prefer to go along with the status quo, keep our heads in the sand, and be deceived.

We should be paying attention and figuring out how Revelation 6:8 and the First Commandment on the Georgia Guidestones in Elbert County, Georgia, USA, signify depopulation from seven (7) billion down to five hundred (500) thousand, will come true; more later. What is going on in the world that will inflict so much death on us? "What technology and health-related biomedical weaponry appear to be emerging on the scene to perpetuate our death?

At the end of 2024, it appears that the next pandemic could be the Bird Flu, affecting farmers whose chickens and cows are causing humans to become ill. This will cause food shortages, famine, higher prices, etc., that will lead to perilous times; Measles, Monkeypox, and others could be on the horizon. God warned us, and now that His Word is unfolding before our very eyes, we still allow ourselves to be deceived. The four horses of Revelation Chapter 6 are riding, the pale horse…death, is pandemically riding through our daily news feeds with ever-increasing intensity, worldwide.

Technology reveals the elite's agenda, for instance, vaccine technology during the pandemic that subjugated us to mandates and law changes. It is for you to test what your government is doing versus the Word of God so that you are not deceived; also, **FEAR NOT** because, in Christ, you have overcome the world that is destined for the eternal second death. Our belief system will be tested by choices that lead to eternal life or eternal death, just as we are in other endeavors. For instance, if we choose to pursue a career, we study and take tests to prove that we can pass the requirements to obtain the degree that we seek. Therefore, since we are here, on Earth, for a second chance at eternal life, our belief system will be tested to determine if our thoughts, choices, actions, or our lifestyle reflect our belief in Jesus Christ or not.

The premeditated planned pandemic with the genetically modified Coronavirus is designed to put the decision about death before you, relative to God's word, the test regarding who you truly love and believe. You probably don't look at this crisis in this way, but it is the same critical test that we failed in the Garden playing out repeatedly… do you believe the word of God or the word of a created being, human or fallen angel? It is this test that separates the sheep from the goats, the believers from the unbelievers, regarding the specific subject of death. Ultimately, it weeds out who will experience the second death sentence, which is eternal.

We may not want to believe it, but that's the way life goes. You must decide whether it is more important to accept what man (a created being) is offering you, i.e., to get your normal life back or a new and even better life. Perhaps they are offering you a solution or cure to aging and longevity, or their version of eternal life, OR will you accept what God (the Creator) is offering you…eternal life so that you do not have to experience eternal death or fear death ever again.

You are being tempted and tested by Satan just as Jesus was in the Garden of Gethsemane, where Satan offered Jesus the whole world if He would simply bow down and worship him: ***"…the devil took him to a very high mountain and showed him all the kingdoms of the world and their splendor. "All this I will give you,"*** he said, ***"if you will bow down and worship me." Jesus said to him, "Away from me, Satan! For it is written: 'Worship the Lord your God and serve him only." Then the devil left him, and angels came and attended him" (Matthew 4:8-11).*** However, one thing is for certain: Satan couldn't offer Jesus the whole world if it didn't already belong to him, right? So, now you know with certainty who rules this world…it's governments, the elite, and the media airways. This is why the Lord tells His believers in John 17:14-16, we are in the world, not of it. Please put your thinking cap on so that you won't be fooled out of your eternal life, yet again!

I know the vaccine can be a difficult conversation to have with others. Right now, it's completely your choice whether you take the shot or not, but it will become forced behavior. However, what you believe about death is a conversation that should be between you and God because only you will stand before Him to be held accountable to His Word, not your word or your feelings, and certainly not your friends or family's word, but God's Word… your Creator. There will be no one else around… just you and the Lord assessing your lifestyle.

We are not at the Mark of the Beast yet; the pandemic is a precursor; it is just the beginning of what is to come. The Word of God is telling you that an image of Satan will be presented to you to worship, and He is revealing and warning us of the consequences: "A third angel… said in a loud voice: ***"If anyone worships the beast and its image and receives its mark on their forehead or on their hand, they, too, will drink the wine of God's fury, which has been poured full strength into the cup of his wrath. They will be tormented with burning sulfur in the presence of the holy angels [Heaven's inhabitants and us, the redeemed from the Earth] and of the Lamb. And the smoke of their torment will rise forever and ever"*** *(Revelation 14:9-11).* He is telling you that there will be a strong deception of lies, signs, and wonders, so be forewarned! Prepare yourself not to be deceived by the false miracles that you may see. And that we all will be present to witness the fate of all unbelievers. **Follow the money and the technology!**

The ultimate death test and reasoning that your mind or your Spirit will ever face is whether to accept "The Mark of The Beast" or not. The answer to this question will be recorded in the heavenly books for all eternity, so prepare yourself now to stand up for your belief in Christ. When the mark comes, the world will be in perilous times, and you or your family may be without food or a place to live, which may cause you to give in to the pressure of the system, so you decide to take the mark. But once you take it and realize that you, once again, turned against God, it will be too late.

However, before your ultimate death test, you will encounter plagues, like the Coronavirus, Bird flu, etc., that cause death and suffering for the sake of your sins and rebelliousness, unless you are forgiven by your belief in Christ, which will transition you back to God upon your demise. The world is now at unrest on a global scale as never before, with increasing birth pains (Matthew 24) that manifest as mass protests erupt, oppression, forced control over society, civil unrest, wars, violence, catastrophic weather and fire events, hearts growing cold, corruption, a great falling away from God's truth and righteousness, etc.

This causes unparalleled worldwide frustration. Recall **Romans 8:14, 20-22, NIV: *"For those who are led by the Spirit of God are the children of God...For the creation was subjected to frustration, not by its own choice, but by the will of the one who subjected it, in hope that the creation itself will be liberated from its bondage to decay [Death] and brought [back] into the [eternal] freedom and glory of the children of God...We know that the whole creation has been groaning as in the pains of childbirth right up to the present time."***

And these birth pains will continue until the war that began in Heaven (spiritual realm) is completed in the Earth (physical realm)... **The War of Armageddon** (Revelation 16:16), because the composition of Man and God, as a Man... Jesus Christ, is made of both Spirit and Flesh. **<u>Jesus Christ will come back to Earth to rule and reign as King, in the glory of a Man, made of both Divine Holy Spirit and Immortal Eternal Flesh.</u>**

Therefore, you must seek Christ and know that you are at war!

Stand on His Truth as your shield, or you will continue to fall for Satan's lies. Truth must be your foundation, no matter what. Even if you have already taken the COVID shot(s), refuse them when you learn the truth of God's Word and become determined to stand on His truth, to the point that you would rather give your life like Jesus Christ gave His Life for you on the cross, rather than bow down to Satan's governmental Beast System. Resist in Jesus' mighty name... pray, remain strong in your faith that death has no hold over you through the risen Christ. Take heed to ensure that you are not deceived out of your eternal life!

DEPOPULATION

"And power was given unto them [Satan's Army] over the fourth part of the earth, to kill with sword, and with hunger, and with death"
*~ **Revelation 6:8***

The former Light Bearer and his elite's plans for depopulation are deeply rooted in Bible Prophecy, and their depopulation agenda is on display at the tourist attraction called the Georgia Guidestones in Elbert County, Georgia. The elite will follow Satan's plan to develop and implement his agendas: the climate change agenda, the gay agenda, the biomedical plague weaponry agenda, the mega-church agenda, etc. (Google them and **wake up!**), and his coming nuclear war technology agenda, lying signs and wonders or Space Force agenda, and all means to deceive and depopulate the Earth. Recall that Christ said, **"And unless those days were shortened, no flesh would be saved; but for the elect's sake those days will be shortened"** *(Matthew 24:22).*

Due to Satan's role within God's redemption plan, He is given authority to kill those who do not accept His grace and mercy that He created through Jesus Christ, therefore, Satan has the right to portray the authenticity of his character… steal, kill and destroy: **"And I looked, and behold a pale horse: and his name that sat on him was Death [Satan], and Hell followed with him [Satan]. And power was given unto them [Satan's Army] over the fourth part of the earth, to kill with sword, and with hunger, and with death, and with the beasts of the earth"** *(Revelation 6:8).* **"So, the four angels [bound under the River Euphrates], who had been prepared…were released to kill a third of mankind"** *(Revelation 9:15).* **"By these three plagues [nowadays: Coronavirus, Bird Flu, etc.] a third of mankind was killed —by the fire and the smoke and the brimstone which came out of their mouths"** *(Revelation*

9:18).

These scriptures reveal what happens to those who have completely removed themselves from God, and therefore, He turns them over to their wickedness and respective consequences. Even now, violence, weather, earthquakes, or natural disasters cause death and destruction to destroy the wicked, while the Lord protects His own. God has given Satan the authority within His Divine Redemption Plan to hurt and kill humans based on unbelief in Christ. Therefore, these scriptures are the root cause of why Satan and his elite have depopulation goals that support the above scriptures. We must analyze what the elite do, follow the money, especially in the context of Climate Change, and be aware of the technology at hand that the elite uses to bring Biblical prophecy into our reality.

The entertainment arm of Satan's kingdom reveals their motives and technology in movies, TV shows, etc., so pay attention! This mindset is under the auspice of their stated-in-stone agenda, and their elite will fulfill their stated goal of DEPOPULATION. Similar to God giving Moses His Ten Commandments, written on stone tablets, so it is that Satan has given man his **Ten Commandments** that are also etched in stone. The former Light Bearer's commandments are 19 Feet (5.87m) tall and written on four thick granite pillars or tablets, back and front, with inscriptions in eight different languages: English, Spanish, Swahili, Hindi, Hebrew, Arabic, Traditional Chinese, and Russian.

The Cherokee Indians say that the monument marks the spot of what is believed to be the center of the universe. The Guidestone's purpose is to explain how to re-establish the Earth in the coming New Age in case of a catastrophic event, like the Rapture. The first commandment is strictly depopulation-specific: "**1. Maintain humanity under 500,000,000 in perpetual balance with nature.**" This means that Earth's entire population will be reduced from 8

A CLOSER LOOK AT LIFE AND DEATH

billion people to 500 million…WOW! I am sure that this number takes into account those who are taken in the Rapture.

The monument was constructed in the 1980s by an unknown architect who used a proxy to provide details and drawings for its erection. However, it has been the subject of much controversy, as many regard it as Satanism because it opposes the Word of our Creator. Subsequently, on July 6, 2022, shortly after the startup of CERN's Large Hadron Collider, the monument was bombed. The mayor states that he plans to rebuild.

Lastly, check out the Apocalyptic 2025 Global Depopulation Forecast that are specific to each country as reported by Deagle Corporation (https://www.deagel.com/), which is reportedly a secretive branch of the United States Military that tracks and collects order data for aircraft (military and non-military), tanks, missiles, launching and combat systems, Space Force satellite weaponry, laser beam, drone and sea systems, and other artillery weaponry and systems. This highly classified data is preserved for the highest-ranked decision makers. They prepare confidential briefing documents for the NSA, NATO, World Bank, United Nations, etc. And surprisingly, they also track and make predictions relative to the world's population growth and depopulation for each country.

A few years ago, their website revealed the world's population for each country, showing specifically the population data for 2017 and 2025, in shocking contrast. To name a few countries:

Country	2017 Population	2025 Population	% Loss
The United States	327 M	100 M	-68.5
France	67.1 M	39.1 M	-41.7
The United Kingdom	63.3 M	14.5 M	-77.1

However, after facing considerable adverse public scrutiny, Deagel removed its depopulation forecast from the internet. Nevertheless, this information can still be found on Archive.org by searching for Deagel. Please view this chilling video for more details: https://archive.org/details/ Rockefeller-cia-connections-to-deagel-depopulation-forecast. And of course, we cannot leave out Bill Gates' TEDx Talk, stating that the mRNA vaccine will reduce the population: https://www.instagram.com/reel/ DKxL3U2IAhq/?igsh=MWQ1c2Jhbjd5YWp2eg==

What in the world do you think their plans will involve that will suddenly and significantly reduce the global population so drastically by 2025? Again, I believe the huge population reduction is the result of the above scriptures by methods of war, including Nuclear War, civil unrest, gun violence, the unpreventable and evitable Rapture of the Church, plagues (Coronavirus was a start), famine, and migration relative to the formation of the end-time **10-Nation Confederacy** as prophesied in **Revelation 17:12.** The resurgence of the **revived Roman Empire** as foretold in the **Book of Daniel, Chapter 2,** God's word will always hold true and will materialize from the pages of the Bible as truth comes to visible life, like Christ did, so for all those who believe the New World Order will rule during the end times and last days, think again.

The bottom line is that now is the time for you to make up your mind, whose side you will be on, like America's 40th President, Ronald Reagan's son, Ronald Reagan, Jr., who wholeheartedly declares that he is a lifelong atheist who is not afraid of "burning in Hell." However, I am sure that if he is home alone and his house catches fire, he will not remain for fear of burning up and thus will evacuate and call the Fire Department. But he expects us to believe he is not afraid of burning in Hell, forever… yeah, right! Ronald, Jr. airs the following commercial on national television periodically throughout the year, especially during major events like the Super bowl:

In the end, like Ronald Reagan Jr., everyone must choose a side based on the lifestyle that they live or their proclaimed belief in Jesus Christ, which determines whom they worship... Jesus Christ or Satan: *"All the nations will be gathered before him [Jesus Christ, who is God], and he will separate the people one from another as a shepherd separates the sheep from the goats. He [God] will put the sheep [believers in Christ] on his right and the goats [unbelievers] on his left" (Matthew 25:31-36).* Those on the left will experience the eternal and permanent Second Death... the Lake of Fire and Brimstone. Therefore, please consider your consequences upon your death and choose a side in this war that is being waged in your thought life...your belief system. Who are you fighting for? You must make up your own mind, no one can do it for you. Remember that your choice is Christ, or default to Hellfire... there is no in between.

If you choose to bow down to Satan, then you must follow the religious figure... the False Prophet, the political figure... the Antichrist, and Satan's Beast System. You must do what they tell you to say and do, including taking the Mark of the Beast. So, it is better to understand your choices now so that you can make an informed decision regarding your life/lifestyle, death, and eternal future while there is still time. The Lord warns us in *Matthew 24:4, "Watch out that no one deceives you!" "The devil, who deceived them [you and me], was cast into the lake of fire and brimstone where the beast and the false prophet are. And they will be tormented day and night forever and ever...Then Death and Hades were cast into the lake of fire. This is the second death"* *(Revelation 20:10, 14).*

A CLOSER LOOK AT LIFE AND DEATH

ALTERNATE UNIVERSES

Is The Metaverse In Bible Prophecy?

"...they could not buy or sell unless they had the mark on their forehead..."
~ Revelation 13:17

Satan's Beast System will have the authority to deny humanity the right to **"buy or sell"** without his mark (666) on their forehead or their hand, ***"...they could not buy or sell unless they had the mark, which is the name of the beast or the number of its name [666]," Revelation 13:17-18.*** One thought that I had regarding the placement of the mark on our hand and on our forehead that is related to shopping is to replace our digital cell phone and credit card payment system with Chip Implants or Digital Quantum Tattoos on our right hand or on our foreheads. These could be administered using a vaccine or microneedle application technology.

Beast = The Entire World = World Ruler = AI Beast System, a Global Ruler = The Antichrist and his total control Beast System, in addition to a religious leader, called the False Prophet

However, with the inception of the Metaverse, you can create yourself as an avatar (incarnation) and create the life that you want without God, or, in essence, "you" become God. This foolishness of vile behavior entices people to virtually purchase fake goods and services, like real estate, clothing, etc., using a headset. Therefore, it is plausible that they will develop a forehead Point of Sale (POS) Payment System that will consist of using an under-the-skin forehead chip or a brain implant (possibly Elon Musk's Neuralink) to bring the buy and sell "Mark of the Beast" of Revelation 13:17 prophecy to our reality. What do you think will require a mark on our forehead?

Moreover, in collaboration with the world's Tech Giants, China is the leader in computer-based technology and the rise of virtual metaverses. I'm sure that the technological development of POS hardware and/or software has already been developed and is probably being produced in China. The technology that has created the totalitarian Beast System that will be used to control the world is based in China.

China's government is the proving ground for totalitarianism. It is not ironic that their national symbol is a Dragon, as Satan is called in **Revelation 12:9, "the great dragon was cast out, that old serpent, called the Devil, and Satan, which deceiveth the whole world."** China has even built temples in worship of the Dragon... Hmm. It is this revelation that prompted me to look closer at **Revelation 13:4, "And they [unbelievers] worshiped the dragon which gave power [through the AI Beast System] unto the beast [The Antichrist/The Papacy or False Prophet]: and they worshiped the beast."** Additionally, it is common knowledge that COVID-19 originated in China as well... Hmm.

After the epidemic began, governments asked us to be six feet apart, which was done to fine-tune their facial recognition system. But get this, China has also created and has reportedly launched an artificial Sun into the stratosphere, and it is said that they will launch a moon too. Google it. Could the reason for this be that the Word of God states, *"But in those days, after that tribulation, the sun shall be darkened, and the moon shall not give her light" (Mark 13:24).* So, will Satan have his own spheres?

China will deploy its totalitarian AI Beast System to the rest of the world. This system will include the evolving use of headsets or headgear to alter our reality, and possibly will be used in worship to the dragon… Satan. You may remember that during the COVID pandemic, supply chains were backlogged; therefore, there was an extreme number of ships that could not dock, so they were held stationary at sea. Of course, the majority of these ships were coming from China. COVID-19 supply chain issues were a cover-up to ship Artificial Intelligence hardware (robots, mainframes, computers, databases, etc.), as well as AI software to be delivered to the USA and other countries in order to prepare for the roll-out of AI technology on a global scale. After the pandemic, we are now hearing about it more and seeing them parade their robots before us. A few months ago, Elon Musk debuted an army of his Tesla robots.

Since COVID is over, you now see evidence of more AI installations being implemented throughout various industries. Of course, this will lead to mass layoffs for humans. Another subtle, but extremely significant achievement that the elite accomplished during COVID was to give power to the World Health Organization (WHO) to simultaneously suspend the constitutions in all countries (195) to make it easy to take control by calling for martial law around the world. A very powerful move that a One World Government Leader, like the Antichrist, will use to exert control over the entire human population.

Furthermore, regarding the coming "Mark" of the Beast (666) System, be on alert for the coming behavior or social score that will replace your credit score, in the US, which will include grading you on your behavior in society… your social media posts, purchases, associations with others and their cashless society will control the flow of your money. The AI-run system will control your spending through a one-world digital currency, possibly providing citizens with a set income or Universal Basic Income (UBI) that they can't access unless they have the mark.

In the new digital monetary system, your money can be activated and deactivated at will; it can also expire or be routed where they want it to go, etc., they are in control. The elite will usher in a Mark of the Beast System that creates a surveillance-enhanced, vaccine-based, and military-driven global society. Citizens will live in the elite's surveilling Smart Cities that will end human rights, void constitutions, eliminate free speech, and more.

Technology, disguised as convenience, will imprison us. The elite already have us purchasing surveilling items that we carry on our person and for our homes (Cell Phones, Alexa, Ring Doorbells, Robot vacuum systems, etc.) over Wi-Fi and global 5G infrastructure. This will propel us to 6G hardware and software for higher AI capabilities. Our supposed "freedoms" will continue to drastically deteriorate. Our world is rapidly deteriorating as we experience increasing atmospheric temperatures, pollution, fires, earthquakes, tsunamis, etc., and volcanic eruptions that release Spirits from the pits of Hell in the form of deadly heat, toxic/demonic clouds of sulfur dioxide, and lava, resulting in death and destruction.

Satan has guided humanity's reckless behavior to erode glaciers, raise sea levels, kill trees, etc., and cause animal extinction so that some species no longer contribute to our ecological system. Recall that this is exactly the devastating state of the Earth that Satan would drive man to create, as prophesied, just before Christ returns, but the elite would rather call it **"Climate Change."**

On top of that, the Book of Revelation foretells of wars and rumors of wars, famine, pestilences, death, martyrs (those killed due to belief in Christ), and the sheer terror of God's wrath will be released upon the Earth as never before seen on Earth or ever shall see again, according to ***Revelation 9:6,*** NLT; it will be so bad that people will be begging to die and cannot die: *"in those days people will seek death but will not find it. They will long to die, but death will flee from them!"* WOW, this is beyond horrific to the nth degree!!!

As far as man's quest to find alternate universes or planets with human life is in futility, because the only other universes out there are those in complete darkness. Recall that William Shatner confirmed this darkness; he didn't see other universes or humans; he witnessed terrifying darkness. Earth is the only universe in the Abyss of Hell, whereby God said, ***"Let there be light…" (Genesis 1:3)*** for the sake of our redemption.

IMPORTANT WARNING... BEWARE!

Satan wants access to your children: The former Light Bearer knows the Bible better than anyone on the planet; he must know it so that he can copy and counter God's every move. However, he didn't understand God's reverence for man, meaning the special love and attention that He gives to humanity. He didn't know that God would come through man, as a man, to die to release the Holy Spirit from His body and transition into the spiritual realm of Hell. Christ destroyed Satan's hold on humanity through death. But he knows now, so his focus is on you, especially your children! The younger Satan can distract and draw your children in, the better...Pay attention!

If Satan can reach your children with the spirit of sexual orientation perversion, then it's game on! You will allow the unstable mind of a child under 13 to have a sex change when they are still in their formative years and incapable of making sound decisions? They change their minds like the wind. You don't even trust them to make adult decisions, like running your household or driving, yet you trust their decision **(No, their "feelings")** to change their sex? REALLY??!!

Statistically, young children who have sex change surgeries suffer from severe depression because they struggle with the God within them, just as adult homosexuals do. They are more likely to become suicidal because of a spiritual war within their heart and minds. This is a symptom of not knowing the Truth of God. How will the children know the truth if the parents or adults don't know? The Lord says: *"My people are destroyed [through depression, suicidal behavior...darkness of the mind] for lack of knowledge. Because you have rejected [God's] knowledge, I also will reject you from being priest for Me; Because you have forgotten the law of your God, I also will forget your children" (Hosea 4:6).* Let that sink in and close your eyes to see your mental darkness, you know the drill!

And if Satan can get you to allow him access to your children under the disguise of "health," you will allow your babies as young as 6 months to be vaccinated using DNA-altering mRNA vaccine technology that has been proven by the US Supreme Court (2013) to make you inhuman? There are minimal to dismal clinical trials, resulting in the population being the guinea pigs. If you pay attention, you will realize that Satan's underlying agenda, as prophesied, is total population control. However, if you voluntarily hand your children over to him, then again, it's game on! We will delve deep into this subject matter as the book series progresses. However, Satan will start early, making your children connect to his Beast System because, again, once he fools you, it's easy access to your children… Hmm…very clever.

A CLOSER LOOK AT LIFE AND DEATH

Recap And Conclusion

We have established that our Spirit, which is our Life, lives forever because of our Creator… God's Holy Spirit made us in His everlasting Divine Image. Thus, we have a **Creator-Created** universal relationship with our Heavenly Father; never forget your place as a created being and that the war we are in is ultimately between light and darkness. However, we sinned and rebelled against Him. We experienced an eternal spiritual death sentence and were cast out of Heaven with the punishment of Eternal Death.

However, God forgave us, but because He extended us a second chance to regain our Eternal Life with Him, therefore, He put off Eternal Death, now called The Second Death, in His plan of redemption, to allow **Natural Death (death #1)** to complete its purpose of redeeming those who believe in Jesus Christ back unto God. However, Lucifer and his inner circle will never be forgiven, and therefore, the **Eternal Second Death (death #2)** or the **Lake of Fire and Brimstone** is their certain destiny.

Satan sinned first and is the father of evil and death, which caused the duality of Eternal Spirit Life Energy or separation and division that created the two opposing forces of good and evil. This defined the choice to have our Soul either filled with God's Holy Spirit (Divine/Light) or Satan (Demonic/Darkness). However, due to the Holiness of God, evil cannot remain in His Presence, as evidenced by our separation from Him. Therefore, these two forces must reside in separate locations… Heaven and Hell. Now, the duality of Eternal Spirit Life Energy flows into all space as positive and negative energy. It is also known as Light Wave Energy… sound waves, tidal waves, musical notes, current, or electricity that powers all things and is displayed graphically in our world as a Sine Wave.

We have established that Sine Waves flow, constantly at various frequencies, to form and produce our thought life as alternating thought waves of good and evil flow through our minds continually; wherefore, you must choose which of the two energies: 1. towards good/peace or 2. towards evil/enrage, that you will yield to at any given moment… in any given decision, situation, or circumstance. Be mindful that whatever you love to do, while on Earth, you will continue to do the same when you leave Earth, as you transition to the appropriate eternal realm that accommodates the behavior that you love. Essentially, if you love doing evil… spreading confusion, hate, and fear, your eternal future will be in Hell.

However, remember that the goal here is for you to determine what you truly believe regarding your life, death, and eternal future before your destined date with death. As certain as your Natural Death is to come, you can be absolutely certain that The Second Death (Revelation 20:10-14) will come. Your eternal future is profoundly serious because your eternal life hangs in the balance. Again, Satan knows that he can never be redeemed back to eternal life with God or exalt himself above God; He will never be able to enter Heaven again, like you, through Christ. So, he wants to ensure that you (and your children) are not redeemed… unknowingly, by default, and of your own volition. But thanks to God's grace and redemption, you can **avoid the Eternal Second Death** through Jesus Christ… It's your choice! We have established that you are a sinner; it is your choice as to whether **you are either a repentant sinner or an unrepentant sinner**. Either way, you are awaiting your turn to die for the sins that you committed in Heaven and on Earth, like me, right?

It is impossible to deny hearing the voice of God. I am certain that a strong thunderbolt or the might of His voice has jolted your heart to tremble in terrifying fear. And you cannot deny the truth regarding your dark, cast down **"Shadow,"** that constantly reminds you of the sinful moment in your Eternal History when you fell from Heaven due to sin, and that you are living in the shadow of death... The Second Death. Neither can you deny God's hard evidence provided here regarding your sinful shortcomings, betrayal, and revolt against Him according to **Jeremiah 33:8.** And most of all, you cannot deny His **(undeserved)** love, mercy, and a time of grace that He has extended to you so that you can save yourself from Eternal Death, by freedom of choice **(Deuteronomy 30:19)**. Therefore, **HEAR THE WORD OF THE LORD** and FEAR His punishments for your sins, which are exponentially, incomprehensibly swift, fierce, and everlasting. But also, know that His overwhelming Love for the righteous yields a life of everlasting peace.

Therefore, you must determine if what you believe is from the Creator (Truth) or a lie from a created being (angel or human), regarding your eternal future, so that you will not end up in Hell or the Eternal Lake of Fire by default. So, stop with the denials, excuses, and lies because the Lord has spoken and has brought us His undeniable truths regarding life and death on Earth. You see the evidence of death happening all around you, and you know that in the back of your mind, you could be next. Again, how can you admit that death exists but deny your Creator who issued you your death sentence?

Remember always that the Lord's Word is as true as your last breath or the last breath of His air that you will take upon your demise. His Truth is written and has been put on display in the life, death, and resurrection of Jesus Christ; so, denying His Truth means that you believe lies that lead to eternal death. Therefore, I urge you to do the research (don't take my word for it); start with the exercises at the end of this book. Also, search your heart so you can make an informed decision about your eternal future before you leave this Earth.

Once again, by now, I hope that you understand your

plight...your wrongdoings towards God, and as well visualize **God's Blueprint** of His Divine Redemption Plan in action... His Word (Jesus) in the flesh, to save you and make you redeemable! Remember to protect your Temple or God's dwelling place within you by blatantly falling for pharmaceutical or biomedical sorcery whereby the elite manufacturers' problems and pandemics then magically execute the solution to the problem that they created. All while telling you that their solution will save your life. Aren't you tired of falling for lies? Stay attuned to what God is doing through prayer and worship to Him in **"Spirit and in truth"** and know His blueprint. Also, know and watch your enemy... Satan and his elite pay attention to what they are really doing behind the scenes; follow the money and their technology... **WAKE UP!**

Christ came as a matter of our eternal life and eternal death. Again, why do you think that when God or Jesus is mentioned, people automatically think of Religion or Church instead of the fact that Jesus Christ came as a matter of our eternal life and eternal death, which applies to everyone on the planet who dies? His coming was not for religious purposes.

Lastly, take one last moment to remember your home in Heaven, imagine yourself standing before the Glory of God's Holy Throne, as you once did. Revel in His Glory with praise. Remember to envision your Home in Heaven when things are not going well in your life, your Victory is in your Praise! God's Throne establishes His sole Sovereignty over all things, and He has defeated death, so fear not. He created, defined, and established the concept of words like everlasting, truth, goodness, love, peace, home, family, security, and Eternal Life... All the things that elude us on Earth, but all these things are in Christ!

God's Redemption Plan in Action

A CLOSER LOOK AT LIFE AND DEATH

WAR IN HEAVEN/YOU! EXPELLED FROM HEAVEN
A CLOSER LOOK AT LIFE & DEATH BOOK SERIES
DOWNLOAD THE ANIMATED VERSION AT
www.FaceEternity.org| IG: @FaceEternity

HEAVEN
AT THE THRONE OF GOD

LUCIFER
ME
YOU

WE WERE CREATED AS ETERNAL SPIRIT LIFE ENERGY TO DWELL IN HEAVEN & IN THE BODY OF MAN ON EARTH

OPENED

Cherubim Angel Lucifer
"I will exalt my throne above the stars of God" (Isaiah 14:13). And ME & YOU believed his lie and followed after him.

WAR IN HEAVEN
"And there was war in heaven: Michael and his angels fought against the dragon; and the dragon fought and his angels [YOU & ME]. And prevailed not...that old serpent, called the Devil, and Satan...was cast out into the earth [darkness], and his angels [YOU & ME] were cast out with him."
~Rev 12:7-8

YOU! EXPELLED FROM HEAVEN
HEAVEN IS CLOSED TO US
NO MORE ETERNAL LIFE HERE

THE ABYSS (BOTTOMLESS) DARKNESS GENESIS 1:2

The totality of Hell is made up of several places: The Earth, The Inner Core of The Earth, The Abyss of Outer Space/Outer Darkness, The Grave, and The Darkness of the Human Mind.

A CLOSER LOOK AT LIFE AND DEATH

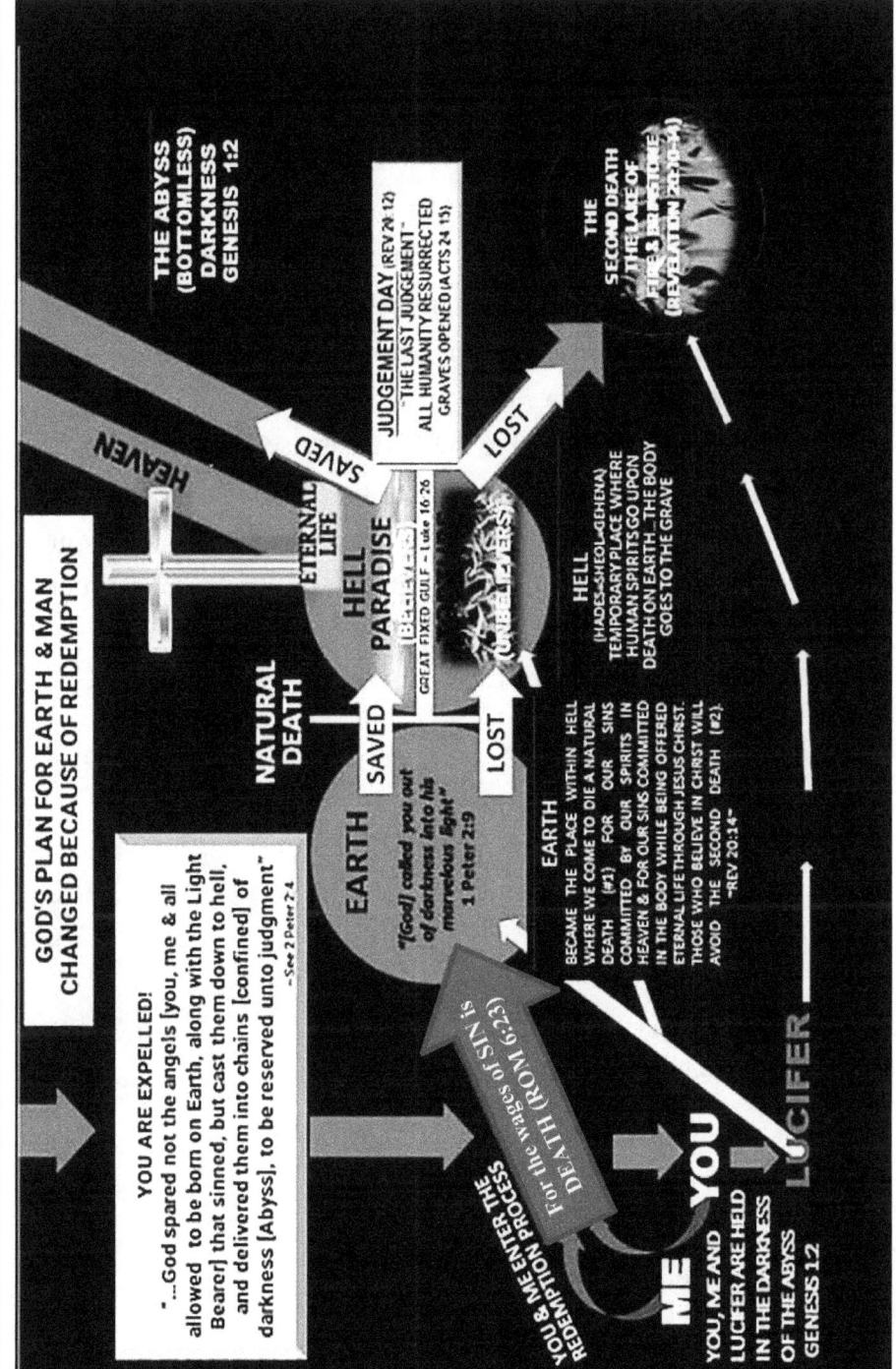

A CLOSER LOOK AT LIFE AND DEATH

EXERCISES

You Need to Know What You Believe!
STUDENTS: See Scholarship Entry Below

1. Go back and select sections of interest and read some of the scripture references. Pull out your digital or physical Bible to gain more wisdom and understanding.
2. Download the Animated Diagram **"War in Heaven/You! Expelled from Heaven"** at www.FaceEternity.org. Study, and proceed to the next exercise.
3. The words listed below require that you take a few moments to reflect on their meaning. Get a dictionary or use definitions from the book to write down your definition of the following:

- God
- Heaven/Holiness
- Spirit/Angels
- Holy Spirit
- Eternity
- Redemption
- Hell
- Lucifer/Satan
- Evil
- Jesus Christ

- Resurrection

- Judgment

- Spiritual Death

- Natural Death

- Truth

- Lie

- Time

4. Explain the **"End Times"** and **"The Last Days"**

5. What is your opinion on the purpose of your eternal life and death, regarding living on Earth, and transition to Heaven, or Hell?

6. What does your **"Shadow"** reveal about you?

7. Explain if you believe, or not, that you evolved from an "Ape" or a Big Bang, and why?

8. **Fill in the blanks:**

   A. God said to Adam and Eve, "Of every tree of the garden you may freely eat; but of the _____ you shall not eat, for in the day that you eat of it you shall surely die" (Gen 2:16-17). Instead, they ate from what tree? _____.

   Based on God's Word above, will you surely die? Yes or No. If you answered Yes, then ALL of God's Holy Word is true.

A CLOSER LOOK AT LIFE AND DEATH

B. "I have set before you [eternal] _____ and [eternal] _____ per Deuteronomy _____."

C. _____ states: "If you confess with your mouth the Lord Jesus and believe in your heart that God has raised Him from the dead, you will be saved. For with the heart, one believes unto righteousness, and with the mouth confession is made unto salvation."

D. _____ is the scripture that tells us that, "the wages of [our] sin is death."

E. _____ came to defeat Death. Therefore, I do NOT **FEAR DEATH** anymore!

F. _____ scripture states: "You believe that there is one God... Even the demons believe —and tremble!"

G. Do you believe that you evolved from an "Ape" or that a destructive "Big Bang" suddenly created your life on planet Earth? Yes or No

H. _____ scripture says, *"Watch out that no one deceives you!"*

I. Is your life (birth) or your death dependent on which religion you belong to or church you attend? Yes or No, **Why?**

STAY TUNED! We have so many more exciting revelations to explore to enhance your understanding regarding your Eternal History and your Eternal Future. For a deeper study, book an online course or attend a live graphical presentation that will bring **"A Closer Look At Life And Death"** into your reality.

Visit:
www.FaceEternity.org
Follow all social media @FaceEternity
Please write a review on our website, on Amazon and on other retail websites.

SCHOLARSHIP ENTRY
Grades 8 to College Grad School!
Please visit our Scholarship Page on our website to register and receive submission entry information for the above exercise. All answers must be written in your own words, no AI answers.

GOD IS PERFECT

IN

LIFE AND DEATH

FEAR NOT!

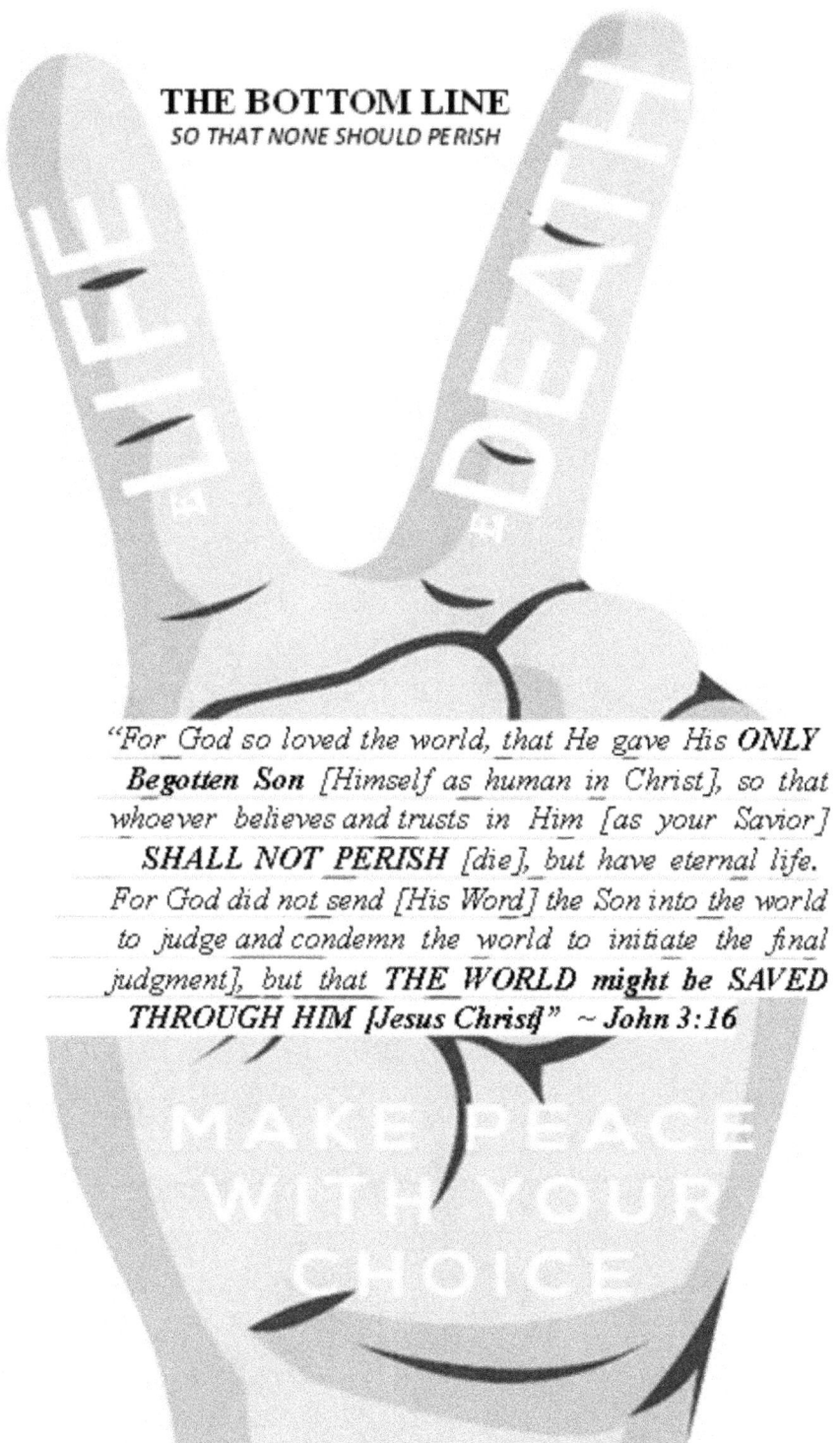

A CLOSER LOOK AT LIFE AND DEATH

www.ingramcontent.com/pod-product-compliance
Lightning Source LLC
Chambersburg PA
CBHW072001150426
43194CB00008B/950